PSST: Please Somebody Speak the Truth

We the People Should Know

PSST: Please Somebody Speak the Truth

Copyright © 2016 by Karen Sloan-Brown

All rights reserved.

No part of this work may be reproduced or transmitted in any form or by any means, electronic or mechanical, including photocopying and recording, or by any information storage or retrieval system, except as may be expressly permitted by the 1976 Copyright Act or in writing from the publisher. Requests for permission should be addressed to Brown-Reflections.com or Karensloanbrown.com.

This book is printed on acid-free paper.

ISBN: 978-1-9444440-02-2

Library of Congress Cataloging-in-Publication Data on file.

Editor: Cornelius Brown

Table of Contents

Introduction .... pg 1

Democracy .... pg 5
- In The Name of Democracy .... pg 7
- The Costs of Containing Communism .... pg 10
- The End of the Cold War .... pg 14
- Spreading Democracy .... pg 15

The Vote, Voting, and Not Voting .... pg 17
- The History of the Vote in the U.S. .... pg 18
- Battle for the Ballot .... pg 23
- State of the Voter .... pg 26

Capitalism .... pg 31
- The Downside of Capitalism .... pg 33
- The Golden Age of Capitalism .... pg 36
- Unfettered Capitalism and Trickle-Down Economics ... pg 38
- The Age of Supercapitalism .... pg 40

Income Inequality, Selfishness, and Greed .... pg 43
- Historical Examples of Inequality .... pg 45
- How Did We Get There and How Bad Is It .... pg 47
- What Are the Consequences? .... pg 50
- What Can Be Done About It? .... pg 51
- Selfishness and Greed .... pg 52

Entitlement Programs .... pg 57
- What Is Really Going On? .... pg 60
- Military Spending .... pg 63
- Foreign Aid .... pg 64

Social Security .... pg 67

 So What's the Problem..pg 71

 What Can We Do About It? ....pg 75

Affordable Healthcare .... pg 79

 What is the Patient Protection and Affordable Care Act..............pg 81

 What Does it Cost? What Does it Save? ....pg 82

 What are the Benefits ....pg 84

 Arguments Against it ....pg 85

 Economic Consequences ....pg 88

Wages vs. Inflation .... pg 91

 Some Wage History ....pg 93

 Minimum Wage vs. Living Wage ....pg 95

 Charting the Path of Wages...pg 98

 Arguments Against Higher Wages...pg 99

 Inflation ....pg 103

Outsourcing and Offshoring .... pg 105

 Jobs Crossing the Border ....pg 108

 Jobs Sailing Overseas ....pg 110

 Benefits to Offshoring ....pg 112

 Consequences of Offshoring..pg 112

 American Workers, Hopeful or Hopeless ....pg 114

Education, the Economy, and Who Should Pay .... pg 119

 Educating More Americans...pg 122

 Financing College Education..pg 124

    Changing Demographics..pg 125

    Are the Jobs Really There? ....pg 126

Affirmative Action... pg 129

    What is Affirmative Action? ....pg 131

    Racism is the Reason ....pg 132

    History of Affirmative Action ....pg 134

    Implementation of Affirmative Action.....................................pg 137

    Challenges to Affirmative Action...pg 140

    Pros and Cons to Affirmative Action ....pg 142

College Athletes, Pay or No Pay...................................... pg 145

    History of College Sports...pg 147

    The NCAA...pg 150

    How Much Money Is Made in College Sports ....pg 152

    Benefits to Schools ....pg 155

    Benefits to Coaches ....pg 156

    Benefits to Athletes ....pg 156

    Support for Paying Athletes...pg 157

    Critics Against Paying Athletes ....pg 158

    Options for Paying Athletes ....pg 159

Victims of the Legal System and Police Brutality .... pg 164

    The History of the Criminal Justice System ....pg 166

    Criminal Justice in the 20th Century...pg 168

    The Lack of Criminal Justice in the 21st Century ....pg 168

    Budget Cuts and Making Up the Shortfall..................................pg 170

    Mass Incarceration and Privatization..pg 172

    Police Policy and Over-policing ....pg 174

    Police Shootings and Brutality...pg 176

Gun Control or Not... pg 180

    What Does the Constitution Say? ....pg 181

    Was it the Wild, Wild West? ....pg 183

    The Business of Guns ....pg 184

    Gun Ownership ....pg 186

    Gun Laws ....pg 187

    Dissenting Arguments Regarding Gun Control ....pg 188

    Gun Violence..pg 189

Global Warming... pg 192

    What Causes Global Warming ....pg 194

    Consequences of Global Warming...pg 195

    Climate Change Denial ....pg 197

    Politics of Climate Change ....pg 199

    Projected Solutions ....pg 200

Greatness, Nuclear Weapons & War.................................... pg 202

    Nuclear Weapons ....pg 205

    Disarming the Danger ....pg 208

    Protests..pg 210

    War ....pg 211

Iraq & Isis .... pg 213

    Brief History of Iraq .... pg 216

    Making the Case .... pg 217

    The Iraq War .... pg 219

    The Aftermath .... pg 220

    Was It About Oil? .... pg 221

    Was It Worth It? .... pg 224

    Iraq Civil War .... pg 224

    Now What? .... pg 226

The Barack Obama Presidency .... pg 230

    The First Year, 2009 .... pg 231

    The Second Year, 2010 .... pg 234

    The Third Year, 2011 .... pg 236

    The Fourth Year, 2012 .... pg 237

    The Second Term, Fifth Year, 2013 .... pg 239

    The Sixth Year, 2014 .... pg 241

    The Seventh Year, 2015 .... pg 242

    The Eighth and Final Year, 2016 .... pg 243

    Bibliography .... pg 245

Introduction

Please Somebody Speak the Truth

I am a firm believer in the people. If given the truth, they can be depended upon to meet any national crisis. The great point is to bring them the real facts. ~Abraham Lincoln

The most sophisticated weapon in the world is the human voice, more often than not it also the most damaging. The power of the voice can be used to bless or to destroy, it can be used to spread truth or lies, to speak peace or violence, to encourage or tear down, to build nations or pillage countries. Instinctively, from the time we are infants we know how to use our voices to gain attention and to have our basic needs fulfilled. Without the power of a voice you can become vulnerable, weak, and helpless. Your thoughts, requests, and protests, go unheard. That's what makes a democracy strong; each person has a voice in their vote. It's the manner that we choose and communicate with our representatives.

Today we are in a precarious position because our leadership is no longer trustworthy. Their voices are loud but they don't tell us the truth, whether it be by omission or blatant lies. Most have gained their elevated positions of leadership through the power of persuasion, deftly convincing us they have all the answers. Politicians are masters of this game. They compellingly communicate all the things we yearn to hear, some are honest, others are downright deceitful. From my perspective, their deeds are more self-centered than noble. In the 21st century, more power-seeking voices have become increasingly brazen, distorting the facts, misrepresenting truths, and threatening to undermine hundreds of years of advancement for personal and privileged interests.

In the political arena, the truth has been stretched and twisted to the extent that it is totally unrecognizable. Adolph Hitler said, *Make the lie big. Make it simple. Keep saying it, and eventually they will believe it.* The reason that most of us are quiet is because we don't possess enough information to participate in the conversation. We need to have a basic understanding of the serious issues facing this country and we can't trust our leaders or the privately owned press to tell us the truth. It's now critical for us to define and clarify our understanding and beliefs on a number of fundamental issues before we can make an educated choice on whom we will listen. We can't continue to cast our votes based on name recognition. The Daily Mirror headline after George W. Bush was re-elected asked the question: "How can 59,054,087 people be so DUMB?" The information from the voices we hear is equally as important as our own. Being more knowledgeable will help us to distinguish the lies from the truth.

We the people are America; we are not cattle to be corralled, not wild animals to be herded, nor a population of geese to be driven out. We are the citizens of the United States. As such, we must become more proactive in addressing the significant issues that affect our everyday lives. The repercussions are dire lest the line between life in the U.S. and life in a third world country becomes blurred and we suffer the issues that concern them, poverty, quality drinking water, hunger, pollution, healthcare, and social and cultural exclusion. It's time to speak the truth! William Faulkner, a great American writer said, *"Never be afraid to raise your voice for honesty and truth and compassion against injustice and lying and greed. If people all over the world…would do this, it would change the earth."*

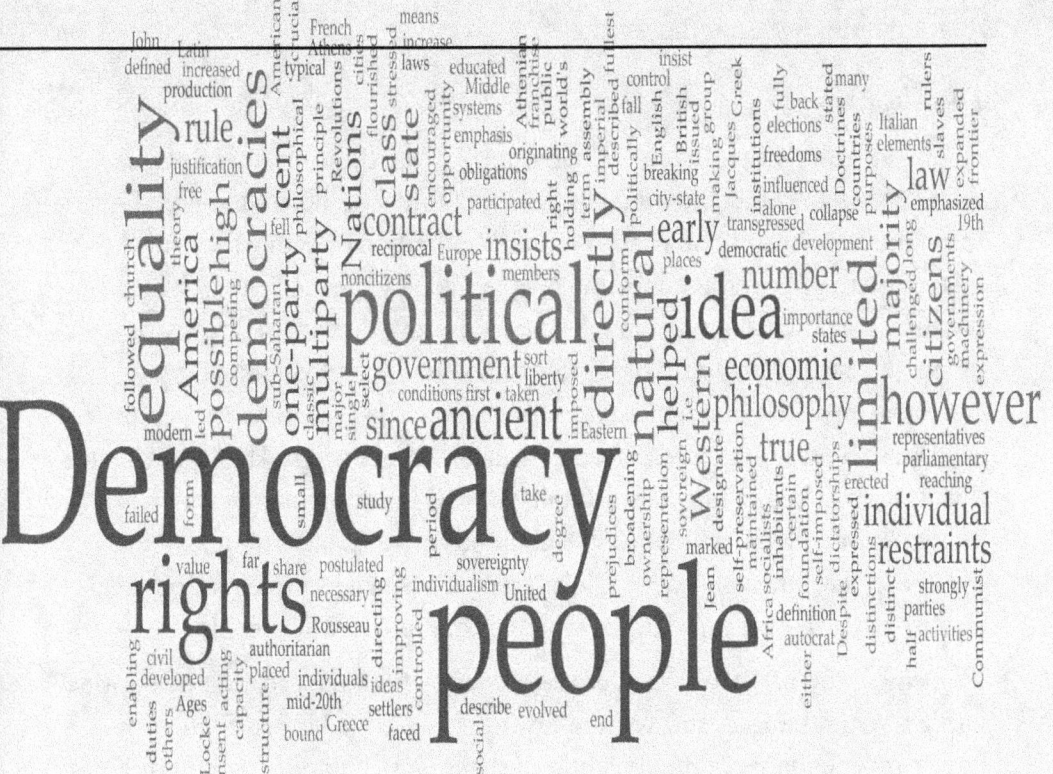

Democracy

Democracy

What is this thing that we Americans say we fight for, this thing that we vow to protect at all costs, and this thing we desire to spread throughout the world? Merriam Webster's definition of democracy says it is a system of government by the people ruled by the majority in which the supreme power is vested in the people, exercised by them directly or indirectly, through a system of representation involving periodical free elections. It sounds so progressive; surely a new age system developed by modern society, however, Democracy is not a new concept. There is evidence that its earliest beginning were around 4000BC in Mesopotamia which is now known as Iraq, Syria, and Kuwait. Thousands of years later, around 507BC in Greece, the Athenian leader, Cleisthenes, introduced a system of political reform that he called demokratia, which meant ruled by the people.

Democracy has evolved over the centuries with the creation of political parties, secret ballots, and written laws. In 1787, the United States, a newly independent country rejecting aristocracy, wrote its democratic constitution establishing a federal system of government. Control was prudently divided among three separate divisions of government to prevent abuses of power. This democracy was to guarantee basic human rights, the right to vote, religious liberty, and freedom of speech. Nevertheless, at this time in history neither slaves nor women could vote. Women gained the right to vote early in the 20th century, for African-Americans it would be almost fifty years later.

The disadvantage of a democratic system is the possibility of unequal representation. Ideally a mixture of classes in any society should represent the people. Regrettably, there is no one system that fits all. The purpose of democracy is to serve the well-being of the greatest number, hence the majority rules. In actuality it doesn't necessarily function in that manner. Whereas it would be thought that most people would vote for the benefit of their class or financial status they frequently don't. In 2015, most of our politicians or representatives are very wealthy people. This is indicative of an aristocracy. In the book, *"Democracy in America,"* authored by Alex De Tocqueville, he wrote, *"When the rich govern alone, the interest of the poor is always in peril."*

In The Name of Democracy

What are the interests of this democratic nation? To form a more perfect union or to spread this good thing that we've found? History has shown presidents wanting a central role, or more aptly, a starring role for the United States on the world stage. More than a few have used democracy as a springboard to become the leading player. World War I was the first time that democracy was used as the reason to declare war. President Woodrow Wilson stated to a special joint session of Congress that, *"We have no selfish ends to serve,"* that the conflict would be a *"war to end war,* and it would *"make the world safe for democracy."* It was sold as a moral responsibility for the United Stated to enter the war but it was probably based more on pride, and wanting to have an interest in the outcome of the war and a voice in the peace conference.

Even while fighting vigorously overseas to preserve democracy in the world, America had not solved its own problem of denying democracy to black people at home. Still, African-Americans were eager to participate in this fight for democracy, believing that if they fought for democracy abroad they would surely be granted with it back in their own country. After the war they demanded the rights they were due as American citizens. They soon realized the hope that their brave contributions would have made a difference was merely a pipe dream. Inequality and racial hatred in America would have a stronghold for the next fifty years even while the fight for democracy abroad continued.

At the end of 1940, Franklin D. Roosevelt, in a presidential speech, said the United States should become the *"great arsenal for democracy... to meet the threat to our democratic faith."* In other words he was saying that it is the responsibility of democracies to fight against dictators. Most of the American people during this time were opposed to entering into the conflict. Needless to say, President Roosevelt lent his support to the British and proceeded to prepare for the nation's entry into the war. He saw it as Democracy's fight against those planning to conquer the world. He spoke eloquently on more than one occasion to convince the American people of the dire consequences of the defeat of democratic nations. He said, *"I would ask no one to defend a democracy which in turn would not defend everyone in the nation against want and privation."*

Psst: Somebody Speak the Truth

At the start of World War II, only 2 percent of eligible African-Americans in the South were registered to vote. Once again, they questioned whether they should risk life and limb for a country that denied them the freedom and democracy in efforts to preserve those privileges for others overseas. In a letter to the editor at the *Pittsburgh Courier* printed on January 31, 1942, John G. Thompson eloquently expressed the timeless sentiments of black people.

DEAR EDITOR:

Like all true Americans, my greatest desire at this time, this crucial point of our history; is a desire for a complete victory over the forces of evil, which threaten our existence today. Behind that desire is also a desire to serve, this, my country, in the most advantageous way. Most of our leaders are suggesting that we sacrifice every other ambition to the paramount one, victory. With this I agree; but I also wonder if another victory could not be achieved at the same time. After all, the things that beset the world now are basically the same things which upset the equilibrium of nations internally, states, counties, cities, homes and even the individual.

Being an American of dark complexion and some 26 years, these questions flash through my mind: "Should I sacrifice my life to live half American?" "Will things be better for the next generation in the peace to follow?" "Would it be demanding too much to demand full citizenship rights in exchange for the sacrificing of my life." "Is the kind of America I know worth defending?" "Will America be a true and pure democracy after this war?" "Will colored Americans suffer still the indignities that have been heaped upon them in the past?" These and other questions need answering; I want to know, and I believe every colored American, who is thinking, wants to know.

This may be the wrong time to broach such subjects, but haven't all good things obtained by men been secured through sacrifice during just such times of strife? I suggest that while we keep defense and victory in the forefront that we don't loose sight of our fight for true democracy at home. The "V for Victory" sign is being displayed prominently in all so-called democratic countries which are fighting for victory over aggression, slavery and tyranny. If this V sign means that to those now engaged in this great conflict then let colored Americans adopt the double VV for a double victory; The first V for victory over our enemies from without, the second V for victory over our enemies within. For surely those who perpetrate these ugly prejudices here are seeking to destroy our democratic form of government just as surely as the Axis forces.

This should not and would not lessen our efforts to bring this conflict to a successful conclusion; but should and would make us stronger to resist these evil forces which threaten us. America could become united as never before and become truly the home of democracy. In way of an answer to the foregoing questions in a preceding paragraph, I might say that there is no doubt that this country is worth defending; things will be different for the next generation; colored Americans will come into their own, and America will eventually become the true democracy it was designed to be. These things will become a reality in time; but not through any relaxation of the efforts to secure them. In conclusion let me say that though these questions often permeate my mind, I love American and am willing to die for the America I know will someday become a reality.

With democracy at the center of his heart, and the decision made to take this country to war and fight in its defense, President Roosevelt signed Executive Order 9066 on February 19, 1942, relocating nearly 120,000 Japanese American farmers on the West Coast to internment camps. Over 60 percent were American citizens and the others had lived in the country for 20 to 40 years and were long-time residents. This was yet another time we failed to practice what we preach. This decision was racially motivated by white farmers in the west who wanted to eliminate the competition. Very few German or Italian Americans were interned at camps during this time.

Japanese American soldiers entered the war wanting to prove their loyalty while African American soldiers hoped that defending democracy abroad would bring an end to the discrimination they suffered at home. When the war ended, the internment of the Japanese Americans was over, yet Black, Latino, and Native Americans found nothing had changed for them. If democracy was as close to the heart as those in leadership proclaimed, why was it in such short supply for its own citizens? Why were the abuses by dictators in other countries so abhorrent to us while we dismissed the abuses within our own nation? Should not our foreign policy mirror the policy by which we govern our own country? Without talking about the lives that have been lost, let's consider the amount of bread and butter that has been spent on the containment of communism during these years.

The Costs of Containing Communism

Tensions between the United States and the Soviet Union continued to increase after World War II prompting President Truman to focus his foreign policy on the containment of communism in this land and on foreign soil. Prompted by the British withdrawing financial support from the Greek government and Turkey, Truman saw an opportunity to stifle the expanding influence of the Soviets. In a speech to congress where he requested $400 million for aid to Greece and the Turkish government, he argued the United Stated was compelled to support "free peoples" in their battles against "totalitarian regimes," to contain the spread of communism which would "undermine the foundations of international peace and hence the security of the United States." This policy would become known as the Truman Doctrine, which established that the United States would provide political, military, and economic assistance to all democratic nations under threat from external as well as internal authoritarian forces (Beschloss, 2006).

Although this foreign policy has no basis in the founding Declaration of Independence or the U.S. Constitution, it has been the cause of much sacrifice for this nation without visible gains. It appears to be the exorbitant price we have to pay to wear the title; "Leader of the Free World." In 1950, President Truman approved $10 million to provide military assistance to France to fight the spread of communism in Indochina, which was also known as French Indochina, a peninsula comprised of Vietnam, Laos, Cambodia, Thailand, Burma, and Malaysia. In the following year he authorized another $150 million to support the French in the fight against communist Viet Minh.

When the Soviet Union invaded Japanese-controlled Korea from the North, the United States moved its troops into the south of the peninsula. Japanese troops in the North surrendered to the Russians and those in the South surrendered to the Americans creating a divided government. In 1950, the North Korean troops invaded South Korea. Truman insisted that America enter the conflict to defend a noncommunist government from attack by communist troops to avert the expansion of communism in a country almost 7000 miles away. Was this mission to stop the spread of communism more about power and position? Was it about these individual countries or more about the Soviet Union and the United States in competition? The cost to the American people, calculated by Commander Richard Miller in dollars equivalent to those in 2005, was $678 billion.

President Eisenhower stayed the course with the foreign policy of containment. In an historical press conference on April 7, 1954 he drove home the significance of Indochina aka Vietnam to the United States with its natural resources. In his final encore he said, *"You have broader consideration that might follow what you would call the 'falling domino' principle."* His theory was that the "fall of a noncommunist government to communism would then in turn precipitate the rapid fall of noncommunist governments in adjoining and adjacent countries. In the worst case scenario it could lead to the disintegration of Southeast Asia."

Seemingly torn in two directions between containing communism and the imminent breaking of the nation's bank, President Eisenhower warned America of the military-industrial complex in his farewell address. The United States and Russia had both developed nuclear weapons and it was already clear where this rivalry was headed. He expressed his worry that an arms race with the Soviet Union would usurp financial resources from other important and vital areas to the American people.

"Crises there will continue to be. In meeting them, whether foreign or domestic, great or small, there is a recurring temptation to feel that some spectacular and costly action could become the miraculous solution to all current difficulties. But each proposal must be weighed in light of a broader consideration: the need to maintain balance in and among national programs – balance between the private and public economy, balance between cost and hoped for advantage – balance between the clearly necessary and the comfortably desirable; balance between our essential requirements as a nation and the duties imposed by the nation upon the individual' balance between actions of the moment and the national welfare of the future. Good judgment seeks balance and progress; lack of it eventually finds imbalance and frustration.

We annually spend on military security more than the net income of all United States corporations. This conjunction of an immense military establishment and a large arms industry is new in the American experience. The total influence – economic, political, even spiritual – is felt in every city, every State house, every office of the Federal Government. Yet we must not fail to comprehend its grave implications. Our toil, resources and livelihood are all involved; so is the very structure of our society.

In the councils of government, we must guard against the acquisition of unwarranted influence, whether sought or unsought, by the military industrial complex. The potential for the disastrous rise of misplaced power exists and will persist. We must never let the weight of this combination endanger our liberties or democratic processes. Only an alert and knowledgeable citizenry can compel the proper meshing of the huge industrial and military machinery with our peaceful methods and goals, so that security and liberty may prosper.

Disarmament, with mutual honor and confidence, is a continuing imperative. Down the long lane of the history yet to be written America knows that this world of ours, ever growing smaller, must avoid becoming a community of dreadful fear and hate, and be instead, a proud confederation of mutual trust and respect. Together we must learn how to compose differences, not with arms, but with intellect and decent purpose. As one who has witnessed the horror and the lingering sadness of war -- as one who knows that another war could utterly destroy this civilization which has been so slowly and painfully built over thousands of years.

Apparently this warning fell on deaf ears as the military industrial complex grew larger. Now foreign policy is influenced not only by presidents and our stature in the world but also by the need for war to fuel the engine of the military industrial complex. No longer is the loss of human life our greatest consideration but the financial gain that continual war brings for corporations that supply arms and military defense equipment.

The second Indochina War was more commonly known as the Vietnam War. The North Vietnamese were again fighting to reunite Vietnam under communist rule. President John F. Kennedy, Eisenhower's successor, was resolute in his commitment to fighting the Cold War. As a U.S. Senator during a speech to the American Friends of Vietnam he said, *"Burma, Thailand, India, Japan, the Philippines and obviously Laos and Cambodia are among those whose security would be threatened if the Red Tide of Communism overflowed into Vietnam."* The current flow of money out of American to aid South Vietnam increased, as well as military advisers, but it wasn't enough. Kennedy became discouraged and said, *"In the final analysis, it is their war. They are the ones who have to win it or lose it."*

He grappled with his decision over the final weeks of his life but in my opinion it was a moment of great clarity.

After JFK's assassination and in the face of much American opposition, President Johnson used the same rationale of communist containment for the United States entry into the Vietnam War. He authorized military offensives in North Vietnam and US forces waged war for nearly eight years until President Nixon reached a peace agreement in January 1973. Two years later North Vietnam invaded South Vietnam and later captured the capital city, Saigon. The war finally ended. More than 3 million Vietnamese were killed. America lost more than 58,000 soldiers, over 150,000 were injured with 21,000 permanently disabled, and 1,626 missing in action. The Defense Department reported that the total monetary cost of the Vietnam War was $173 billion (equal to $770 billion in 2003 dollars). Vietnam veterans' benefits added another $250 billion ($1 trillion in 2003 dollars).

The End of the Cold War

The policies of glasnost and perestroika, introduced under Mikhail Gorbachev in the Soviet Union beginning in the mid-1980s, ushered in the democratization of the political system in the country. His initial aim was to revitalize their stagnant economy but the reforms and open elections led to the fall of one communist regime after another in East Germany, Poland, Hungry, and Czechoslovakia, similar to the domino effect described by Harry Truman. The Berlin Wall fell and East and West Germany were reunified. In December of 1991, the Soviet Union was dissolved; the Iron Curtain had been shredded. The Cold War was over.

The United States' preoccupation with the preparation for a monumental war with the Soviet Union was thus anticlimactic. Trillions of dollars had been spent in the build-up but thankfully the human loss had been avoided. America's policy of containing the threat of communism, the concept that had defined foreign policy for almost a century, had lost much of its vim and vigor. What would now be the frame for our foreign policy? Possibly this might be the time to shift our focus and resources to domestic issues like improving the economy, education, technology, or the aging infrastructure. In the words of Star Trek's Spock, "Negative, Captain."

Spreading Democracy

The other side of the 'containment of communism' coin is the 'spread of democracy.' The question was; in view of the past sacrifices of lives and money, and the ineffectiveness in the last three attempts, is it in the United States interest to spread democracy? The answer was; that it is in the strategic interest of the US to urge our autocratic allies toward democracy. We also have a moral responsibility as the only surviving superpower to protect human right and civil liberties around the world. So began our international mission to spread democracy, but it was not without criticism.

Political realists have argued against the fervor of spreading democracy through military force or covert actions. They believe that democratization comes from internal forces and that any outside entity has little ability to influence that process. Realists think that change by force can lead to instability in some regions. The perfect example of this was George W. Bush's invasion of Iraq to spread democracy in the Middle East. There is also the assumption that terrorists fear democracy. President Obama could be categorized as a realist for showing restraint in intervening in conflicts around the world.

Then there is the most important question for the people: Is it our role to spread democracy? Sean M. Lynn-Jones answers in his discussion paper (1998), "First, as human beings, Americans should and do feel some obligation to improve the well-being of other human beings. The bonds of common humanity do not stop at the borders of the United States." Dove Ronen wrote in the *New York Times* (April 30, 2013), "The ideological campaign to spread democracy around the world must be stopped. Instead, there should be a commitment to the promotion of a new global order based on the exercise of the right of ethnic groups and nations to self-determination in politically autonomous entities, and to the true version of democracy: people's rule." The most common response is that we in America should take time to fix our own backyard before we venture out into someone else's.

All that being said, it is the policy of the U.S. Department of State to promote democracy as a means to achieve security, stability, and prosperity for the entire world. The commitment to this foreign policy seems to overshadow our domestic issues. Our elected leaders are more concerned with controlling the rest of the world versus the concerns of their own fellow citizens. This isn't practical, particularly at this historical time where we wrestle with the fundamental values of religious freedom (Muslims), a living wage for all workers, and healthcare. It's extremely difficult for one to teach a concept they haven't mastered.

As a parent I have been humbled by the inability to influence and change the opinions and behavior of my own children. As they grew older, my threats of punishment lost their verve. In foreign policy we don't have the advantage of dealing with children. We have to remember that we are dealing with adults, people who have their own philosophies, experiences, and culture. Implanting our thoughts and beliefs within their hearts and mind is virtually impossible. I would fall back on the solution I used to deal with my children. I lead by example.

YOU HAVE A VOICE

The Vote, Voting, and Not Voting

The Vote, Voting, and Not Voting

De Tocqueville wrote, "In the English aristocracy the good of the poor has often been sacrificed to that of the rich, the rights of the greatest number to the privilege of some resulting in extreme fortunes. Those of aristocracy tend, on the contrary, to monopolize wealth and power in the hands of the few because aristocracy always forms a minority."

In the United States and other democratic societies, the only aspect in which all men and women can exercise their voice equally is through their one vote. Voting is our ultimate defense against those who want to control us. We have the power to take away their influence. Presently there are numerous issues of importance that require us now more than ever to wake up and vote. There are the never ending attacks on the Affordable Care Act, the resistance to raising the minimum wage, efforts on protecting the environment, the decisions on whether we remain the world's police, the policy of our local police, the future of education, the cost of education, and the preservation of Social Security. To fully understand the need and the obligation for all the citizens of this nation to vote we must look at the history of the vote in America.

The History of the Vote in the United States

Although most Americans take voting for granted, it's something that we should never take lightly. The right to vote has been fought for from the time the forefathers of this country wrote the Declaration of Independence. Believe it or not, in 1776 the privilege to vote was reserved only for white Protestant men who owned property or paid a specified amount in taxes. Needless to say, African-Americans were not included. The U.S. Constitution, ratified in 1788, did not detail who was eligible to vote. Without a specific federal law each state has the discretion to establish the qualifications for suffrage or the right to vote.

It wasn't until 1790, when the religious requirement was eliminated: that Catholics, Jews, and Quakers were permitted to vote in most states. Free African-Americans were able to vote in six states, Maryland, Massachusetts, New York, North Carolina, Pennsylvania, and Vermont.

A few years later in 1792, New Hampshire eliminated the property requirements for white men. White women property owners in New Jersey were enfranchised from 1797 until 1807 when the Assembly passed a law to clarify the right to vote to "all inhabitants." The vague wording of the law could have allowed slaves and aliens the right to vote. Hence this was corrected and suffrage was then limited to free white males.

Early in the 18th century, the country was young and growing with immigrants who wanted to register to vote. Several things stood in their way. There were restrictions among the states that excluded paupers and felons and literacy tests. To add to those limitations, there were long residency requirements imposed. Consequently, Asians immigrants were not allowed to vote. Mexicans who were living in the territory now known as Arizona, California, New Mexico, Texas, and Nevada were declared American citizens but they were not granted the right to vote. They did not fulfill the property requirements and they failed the English proficiency and literacy. If those reasons weren't enough, violence and intimidation also limited the right to vote.

The 1857 landmark decision by the Supreme Court in the Dred Scott vs. Sanford case ruled that African-Americans were not citizens; therefore they had no right to vote. The following year in an address to Congress, Abraham Lincoln, said, *"A house divided against itself cannot stand. I believe this government cannot endure, permanently, half slave and half free. I do not expect the Union to be dissolved... It will become one thing, or all the other."* In 1860, Lincoln was elected president. The South seceded and the Civil War began. The Union prevailed and the Thirteenth Amendment abolishing slavery was ratified on December 6, 1865. The Civil Rights Act of 1866 granted the newly freed slaves with citizenship stating:

> That all persons born in the United States and not subject to any foreign power, excluding Indians not taxed, are hereby declared to be citizens of the United States; and such citizens, of every race and color, without regard to any previous condition of slavery or involuntary servitude,

except as a punishment for crime whereof the party shall have been duly convicted, shall have the same right, in every State and Territory in the United States.

At last slavery had come to an end, black people were emancipated. Except freedom wasn't enough, animals are free. You must have a voice in rules and laws that govern your life as a citizen. Frederick Douglass articulated it saying:

> "It is said that we are ignorant; admit it. But if we know enough to be hung, we know enough to vote. If the Negro knows enough to pay taxes to support government, he knows enough to vote; taxation and representation should go together. If he knows enough to shoulder a musket and fight for the flag for the government, he knows enough to vote ....What I ask for the Negro is not benevolence, not pity, not sympathy, but simply justice."

The Fifteenth Amendment giving African-American men the right to vote was adopted into the Constitution on March 30, 1870. It read; "The rights of citizens of the United States to vote shall not be denied or abridged by the United States or any state on the account of race, color, or previous condition of servitude."

For every law instated to grant and protect the right to vote another was passed to get around it. In 1882, the Chinese Exclusion Act restricted Chinese immigration and excluded the Chinese from becoming citizens and gaining the right to vote. Needless to say, a long laundry list of discriminatory methods, including the Grandfather clause, poll taxes, and literacy tests were used, not to mention violence, particularly in the South, to prevent African Americans from voting.

American women were finally granted the right to vote in the 19th Amendment in 1920 after a long hard-fought battle for women's suffrage that had lasted for over 70 years. The timing was most likely due to the irony of the fight for democracy in World War I. Opponents against women voting had argued that it would cause problems in families, that it would blur the separation between masculinity and femininity, and would degrade women by exposing them to the corruptness of politics. It's hard to believe that this country denied women the right to vote for more than 140 years after the Declaration of Independence.

In 1924, Congress passed the Indian Citizenship Act that declared all non-citizen Native Americans born in the United States were indeed full citizens. However, the privileges of citizenship were governed by state law and they were still denied the right to vote in many states. It wasn't until the 1940s that state laws denying Native Americans the right to vote were finally overturned and the Chinese living in American were eligible to become citizens and vote. The timing of this was probably related to China being an ally in World War II.

After fighting and serving for their country in World War II, African-American veterans demanded the right to vote that was consistently being denied in the South. Blacks that attempted to cast a ballot were forced to leave by gun-point or beaten, some were even killed. In 1947, Truman, bothered by the manner in which black veterans were being treated established the President's Committee on Civil Rights to strengthen and protect the civil rights of American citizens. It was a nice gesture but it wasn't effective. However, in 1952, first-generation Japanese Americans were recognized as citizens and given the right to vote.

Ten years after the executive order by Truman, only 20 percent of African Americans were registered to vote. On May 17, 1957, The Prayer Pilgrimage for Freedom, organized by A. Philip Randolph and a number of other national civil rights leaders, took place on the steps of the Lincoln Memorial. Martin Luther King, Jr., as the last speaker, gave his first speech to a national audience urging the President and Congress to "Give us the Ballot:"

> "All types of conniving methods are still being used to prevent Negroes from becoming registered voters. The denial of this sacred right is a tragic betrayal of the highest mandates of our democratic tradition. And so our most urgent request to the president of the United States and every member of Congress is to give us the right to vote.

Give us the ballot, and we will no longer have to worry the federal government about our basic rights.

Give us the ballot, and we will no longer plead to the federal government for passage of an anti-lynching law; we will by the power of our vote write the law on the statute books of the South and bring an end to the dastardly acts of the hooded perpetrators of violence.

Give us the ballot and we will transform the salient misdeeds of bloodthirsty mobs into the calculated good deeds of orderly citizens.

Give us the ballot, and we will fill our legislative halls with men of goodwill and send to the sacred halls of Congress men who will not sign a "Southern Manifesto" because of their devotion to the manifesto of justice.

Give us the ballot, and we will place judges on the benches of the South who will do justly and love mercy, and we will place at the head of the southern states governors who will, who have felt not only the tang of the human, but the glow of the Divine.

Give us the ballot, and we will quietly and nonviolently, without rancor or bitterness, implement the Supreme Court's decision of May seventeenth, 1954."

Introduced under Eisenhower, the 1957 Civil Rights Act was to ensure that all African Americans would be able to exercise their right to vote. The U.S. Attorney General was authorized to file suits on behalf of those who were denied their right to vote. The bill had loopholes and only served to escalate the pushback in Southern states to prevent blacks from voting. Churches and schools were being bombed to intimidate African Americans from exercising their rights. To protect Mexican and Black voters at the polls, Eisenhower responded with the 1960 Civil Rights Act, which brought forth penalties to be charged against anyone who obstructed another's ability to register to vote or cast their vote. Subsequently, only an additional 3 percent of African Americans were added to electoral rolls from the passage of both civil rights acts.

The Battle for the Ballot

"America will never be destroyed from the outside. If we falter and lose our freedoms, it will be because we destroyed ourselves." ~ Abraham Lincoln

Most of us think that the Civil War in this country ended in 1865, except for all intents and purposes it raged on for another 100 years and in some ways continues to be fought. The rights established in the 13th, 14th and 15th Amendments of the Constitution after the Civil War had never been enforced. Halfway into the 20th century, Southern states were still using literacy tests and poll taxes to keep Blacks from voting. It was the Civil Rights Movement with its protests, demonstrations, and law suits, met with violence and retaliation that stirred American political leaders to act, or possibly it was the embarrassment on the international stage of the questionable democracy we practiced at home. President Kennedy initially proposed, and then President Johnson passed, The Civil Rights Act of 1964, banning discrimination on the basis of race, national origin, gender, or religion in voting, employment, schools, and in public areas.

Southern states refused to accept defeat, specifically because of the large populations of blacks who could affect the results of an election. African American voters were blocked and battered to keep them from registering and casting their vote. After a contentious seven-week voter registration drive in Alabama without adding one new registrant, Martin Luther King, Jr. led a group of demonstrators on a voting rights march from Selma to Montgomery, Alabama in March of 1965. They were viciously attacked by state troopers in the first two attempts. The brutal incident of Bloody Sunday was broadcast around the world prompting President Johnson to call for comprehensive voting rights legislation. The 1965 Voting Rights Act, introduced during the successful march to Montgomery, prohibited any election practice that denies the right to vote to citizens on the basis of race, poll taxes, and literacy tests. Federal examiners were sent to register black voters in seven Southern states. In a year's time 450,000 African American were registered in the South.

Section Five of the 1965 Voting Rights Act was designated to ensure that the changes in the election practices in each jurisdiction were determined to be favorable and would not have a discriminatory effect. This requirement was enacted as temporary legislation, applicable to certain states, and would expire in five years. The states affected would be the ones where less than 50 percent of eligible voters were registered and where less than 50 percent of those of voting age voted in the preceding presidential election.

Historically, the voting age in the United States had been 21 years, but from the time of World War II up to the Vietnam War this was a subject for much debate. In response to the slogan, "Old enough to fight, Old enough to vote," President Roosevelt lowered the voting age from 21- to 18 years. President Eisenhower in his 1954 State of the Union address affirmed, "For years our citizens between the ages of 18 and 21 have, in time of peril, been summoned to fight for America. They should participate in the political process that produces this fateful summons." During the Vietnam War with so many young men dying, youths protested the hypocrisy of being drafted into the war without the right to vote. When the 1965 Voting Rights Act was extended and amended in 1970 with discrimination still an issue, one additional provision lowered the voting age in federal, state, and local elections to 18 years. The 26th Amendment prohibited the states and federal government from denying anyone 18 years or older the right to vote.

Five years later in 1975, it was determined that the special provisions to limit discrimination in Section Five of the Voting Rights Act were still necessary and it was renewed. The voting act was also broadened with Section 203 in 1975 to include jurisdictions that had 'English only' ballots to protect language minorities and then extended another seven years. In 1982, Section 5 was extended for 25 years, and Section 203 due to expire in 1992 was extended for another 15 years, and then again for another 25 years in 2006.

Another debated topic that leads to the disenfranchisement of voters is the conviction of a felony. Early democracies in Greece disenfranchised persons who were convicted of felony crimes as part of their punishment, a civil death, where they were stripped of all their civil rights. In the Fourth Amendment of the U.S. Constitution, States were given the right to determine their own rules for disenfranchisement for criminals. As a result, the rule for disenfranchisement varies greatly among the states. Only Maine and Vermont have no restrictions with felons never losing their right to vote. Felons in Florida, Iowa, and Virginia are permanently disenfranchised. Objections to disenfranchisement say that it is antidemocratic, and that the correctional system is deemed to rehabilitate those who have paid their debt to society. Most other democracies around the world give ex-offenders the same voting rights as their other citizens.

The concern is that these disenfranchisement laws disproportionately affect minorities, as they are more likely to be arrested, convicted, and consequently denied the right to vote. Data compiled by *The Sentencing Project* show an estimated 5.85 million felons were prevented from voting in the 2012 election as a result of the combined state felony disenfranchisement laws, increasing the number of 1.2 million in 1976. This number is 2.5 percent of all potential voters and 8 percent of African American potential voters. Three million of those disenfranchised live in six Southern states, Alabama, Florida, Kentucky, Mississippi, Tennessee, and Virginia. Florida has the highest number of disenfranchised with 1.5 million, rendering 23 percent of Blacks there unable to vote. Virginia is the next highest with 20 percent of Blacks living there without the right to vote.

The injustice is that after all the battles for the right to vote, all the lives that were sacrificed by poor black and white males and females, Catholics and Jews, immigrants, Asians, Native Americans, and Mexicans, most of us don't even bother to exercise that right. Sadly, in states and cities all across the United States, we the people aren't using our power as voters to improve the problems that most concern us. The biggest question is why do we as voters, with a median household income of $51,939, choose the very wealthy to represent us and our interests. Why would a relatively poor state like Tennessee would choose a billionaire governor to represent them? How can Donald Trump be a front runner in the 2016 Republican Primary? The poor and the rich have completely different needs and requirements from the government. The poor want to share the wealth and the rich want to keep it all.

State of the Voter

The historic view of how vigorously the right to vote has been fought and contested demonstrates how meaningful and significant voting is in the United States. The historic view has also shown that no American should take that right for granted and abstain from voting, not white men who don't own property, women, black people, Asians, Latinos, Native Americans, or young people. We owe a debt to those who have sacrificed their time, energy, and even lives for us all to have that right. We all have interests to protect and our voice is our vote. Now we must ask: How are we exercising our civic responsibility?

Numbers from the Statistic Brain Research Institute are:

- Total of Americans eligible to vote   218,959,000

- Total of Americans registered to vote   146,311,000

- Registered Americans who voted in the 2012 Presidential election 57.5 percent

Demographic data of voters shows:

Male	69.1
Female	72.8
White	73.5
Black	69.7
Asian	55.3
Latino	59.4

- Voter participation increases with age

- The higher the education level, the higher the voter participation.

- Home owners vote at a higher percentage than renters.

- Voter participation grows higher with income up to $100,000.

The voting rates for the presidential election of 2012 were an upward blip on a downward pattern. The voter rates in the 2014 Congressional election were well below par. Only 41.9 percent of those registered voted. Census data of voters by race and ethnicity show: Whites at 45.8 percent, Blacks at 40.6 percent, and Hispanics at 27.0 percent. Less than 25 percent of adults in the 18 – 34 age range participated. Census data collected from 1978 – 2014 show voter rates have continued to fall over the years. Statistical data shows that there is more participation during the years of a presidential election. The simple truth is it's not enough to vote for the president we desire for change, we also have to vote in midterm elections for a Congress that won't tie his hands and sit on their own.

The United States voter turnout is characterized as "dismal" when compared to other democratic states. Of the countries counted by the Organization for Economic Cooperation and Development, the U.S. ranked 31st out of 34 countries. The inconsistency and the irony in the state of voters in the United States is in view of the fact that we have touted democracy all over the world, and have spilled much blood in its name, yet as a people we neglect to practice what we preach. Democracy is not a theory it's an action, it can't function properly when the majority of eligible voters fail to cast a ballot.

There really are no excuses for not voting due to mail-in ballots, absentee ballots, and early voting opportunities. Still, there are many reasons non-voters have for their lack of participation. A 2012 poll by *USA Today* found that 59 percent of non-voters were frustrated by the fact that "nothing ever gets done" in government, 54 percent mentioned corruption, 42 percent blamed the lack of contrast between the Republicans and Democrats, and 37 percent felt that politics doesn't make much difference in their lives. While most of us don't believe that the government works to benefit us all (80 percent), voting is the only recourse we have in choosing a government that will work for the betterment of the middle- and lower classes.

I've heard the phrase "take our country back" on many occasions in the last seven years without the clarification of whom it is to be taken back from. Without saying where this phrase may have been directed, I would like to agree with those who say our democracy has been hijacked by corporations and donors with large caches of dollars to purchase candidates to do their bidding. There is a cornucopia of important issues at the forefront for this country, foreign policy and the policing of foreign nations, domestic police brutality, gun control, the future of Social Security, healthcare, raising the minimum wage, affordable housing, high quality clean water, education, college costs and student loans. The voting booth is where we can best address these issues.

Then there is the issue of gerrymandering, where districts are cut and divided with political boundaries that give one party a numeric advantage over the opposing party. Gerrymandering is used as a tool to disenfranchise voters, particularly minority voters. Despite comprising the majority population in quite a few counties and Congressional districts, African Americans and Latinos are not being elected. Districts can be cut to prevent the majority from ruling. Texas, described as a non-voting state, is one of the more ethnically diverse states in the nation. Yet it has a white Republican governor, white Republican senators, and majority white and Republican elected office holders. This is a result of gerrymandered districts with low Latino turnout included with high-voting Republicans. Sam Wang wrote an opinion piece in the New York Time saying, "Politicians, especially Republicans facing demographic and ideological changes in the electorate, use redistricting to cling to power. It's up to us to take control of the process, slay the gerrymander, and put the people back in charge of what is, after all, our House."

The United States will continue to become more diverse as the years go on, and this diverse population should participate in the political process, not only as voters but as candidates as well. I'm weary of the old names and faces. We need fresh faces and new ideas. None of that can be attained until we make our voices heard from the ballot box. The National Voter Registration Act requires all states to permit mail-in voter registration, registration services at unemployment offices, at the Department of Motor Vehicles, and other state agencies.

"Politicians are like diapers. The both need changing regularly and for the same reason."

~Mark Twain

kan_khampanya / Shutterstock.com

Capitalism

"The end of democracy and the defeat of the American revolution will occur when government falls into the hands of lending institutions and moneyed corporations."
~Thomas Jefferson, 1816

Capitalism

The United States is more often described as a capitalistic society than a democratic one, and the success of this country is most attributed to capitalism than its commitment to democracy. The coexistence of these two concepts is a prime example of the unity of opposites. "Democracy seeks greater equality, while capitalism requires inequality. Democracy seeks restraint and prudence, while capitalism requires unrestrained action and self-interest (Curran, 2016)." So what exactly is capitalism? Merriam-Webster defines it as an economic system characterized by private or corporate ownership of capital goods, by investments that are determined by private decision, and by prices, production, and the distribution of goods that are determined mainly by competition in a free market. The Oxford dictionary puts it simpler: An economic and political system in which a country's trade and industry are controlled by private owners for profit, rather than by the state.

The notion of capitalism is that wealth is used to create more wealth. Thus, historically those who were landowners and those who were moneylenders were the only ones to accumulate wealth. That's how it was before the Civil War. Then the Industrial Revolution changed the world. The rural farming communities of America became industrial urban cities. Making things in the home with hand tools and basic machines was then shifted to factories and mass production. Larger and larger amounts of goods were being factory-produced. A national economy was created. More banks were spawned along with industrial financiers, and the New York Stock Exchange was established. There was a wider distribution of wealth creating middle and upper classes, however, the poor and working class suffered under low wages and hazardous working conditions. So was the birth of industrial capitalism and the struggle between the employer and the worker in the share of profits.

Adam Smith, author of *Wealth in Nations* (1759), gave this theory:
> Every man is rich or poor according to the degree in which he can afford to enjoy the necessaries, conveniences, and amusements of human life. But after the division of labour has once thoroughly taken place, it is but a very small part of these with which a man's own labour can supply him. The far greater part of them he must derive from the labour of other people, and he must be rich or poor according to the quantity of that labour which he can command, or which he can afford to purchase.
> The rich only select from the heap that which is most precious and agreeable. They consume little more than the poor, and in spite of their natural selfishness and rapacity, though they mean only their own convenience, though the sole end which they propose from the labors of all the thousands whom they employ, be the gratification of their own vain and insatiable desires, they divide with the poor the produce of all their improvements. They are led by an *invisible hand* to make nearly the same distribution of the necessaries of life, which would have been made, had the earth been divided into equal portions among all its inhabitants, and thus without intending it, without knowing it, advance the interest of the society, and afford means to the multiplication of the species.

The Downside of Capitalism

Capitalism's first epic failure in the United States was manifested in the Great Depression. With a crisis of grand proportions there was plenty of blame to go around; however, the vast uneven distribution of wealth between the rich and the poor probably bore the brunt of it. It was eloquently summed up in the Transcript of the Copy of Great Depression/

New Deal:
> The problem with American capitalism in the 1930s was that there was too much of everything! Why?! Too much supply, not enough demand. Too many automobiles, and not enough workers who could afford to buy them. Too much cotton, too much corn, too much pork, too much beef, too much wheat, and not enough buyers able to pay a price that made the crops worth harvesting. Too many workers needing jobs, and not enough employers to hire them.

Anna Rochester, a labor reformer wrote about these years, *"The flaunting extravagance of the new industrial ruler and their Wall Street brothers covered depths of mass poverty and suffering. Both the crowded tenements and scattered farms were cruelly exploited in this onward march of capitalism."* Workers discovered they had no leverage to protest the paltry wages, miserable working conditions, and the demand for longer work days. They had no choice except to form unions. Local unions and then national labor unions were organized to help balance the power of employers in the struggle for higher wages, worker benefits, and improved working conditions.

Those with money and means sometimes forget that for the economy to grow and the rules of supply and demand to operate properly, the wealth must be shared. Without supplying workers with decent salaries demand for goods dries up. We can't spend that which we don't have. This predicament was temporarily resolved with the new concept of buying-on time or credit installments. Convinced that we needed the new technologies of radios, electric appliances, and cars to survive, we bought them all doing our best to make the payments. The manufacturers reaped huge profits which they did not share with the workers, increasing the growing disparity between the wealthy and the working classes. A Brookings Institution study found that in 1929 the very wealthy (the top 0.1 percent of Americans) had a combined income equal to the bottom 42.0 percent. That same wealthy class in 1929 controlled 34 percent of all bank savings, while 80 percent of Americans had no savings at all.

"By the end of the 1920s, about 60 percent of cars and 80 percent of radios were purchased on credit installments. Between 1925 and 1929, the total amount of outstanding installment credit more than doubled from $1.4 billion to around $3 billion." Nevertheless, credit is not income. Many, if not most, had purchased items that they could not have normally afforded. Their monthly expenses were increased with installment payments eliminating disposable income and digging them deeper in debt. The labor union movement did not yet have the power to demand higher wages and the cheap labor had produced a glut in the supply of goods. The economy was off kilter and headed for collapse.

The Stock Market crashed on October 29, 1929 triggering the Great Depression. In Franklin D. Roosevelt's acceptance of the Democratic nomination for president he offered a solution to the economic crisis: the New Deal. *"Throughout the nation men and women, forgotten in the political philosophy of the Government, look to us here for guidance and for more equitable opportunity to share in the distribution of national wealth... I pledge myself to a new deal for the American people. This is more than a political campaign. It is a call to arms."*

The New Deal became the hand-up to the working class while challenging the philosophy of the "invisible hand." Frances Perkins Wilson, President Roosevelt's U.S. Secretary of Labor, was instrumental in the implementation of the Social Security Act which established unemployment benefits, pensions, and welfare for the handicapped and children in need without a father in the home. Through the Fair Labor Standards Act she established the first minimum wage, defined the standard forty-hour work week, overtime laws, and child labor laws. Through the Wagner Act government policies for working with labor unions were drawn up guaranteeing workers the right to collective bargaining which helped strengthen the unions and alleviate strikes. Union membership grew dramatically comprising the American Federation of Labor.

Bank failures paid a significant role in the decline of the economy as well, more than 5000 failed during the Depression. Thus began the dreaded interference by government through federal regulations on banking and the stock market. Congress passed the Banking Act of 1933, also known as the Glass-Steagall Act, to remedy the previous abuses. Banks would be permitted to take deposits and make loans and brokerage firms would be allowed to underwrite and sell securities. Neither of these businesses could do both due to conflicts of interests and added risks to now insured deposits. The Federal Reserve created the Federal Deposit Insurance Corporation (FDIC) to insure deposits and had the assignment to regulate national banks.

Regulations were put in place to eliminate monopolies, keep prices in check, and to control dangers. These additional regulations included the railroads, telephones, utilities, and energy suppliers. The government put in price supports, subsidized highways, and supplied federal loans. As to the issue of redistributing the wealth, President Roosevelt established a corporate income tax and instituted the Wealth Tax Act. The bill called for an income tax of 79 percent on incomes over $5 million. That tax bracket included one man, John D. Rockefeller. The real game changer was the war effort in World War II.

The Golden Age of Capitalism

The postwar economic boom, which some refer to the Golden Age of Capitalism and others as the not so Golden Age of Capitalism, began in 1945 after World War II and lasted until the mid-1970s. Industrial production to supply the war effort started the dynamic growth in the economy. Factories were amped up and employing higher numbers of workers. This was a unique time when growing technology actually created jobs instead of eliminating them. The U.S. labor force was fully employed. It was a mutually beneficial situation between the employers and employees that created a robust economy fed on the increased income and investment. Higher productivity was needed domestically and for export.

The boon was shared by all as a result of the strength of labor unions during these years; one-third of the workforce belonged to a union. A significant amount of the growth was seen among low-income farmers migrating to cities for the lucrative factory jobs. High productivity and huge profits were shared with workers in higher wages. These years marked the highest degree of income equality ever measured. The middle-class grew as did their demand for the mass-produced goods. Things were good for the most part, despite the fact that minorities and women were basically left out with no political equity and fewer economic opportunities.

As the economy thrived the economic controls that were put in place to deal with the Great Depression were removed and the tax rates were cut. Opponents to the welfare-state capitalists began their attack to reverse the New Deal; they demonized unions, socialists, and communists. They also began to demonize the government, blaming it as the cause of social ills, adding that the cure to those ills called for the elimination of the government's intrusion on individual freedoms. These intrusions were the New Deal laws and regulations.

The Golden Age of Capitalism ended in the early 1970s, about the same time as the Vietnam War. There was an energy shortage or oil shortage and the price of gas more than tripled, choking off the American economy that was already suffering from globalization. Manufacturing competition from Europe and Japan reduced the power of American companies to raise prices. This led to declines in profits and productivity and more rises in inflation and unemployment. Companies resorted to layoffs to cut costs. This combination of 11 percent inflation coupled with 9 percent unemployment and a lagging economy was called "stagflation." The stock market crashed again losing 48 percent of its value from 1973 into 1974 leading the nation into a recession.

President Nixon's reaction to the stifling inflation was to impose wage and price controls. After he resigned without the controls making any difference, his successor Gerald Ford, believing in less government, thought deregulation was the answer to curb inflation. Despite opposition from labor unions he convinced Congress to partially deregulate oil and gas, and the railroads. Carter completed the deregulation of oil, natural gas, and the railroads, and added the deregulation of the airlines, transportation, and savings and loans.

The 1970s started a new era of fewer jobs, not only because of more women in the workforce, the growing number of immigrants, and computers and automation, but because of the outsourcing of jobs for cheaper labor. Unions came up against stronger resistance in their negotiations with companies starting to replace striking workers and firing union organizers.

Unfettered Capitalism and the Trickle-Down Economics

Ronald Reagan's philosophy of democracy is capitalism, and the idea that government intervention threatens our individual freedoms, ignited a surge in capitalism with reductions in the New Deal. He won the election in 1980 promising to restore the country to prosperity by getting "the government off the backs of the American people." He said there were too many taxes, too much government spending, and too many regulations. In other words, the wealthy were tired of all the taxes, why was so much being spent on programs for the poor, and the regulations are keeping companies from making a killing. His solution was called the trickle-down theory. Tax rates for the rich were drastically lowered, social programs were cut, and regulations to hold companies accountable to the consumer, the worker, and the environment were removed.

Contrary to Roosevelt's trickle-up policy of taxing businesses and the wealthy to pay for social spending that benefited the disadvantaged without increasing the deficit, Reagan distributed the benefits at the top while slashing domestic programs that provided assistance to the poor. Military spending knew no bounds without consideration of creating deficits; they actually tripled under his leadership. The burden of federal taxation was shifted from the corporation to the individual and from the upper-class wealthy to the middle-class. Supposedly, the tax cuts for the wealthy would allow them to invest in new ventures that would create more jobs and higher wages for those less fortunate.

Weakening the unions and their bargaining power would also leave business and the wealthy with more money in their pockets. A prime example was Reagan breaking the air traffic controllers union with the firing of 11,345 controllers, invoking the law that striking government employees forfeit their jobs. His actions gave credence to the legal right of private employers to use their own discretion to both hire and discharge workers.

The recession seemed to abate, at least for those at the top of the food chain, with the start of another bull market with the same exuberance of the 1920s. Not surprising, because like a time machine it took the country back fifty years to the times where the gap between the wealthy and the workers widened with the uneven distribution of benefits. Similar to the roaring twenties, some remember the eighties as a time of great prosperity where others saw it as years of want. New words were introduced into our vocabulary, homeless, shelters, government butter, and government cheese. The rise in wages came to a screeching halt. The good-paying blue-collar manufacturing jobs that sustained the middle-class quickly headed overseas.

So began the process of the "financialization" of the United States economy (Foroohar, 2016). The financial market dominates and its interests dominate over the industrial and agricultural economies. The rich no longer build factories and employ people. Greta Krippner of the University of Michigan explained that financialization is merely "a pattern of accumulation in which profit making occurs increasingly through financial channels rather than trade and commodity production." Simply put by Steve Denning in *Forbes* magazine; "The focus by elites of "making money out of money" rather than making goods and services…" Unfortunately this has only increased the wealth for the very few. During the Reagan years the top 20 percent of American households had income increases of 14 percent while the bottom 20 percent had their income decrease by 24 percent. The income level for the 60 percent in the middle never moved.

Financialization and deregulation under Reagan allowed Savings and Loans to expand outside of making home mortgages into commercial real estate speculation. The once conservative and fiscally responsible industry was mismanaged, became corrupt, and then insolvent. More than 1000 of the S&Ls collapsed. The government clean-up ultimately led to a taxpayer bailout. Rep. Jim Leach (R-Iowa), chairman of the House Banking Committee gave the final assessment of the S&L industry from the General Accounting Office:

> "The bad news in this report is that the cost of the failure of many thrift institutions, with interest, approaches a half trillion dollars and that taxpayer accountability due to bonds issued will continue through the year 2030," he said. "The good news is that America's financial institutions today are stronger and sounder than in many years, that the banks and savings and loan insurance funds are positively capitalized and that prudent regulation is in place."

The Age of Supercapitalism

In Robert Reich's book titled *Supercapitalism* he notes, *Capitalism and democracy seemed to be working in such remarkable tandem that they come to be seen as one system.*" More accurately capitalism has been strengthened by the association and democracy has been weakened. Beginning with Reagan, big businesses supported the Republican Party in return for their promotion of a pro-business agenda. It worked out better than they could have hoped. For the richest the tax rate was decreased from 91 percent to 35 percent while the taxes for Social Security and Medicare from paychecks were increased. With that result, more and more money continues to flow into politics. Democrats and Republicans are so concerned with attracting money that they all cater to big business. Companies now have more political power than citizens. They influence the political process through donations and campaign contributions. They hire lobbyists. The working class are unable to purchase this influence. Legislation goes to the highest bidder. The biggest problem is the reality that you can't be a legitimate contender running for a political office without a small fortune at your disposal.

Somehow like unruly children, we never seem to learn from our mistakes. In 1999, at the request of big banks, Congress passed the Gramm-Leach-Bliley Act to repeal two provisions of the Glass-Steagall Act that restricted affiliations between banks and security firms. Up to this point there had hardly been any bank failures since 1933; the law was working effectively. The Bank Holding Company Act was amended to allow affiliations between financial services companies, which included banks, securities firms, and insurance companies.

    Looking at the eight years that followed was almost like a flash back to the 1920s collapse. We the people can't afford the higher cost of homes and cars. There is less disposable income to fuel the mammoth machine of our economy that runs on the gains of Wall Street and the financial markets. When we don't have the money they loan it to us and sell the bad debt. That brought us to the familiar combination of rising debts coupled with low or stagnate wages for the poor and middle-class. Banks were playing fast and loose with the free-hand they were given. They made subprime and illegal loans and sold them as securities to unsuspecting customers. This created a huge financial bubble that burst in 2008 as borrowers defaulted and lenders defaulted taking the rest of the economy out with them.

    CEOs rushed to Washington begging for a trillion dollars of assistance, government welfare, wanting to be subsidized but remain private entities. The government's answer to them, The Great Recession, the growing foreclosures, and increasing unemployment, was tax-payer financed bail-outs for banks and big business, and to cut back on social programs. The Troubled Asset Relied Program (TARP), established by Bush and Congress, contained $787 billion to buy troubled assets from banks. The economic stimulus for low- and middle-income families was a $600 tax rebate. There were no New Deal programs passed, no federal jobs created, and social welfare spending was rolled back.

    Historically, Americans are believers of "no taxation without representation." This notion was at the root of the American Revolution. The question is what do we think about all the representation without taxation for corporations? The advocacy group **Citizens for Tax Justice** released a report naming Fortune 500 companies that don't pay any taxes. The list included CBS, General Electric, Interpublic Group, JetBlue

Airways, Mattel, Owens Corning, PG&E, Pepco Holdings, Priceline.com, Prudential Financial, Qualcomm, Ryder System, Time Warner, Weyerhaeuser and Xerox. As a whole, the 15 companies paid no federal income tax on $23 billion in profits in 2014, and they paid almost no federal income tax on $107 billion in profits during the past five years. All but two received federal tax rebates in 2014. The list of companies that pay no income tax is much longer including Goodyear, Tyco International, Royal Caribbean, and Wynn Resorts.

The wages for the majority of workers have been stagnant for over 30 years. At the same time profits have grown in an upward trajectory. The unions, the workers best defense in the battle with capitalism, have been mortally wounded. Socialism and communism are not viable alternatives. Robert Reich wrote, "*Genuine reform will occur only if and when most citizens demand it. In order for that to happen the public must understand several truths about the present system that are now obscured. The most effective thing reformers can do is reduce the effects of corporate money on politics and enhance the voices of citizens.*"

In an ideal world we wouldn't need regulation. CEOs would do the right thing if left to their own devices, except this is the real world. We make laws not to impose on those who do the right thing but to counteract those that don't. We don't say get rid of speed limits just because most people drive at safe levels.

a katz / Shutterstock.com

Income Inequality, Selfishness, and Greed

Income Inequality, Selfishness and Greed

"All politics is rich people screwing poor people. Poor people are too stupid to know they're just chess pieces in a game. All the poor white people, all the poor black people, all the Hispanics, they're all in the same boat." ~Charles Barkley

It sounds harsh but there's a lot of truth to it. One of the consequences of capitalism without regulation is widening income inequality. Income inequality is a rising dilemma economically, not only in this country but around the globe. According to the Organization for Economic Co-operation and Development, (OECD), the United States ranks the highest in wealth inequality among developed nations. Bernie Sanders speaks the truth when he says, "The issue of wealth and income inequality is the greatest moral issue of our time, it is the greatest economic issue of our time, and is the greatest political issue of our time." It is the very thing that threatens our precious democracy. I can't say I have much hope for any resolution on this situation when all of Congress is wealthy and motivated by their allegiance to the very rich (corporations included).

The Declaration of Independence, which says that all men have the right to life, liberty, and the pursuit of happiness, is based on egalitarian principles. That's what made America so attractive to the outside world. Even if you weren't born with a silver spoon in your mouth, it's possible through hard work to be able to buy one for yourself. The setback is that things have changed, the conditions that enabled the common man to improve his circumstances, education, income growth, and the ability to save, are being harder to attain. When the opportunity for social mobility are limited or almost non-existent that goes against the principles and creed that this country has been founded upon. When political favor shines on the very wealthy and disadvantages the poor the environment becomes more inegalitarian, marked by increased disparities in economic and social standing.

For those fortunate ones who may not understand what income inequality is; it's sometimes called economic inequality or wealth disparity, and is the difference in the economic status of individuals in a group, among various groups in a population, or among countries or regions of the world. Economic status is measured in several ways, by wealth, income, and consumption. Wealth is the value of your property and assets minus your debts. Income is the money you receive from work or investments. Consumption is the purchase of goods and/or services. Simply put income inequality is the gap between the rich and poor, or the difference between the haves and have-nots.

Income inequality dates back as far as the existence of mankind on earth. In ancient societies there have always been the aristocrats as the upper-class, the skilled workers and landowners as the middleclass, and the unskilled workers and slaves as the lower-class. In this common structure the wealth was distributed unequally. For the most part your birth dictates your economic status, although that's where the United States is supposed to be different. The American Dream is the thought that every US citizen has an equal opportunity to achieve success and prosper through hard work and determination regardless of where they were born or what class they were born into. In other words we have to play the game the best way we can with the cards we're dealt. Yet, it's becoming a lot harder with a stacked deck. The dream is becoming is just that, an idea very far from reality. It brings to mind the question Langston Hughes put forth in his poem, *"What happens to a dream deferred? Does it dry up like a raisin in the sun?"*

Historic Examples of Income Inequality

The wise words of George Santayana, *"Those who fail to learn from history are doomed to repeat it,"* continue to fall on deaf ears. There is no dearth of instances where the downfall of powerful empires is due to income inequality. One prime example is the Han Dynasty, one of the great Chinese Empires that ran from 206 BC to 220AD. A world power during its time, its organization was highly structured, not very different from those of more modern times with three social classes. Below the emperor at the top were the aristocracies, in the middle, skilled workers and farmers, and the bottom, unskilled workers and slaves. Once very successful, things began to fall apart as the rich landowners gained power and began to evade payment of taxes. That burden was shifted to the poor who had no opportunity to hold political positions. Tensions from the uneven distribution of wealth grew, civil wars were fought, and the dynasty fell apart.

Looking at the fall of the Gupta Dynasty in India it was basically the same thing. It had a huge and complex system of government. The price of frequent war is higher taxes on the people. Typically those with means have some power and they use it to protect their assets. This is exactly what the regional lords in Gupta did. As time went on they gained more power and increased their autonomy from the emperor, and refused to pay taxes. They became richer, the poor poorer and the unequal distribution of wealth caused civil war.

France made the same mistakes more than a thousand years later. More wars and high living by the nobles and clergy demanded more taxes. King Louis XIV made a deal with the nobles that he could raise taxes as long as he didn't tax them. This sounds familiar. The peasants paid most of the direct taxes while the bourgeois got exemptions. The gross wealth inequality started a revolution. The one thing common in each of these empires was the redistribution of money from the poor through regressive taxes and funneled to the rich.

How Did We Get Here and How Bad Is It?

Distribution of Household Income

The years following World War II and up to the 1970s were a period of substantial economic growth for the United Sates. The prosperity and income growth was shared proportionately on all rungs of the income ladder. The gap between the income spread didn't fluctuate. Earnings on the top, the middle, and the bottom all grew at a similar rate. Then there was a recession. Inflation or the prices of things was high and so was unemployment. This is when the fortunes of the middle- and lower-income began to move in a different direction than those with upper-income. It went from bad to worse when Ronald Reagan became president.

Ronald Reagan ushered in a time of antagonism for social programs and hostility towards labor unions, two key vehicles necessary for social mobility. So while he was slashing budgets for education, job training, employment programs, AFDC, and Medicaid, he was also slashing taxes for the rich from 80 percent down to 25 percent. Roosevelt's New Deal was practically undone. During the Depression, taxes were progressive, where the rich paid a higher rate to support programs that would put the country back on its feet. Reagan did the opposite during the recession; he cut the programs that assisted the middle and lower-income groups and gave all the benefits to the upper-income groups, effectively chopping the country off at the knees telling us that the wealth would trickle down.

Unsurprisingly, only shiggity rolls downhill, the boon to the wealthy wasn't shared. The minimum wage never changed, the rich shielded their money, and the government had given up the revenue needed to pay for domestic programs. The incomes for workers stagnated as the unions were weakened and CEOs starting demanding outrageous compensation and stock options. Reagan's policies only served to widen the gap between the rich and everybody else. Where Roosevelt had acted as a "Robin Hood," taking from the rich to give to the poor, Reagan was the epitome of a slumlord, ignoring the deteriorating conditions of his poor tenants.

Fast-forward to the 2000s and the jobless recovery under George W. Bush, and you find there has been a huge transfer of wealth from the middle- and lower-class workers to the richest people in America. This was a perfect example of income redistribution. It's seems to be an abomination to give to the poor, money should only be given to those who already have it. Whether the money flows to the top or the bottom, it's a redistribution of wealth, nonetheless.

Psst: Somebody Speak the Truth

What the Great Depression of the 1930s and the Great Recession in 2008 had in common was they were both preceded by sharp rises in income inequality. Housing bubbles burst and the financial markets nearly collapsed. Once the bailout stabilized the markets, the wealthy recuperated while the rest of the country battled unemployment and home foreclosures. I think the bulk of people tolerated the situation believing it would be temporary but with each passing year it seems that this is the new normal. The truth is, most people don't consider themselves among the unfortunate because they have cars, televisions, and cell phones. It is much harder to distinguish the poor because most of us have roofs over our heads and clothes on our backs, and food on the table, but we have no job security or golden parachute to catch us when we fall.

The consensus is that the United States has more wealth disparity and income inequality than any other major developed country on earth. This gap between the extremely wealthy and the rest of us is reminiscent of the Gilded Age of the late 1800s and roaring 1920s. By some statistics the top 1 percent has more wealth than the bottom 90 percent. In a research study from U.C. Berkley, from 2009 to 2012, the top 1 percent benefited from 95 percent of all income gains (Saez, 2013).

Wealth Is Even More Concentrated Than Income

Distribution of before-tax income, 2013

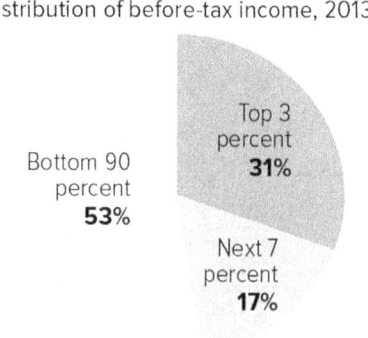

Bottom 90 percent **53%**

Top 3 percent **31%**

Next 7 percent **17%**

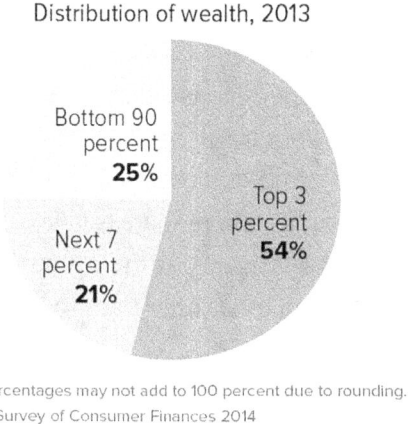

Distribution of wealth, 2013

Bottom 90 percent **25%**
Next 7 percent **21%**
Top 3 percent **54%**

Note: Percentages may not add to 100 percent due to rounding.
Source: Survey of Consumer Finances 2014

CENTER ON BUDGET AND POLICY PRIORITIES | CBPP.ORG

In the years after the 2008 financial crash, the rich have increased their wealth at a faster pace than ever while the standard of living for the rest of the population is declining. Between 2009 and 2013, 95 percent of all income gains went to the top 1 percent in the US. Half of the wealth in this country is held by 400 people.

During this 2016 election season, wealth disparity has become a political football. Even more worrisome is when Republicans start throwing around the words, income inequality, it must be really bad. President Obama's feelings about the disparity in wealth have not been a secret. He alluded to it in a lecture at Loyola in 1998, spoke about income injustice in a public radio interview as a state senator in 2001, and it was a hallmark in his 2012 re-election campaign. When he mentioned redistribution of wealth in his 2014 State of Union Address he was called a socialist, a fascist, and a communist. It's amazing how one man can be so many things to so many people. Obama's statements weren't an attack on capitalism, *"But if you're making more than $1 million a year, you can do a little more. This is not class envy. This is not class warfare. This is basic math—that's what this is."* The unfortunate truth is that his time in the White House is limited. The issue of income inequality will be here long after Barack Obama leaves office.

What are the Consequences?

The vast differences between the income and wealth of the rich, the waning middle-class, and the poor create significant problems for the national economy. The wealthy don't put much of their money back into the economy and the middle-class and poor don't have enough disposable income to spend that would grow the economy. Without increased taxes on the rich there aren't resources to improve infrastructure across the country, to reduce education costs, to provide healthcare and other important social services.

People probably don't believe it but the truth is; Democratic administrations have consistent records of sustained economic growth for all classes of people. Republican administrations tend to have policies that enrich the wealthy at the expense of the poor. The relentless commitment of conservatives to trim the fat from the poor by cutting social programs is more baffling than anything. The rich never suffer from the progress of the less fortunate. As said many times before, "let's lift all boats, not just the yachts."

Even though most of the blame for the Great Recession belonged to the banks, they were the one's chosen to be rescued. We were told they were too big to fail. Yet millions of American families lost their jobs and their homes in the aftermath and there wasn't a rush to come to their aid. That's the unfairness of our system that values corporations more than people, and shows more concern for those who have plenty than those who have little. Instead of making corrections and addressing the cause of inequity, policymakers increased the access for loans to low-income households to support spending, particularly home purchases. The borrowing of the middle-class skyrocketed creating a temporary boom for a while, but it's not sustainable. Income is not keeping up with the level of debt.

The most negative effect of income inequality and the problem with the growing gap is that more people are being pushed into poverty as the middle-class shrinks. With 70 percent of the U.S. economy coming from spending, it's the middle-class folks who keep the ball rolling. As their numbers shrink there are fewer people to buy the products. Suffering from flat wages, middle-income families sink deeper into debt trying to maintain their standard of living. The excess debt creates instability. In Thomas Piketty's book,

Capitalism in the 21st Century, he makes the point that no economic system can sustain the imbalance that we have and stay at equilibrium. America can't progress if its people don't progress. High income inequality is directly related to low economic growth.

The major vehicle for success in the United Sates is education, a college degree. Higher education correlates to higher earnings. The problem is that the costs of higher education have risen to the level where most people are priced out, their only option is burying themselves in student loans. Student loan debt is also becoming a drag on the national economy. High monthly payments delay or dismiss home purchases for first-time buyers. In essence, you're damned if you do, and damned if you don't. This is a part of the vicious cycle that keeps so many people at the low end of the totem pole. Still, if we don't make education a priority then we only further income inequality.

What can be done about it?

Emmanuel Saez, economist, and winner of the 2009 John Bates Clark Award, warns that income inequality will remain persistently high "unless drastic regulation and tax policy changes are implemented." What the president and many others have suggested in "redistribution" is taxing the very wealthy more and putting those resources back into the economy (Saez, 2010). The backlash from this suggestion is so intense, even by those who would not be affected, that you would have thought it meant going into rich people's home and robbing them of their money at gunpoint and giving it to undeserving poor people as a handout. The idea is to return the tax rate back where it was before the concentration of wealth took place. Thomas Piketty advises that the tax rate for the top 1 percent should return to a top margin of 80 percent. The revenue should be used to create jobs as FDR did to stimulate the economy instead of the super-rich continuing to use it to buy political influence to ignore the public demands for greater equality.

The truth is if we need more revenue to run the country for the benefit of everyone, then the solution lies with the people who have the most, they can spare the most. It's simple mathematics. The argument is whether the wealthy are paying their fair share. We have been told that you don't tax the wealthy or corporations because they are the creators of jobs. The fact is we the consumers, the 47 percent, or the 99 percent, are the job creators. We create the demand for supplies. We make corporations profitable not CEOs. Without us there is no economy. Better paying jobs need to be created and the people have to be educated to fill them. Tuition at public colleges and universities in the U.S. should be nominal if not free. Higher education should be available to everyone in the country regardless of their income level.

Democratic Senator Charles Shumer in a statement to the *Washington Post* said, "The focus has to be on how to get middle-class incomes up, rather than drive other people's income down." Where was this concept when employees were being laid-off, jobs outsourced, and wages held down? We need to get over the notion that we must protect the income of the wealthy, they do that job quite well by themselves. It's the worker that needs support now. Support for higher wages and respect for their right to collectively bargain. If we can't bring ourselves to tax the rich and wealthy corporations then we'll all have less. History will repeat itself again. We're all insane; we keep doing the same thing over and over and expecting a different result.

Selfishness and Greed

Income Inequality, Selfishness, and Greed

Is it human nature to be greedy? Are we like the dog that sees his reflection in the lake with the meat in his mouth and drops it to take the piece from his own reflection? Is it an American trait to be greedy? Is greed synonymous with ambition? Does greed foster selfishness? Why all the objections to raising the minimum wage? Why all the opposition against diluting the concentration of wealth? Have we bought into the Gordon Gekko philosophy from the movie "Wall Street," that "greed -- for the lack of a better word – is good. Greed is right. Greed works. Greed clarifies, cuts through, and captures the essence of the evolutionary spirit." In truth, there is nothing wrong with generating wealth; the issue is with the distribution of the profits.

When we think of greed, we think of investment bankers and fund managers on Wall Street who make their money off of money without real goods or services. It's driven by an insatiable desire for profit. Then there are the CEOs and senior top executive who think more of themselves and shareholders than they do about their employees who keep the company running. To increase profits they have practically eliminated provisions for health and retirement benefits, and held wages flat for decades. Meanwhile their compensation has gone up astronomically. Not to mention the elimination of every position that could be replaced by a computer or robot. A look at the earning numbers tells us that profits are up. If a worker contributes to the production, then they should share a fair portion of the earnings, but that's not happening.

There is an indelible line that we seem to be crossing between healthy ambition and rewarded success and outright diabolical greed. I would argue that most of us don't have a problem with a superstar being richly paid for his or her unique abilities. If you are able to fill stadiums and arenas and showcase your talents to millions, then you deserve to be paid millions of dollars. That is an ability that is rare and reserved to very few. As someone who has worked her whole life, I believe that compensation should be based on the EAR, Education/experience, Ability level, and Responsibility. What I don't understand is how a CEO or other upper-management can justify salaries at 1000 times of their workers. If Prince didn't come to his concert, there wouldn't have been a show, if Lebron doesn't play well, the team loses. If the factory workers don't show up at the job, nothing is produced. If the CEO doesn't come to the office for weeks, the beat goes on. So why are they valued so much more than the worker. His talent is to cut corners and increase shareholder value. I would think him valuable and worthy of great pay if he could do this while maintaining quality and not cutting his workers to the bone.

United States corporations spent $400 million in 2013 lobbying Congress to pass laws that favor them. That money would have been greatly appreciated by their employees. Evidently no price is too high to keep from paying a living wage. There are no shortages of politicians or executives weighing in on the minimum wage debate. However, it's virtually impossible to get a conversation going about the fairness of CEO and executive pay. Why is it that one man is barely worth $7.50 an hour or $15,600 in a year but another man working in the same company is worth $7,500 an hour or $15,600,000? The Federal Reserve is puzzled with low unemployment, low interest rates, and the lack of wage growth. Why can't we utter the words, corporate greed? Their earnings have skyrocketed. That money has to come from somewhere, namely higher prices and lower wages. Companies should pay higher wages or higher taxes.

Surprisingly, there are objections from the workforce about raising the minimum wage. More interesting is the average person's objections are not based on whether the wage is adequate to support one's self above the poverty level or whether someone deserves to be paid that much for flipping burgers, it's generally based on what that person's wages happen to be. If I'm a professional with three degrees barely making $22 an hour then it is somewhat of an insult to me for the person frying chicken to make almost as much as I do. The problem is that most of us are inadequately paid or underpaid for the services we render. Why do we hold up what someone makes in China as the standard to make us feel better when the companies can afford to pay better wages?

A 2011 study conducted by Paul Piff and Dacher Keltner and published in *Scientific American* found that as people climb the social ladder, their feelings of empathy and compassion for others declines. It's antithetical to what you might think. Naturally you might suppose that one who has less would tend to be more selfish than one who has abundance but their data contradicts that theory. Herein lies the problem with political leaders who have immense wealth making decisions that affect the poor and disadvantaged. The worker is not being heard with the unions being quieted, our voices are small in comparison to that of a corporation. It must be reiterated again and again that corporations are not people and should not have the equivalent rights as people to be represented in a democracy.

An important concern in the 2016 presidential election is whether taxes should be increased for those at the top and the future of entitlement programs for those at the bottom. Bernie Sanders said that his campaign is sending a message to the billionaire class:

> "You can't have it all. You can't get huge tax breaks while children in this country go hungry. You can't continue sending our jobs to China while millions are looking for work. You can't hide your profits in the Cayman Islands and other tax havens, while there are massive unmet needs on every corner of this nation. Your greed has got to end. You cannot take advantage of all the benefits of America, if you refuse to accept your responsibilities as Americans."

I've heard so many say that the United States is a Christian nation. Maybe our governing political leaders need to be reminded of Proverbs 22:16, "Whoever oppresses the poor to increase his own wealth, or gives to the rich, will only come to poverty." Let's stop going down that road. It only leads to a place none of us wants to go.

Entitlement Programs vs. Military Spending and Foreign Aid

Entitlement Programs vs. Military Spending and Foreign Aid

Many people consider the things which government does for them to be social progress but regard the things the government does for others as socialism. ~Chief Justice Earl Warren 1952

The top expenditures for the federal government are entitlement programs and defense spending. We are told that Social Security and Medicare trust funds are steadily approaching insolvency. Then there is the non-negotiable cost of the War on terrorism. Meanwhile the U.S. national debt is over $19 trillion. Something has got to give. The blame and the solution to the crippling deficits have led to quite a bit of finger pointing from both sides of the political aisle. Liberals feel that the corporations and the wealthy don't pay their share of taxes; Conservatives feel entitlement programs are huge drains on the federal budget. Military spending is rarely questioned.

Entitlement programs are the usual suspects when the subject of deficits and the national debt are discussed. An entitlement program by definition is a government program that guarantees certain benefits to a particular group or segment of the population based on rights or legislation. These programs were initially called "entitlement" programs because workers paid into them and hence were entitled to receive benefits from them. The term has been expanded to include other programs where the eligible recipients have not paid into them.

The government programs that fall into the category of entitlements are Social Security, Medicare, unemployment insurance, most Veterans' Administration programs, federal employee and military retirement plans, SNAP (formerly the Food Stamp Program), SSI (Social Security Income for Disabled Persons), Temporary Assistance for Needy Families (TANF), the school lunch program, the Children's Health Insurance Program (CHIP), Earned Income Credit, the Child Tax Credit, low income housing programs, WIC, and Low Income Home Energy Assistance Program (LIHEAP). Generally these programs were born out of President Roosevelt's New Deal though there were several social programs offered in the United States before the Great Depression.

These programs varied from state to state but most were to assist the veterans of war: there were hospital and medical care benefits, pensions for widows and handicapped veterans, and free grants of land. State and local governments provided retirement programs for teachers, police officers, and firefighters. Sources of what we consider to be safety nets were offered through worker's compensation, sick leave, life insurance, churches, and charities. When the Great Depression followed the stock market crash these programs were grossly insufficient to handle the poverty and despair that it wrought. The hungry and desperate were raiding stores and looting to survive. Private organizations, and even state and local governments, lacked the resources to help due to the economic downturn. With employment near 25 percent, only the Federal government had the means to deal with the pressing needs of the people.

Franklin D. Roosevelt proposed a number of federal social relief programs, including unemployment insurance and old age pension, to Congress for approval in 1935. In 1940, the Aid to Families with Dependent Children was established. Prior to this time it was believed that it was not the government's responsibility to provide relief to the poor. However, with a national crisis how could the federal government not be compelled to respond? The Roosevelt administration implemented reforms that enlarged the role and the responsibility of the federal government in the social welfare of the American people. The Social Security Act of 1935 contained Old Age Assistance, Aid to the Blind, and Aid to Dependent Children. This New Deal meant that poor relief became the right of an American citizen who met certain financial eligibility standards.

The New Deal created deficits in spending and there were many objections from conservatives against it. For others it felt too much like socialism, and then some felt it made the poor lazy and discouraged them from working when there were jobs available. Thinking about this it seems as if in some ways time did stand still; those sentiments haven't changed much at all. In 2016, the complaints about the deficits and debt that continue to grow to fund entitlements are the same, some continue to say it feels like socialism, and many conservatives think it makes slackers out of people who can work.

What Is Really Going On?

The federal budget for 2015 was $3.8 trillion. Federal spending is divided into three groups, mandatory spending, discretionary spending, and interest on the debt. Mandatory spending is funding for programs that are required by law and continue from year to year. Discretionary spending must be approved each year in appropriation bills that become part of the federal budget. According to data from the Center on Budget and Policy Priorities (CBPP), 59 percent of mandatory federal spending goes towards entitlement programs, 24 percent for Social Security, 24 percent for Medicare, Medicaid, CHIP, and market place subsidies, and 11 percent for safety net programs. Half of the discretionary spending is on the military. The other half is spent on the central work of government, including veteran's medical care, research, education, housing, federal law enforcement, National Parks, NASA, the EPA, job training, and other social services.

U.S. Federal Spending – Fiscal Year 2015 ($ Billions)

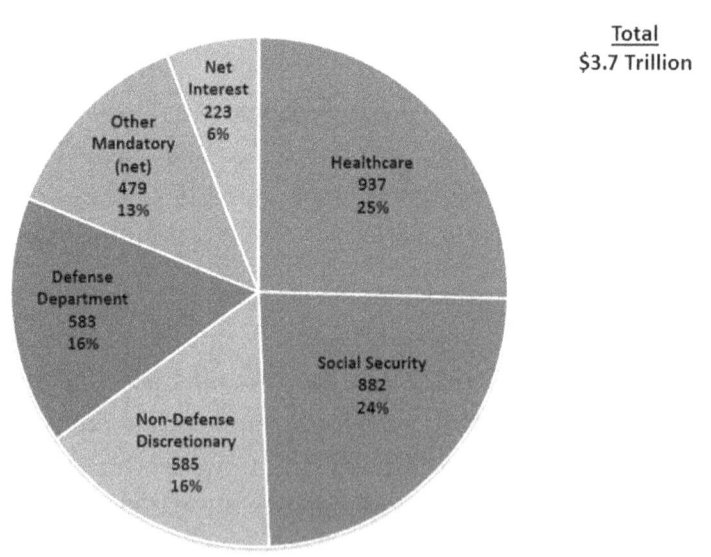

Entitlement Programs vs. Military Spending and Foreign Aid

Garnering the bulk of the federal budget; entitlement programs, particularly Social Security and Medicare, are a "hot button" political topic. The message we hear most of the time is how exorbitant the costs are and how they will eventually consume all of the nation's revenues. Conservatives expound on how these programs should be reformed, privatized, some even dissolved, that they are too expensive, mismanaged, and full of corruption. This is a complicated subject with only half-truths being represented. Social Security basically funds itself and would do even better without the salary cap. The problem is Medicare and the high costs of healthcare, a subject that no one seems to want to broach.

Before we talk about cutting or eliminating programs, we need to know to what extent does the population depend on these programs. Census Bureau data shows that 49 percent of American households are receiving some kind of entitlement benefit, and 90 percent of the benefits through entitlement programs go to people who are elderly, who are certified disabled and unable to work, and working households. This doesn't sound like something we can limit without serious repercussions being felt by large numbers. Despite the fact that most people think the recipients of Temporary Aid for Needy Families (TANF) are largely African American, the 2010 research data from CBPP shows that white families received 69 percent of entitlement benefits while being 64 percent of the population, black families received 14 percent of the benefits while being 12 percent of the population, and Latino families received 12 percent of the benefits while being 16 percent of the population.

Entitlement programs make for a "Catch 22" situation. You're damned if you do and damned if you don't have them. In the 1930s, some feared that the scarceness of jobs and the abundance of hunger and hopelessness had the country ripe for a revolution. We definitely don't want to go that route. Much has been said about the poor becoming dependent on the government, that it makes the needy lazy, destroys the work ethic, and creates a class of Americans who would rather collect government benefits than work. The truth is that between Ronald Reagan's tax cuts and Bill Clinton's welfare reform during the 1980s and 1990s the assistance to the unemployed poor has been greatly reduced. More accurately, it's the working poor who benefit from the safety nets. Discretionary spending on education has also been a place where funds have been reduced and that defeats the purpose of preparing the youth to participate and compete in the global economy. If you don't have an educated society how do you expect them to be independent and not rely on safety net programs?

    The costs and the effects that entitlement programs have on the future of this country are constantly debated. The wealthy always object to entitlement programs unless it benefits them, lest we forget the bailout. We seem to be more comfortable with corporate welfare than taking care of the poor. One prime example is the 2014 Farm Bill which authorizes nearly $1 trillion in spending over the next decade. The farm bill was initially passed in Congress as part of FDR's New Deal to give financial assistance to farmers who were suffering with excess crops that lowered prices, and to guarantee food supply. Over time part of it evolved into subsidies for farmers and landowners whether they grew crops or not.

    In exchange for elimination of these direct-paid farm subsidies, SNAP, better known as the food stamp program, was cut by $8.7 billion. According to an article in the *New York Times*, that means 850,000 households will lose $90 per month in benefits (Nixon, 2014). The unfairness is in the $7 billion increase to $90 billion over the 10 years for federally subsidized crop insurance. Essentially, money has been cut to feed families to pay for corporate welfare. The federal government feels more comfortable covering losses from poor yields and declines in revenue for large corporate farmers along with new subsidies for rice and peanut growers. Let's not forget the private insurance companies who love to feed at the federal trough.

    Drifting off on a side issue for a moment is the fact that these subsidies are basically for the farmers of corn, wheat, soybean, cotton, rice, peanuts, and dairy producers. Smaller farmers who grow most of the fruit and vegetables are not subsidized. They have to deal with the fluctuations in yield and pricing by themselves. That explains the higher prices of fruits and vegetables in comparison to the other commodities. On one hand, people who receive benefits from SNAP are encouraged to eat more healthy foods, which is also the more expensive food, while we subsidize the less healthy and cheaper food.

Military Spending

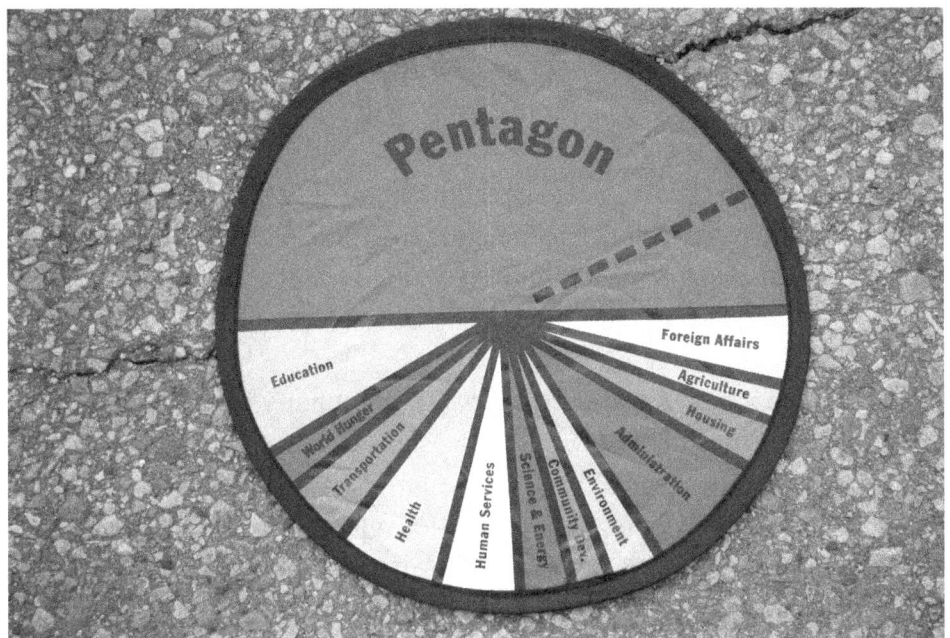

Joseph Sohm / Shutterstock.com

There's one thing that we rarely fight about in this country and that is military spending. It's the one thing that on which we feel no expense should be spared. After much compromising, President Obama signed the 2016 military spending bill with a $1.1 trillion budget, a $26 billion increase from the previous year. In 2015, the amount spent was 54 percent of the discretionary budget, $598.5 billion. This is roughly the same amount spent by the next six highest spending military budgets combined which include China, Russia, Saudi Arabia, France, the UK, and India. Most people might not be aware that the military spending in this country has gone up 50 percent since September 11, 2001. The two wars in Iraq and Afghanistan, and the War on Terror were part of the escalation. Prior to that time military spending was going down.

With the two wars ending, military spending should be winding down as well, but don't bet any money on it. War hawks and cheerleaders are shouting about dangers and threats of terrorism that require us to ratchet up and respond militarily. Add to that the fact that Congress continues to ignore any recommendations for more military base closures speculating that they might be needed in the future. In an article in *Army Magazine*, Lt. Gen. David D. Halverson, commanding general and assistant chief of staff, explained his request for another round of base closing, stating that the army can't afford to waste money maintaining infrastructure that they don't need. The estimated $480 million a year spent on maintaining unneeded bases could be better spent on training and the readiness of troops, and the upkeep of needed facilities. Leaders in Congress disagree and have denied any Pentagon funding allotted for planning closures.

Foreign Aid

There is so much said about citizens of this country being independent from government assistance while at the same time we send so much money out of our borders to aid other countries. The federal government spent $35 billion in foreign aid in 2014. It's admirable for this country to help other countries that are in need, especially when it comes to feeding the hungry, which is definitely worthy of sacrifice. My concern is when foreign aid is spent to finance military actions by other countries. Israel receives $3.1 billion that is used for military activities. For 2016 they have increased their request for aid up to $5 billion. In Egypt, $1.3 billion was used to finance military actions. As a country do we really want the responsibility of paying the costs for another country to wage war on their enemies?

The foundation of our foreign policy is based on the Truman Doctrine, which dictates "the policy of the United States to support free peoples who are resisting attempted subjugation by armed minorities or by outside pressures." In other words, the U.S. should provide political, military and economic assistance to all democratic nations that find themselves under the threat of internal or external dictatorial forces. This policy is a remnant of the cold war and the fight against the spread of communism. Surely we have moved on from this stance. President Obama has stated that we cannot continue to act as the world police, and that we should return to our policy of withdrawal from regional conflicts that do not directly involve the United States.

Now that the nation is suffering under huge deficits and fiscal problems from a sputtering economy this would be an appropriate time to re-evaluate some of our spending policies and actually see where this notion of our "values" really lies. War is a luxury we cannot afford. The days of nation building are behind us. As a "Christian nation," we should know what the Bible tells us. Charity begins at home, give from your overflow not what you've borrowed. Maybe it's time to be a little selfish and make sure that our own needs are met, that our children are fed, that they receive a quality education, and that they are not in debt up to their ears to pay for it. Maybe we should ensure that our elderly are cared for in a way befitting to the United States. Social Security does not provide enough for most of them to live on. Should they be punished for the inflation factor? Shouldn't we upgrade our infrastructure and mass transit throughout the country? Shouldn't we stop arguing over healthcare and make sure we all have it. Is there anything wrong with creating jobs for our own? It's time to put the people of this country and their needs at the top of the priority list instead of the bottom.

Social Security

Social Security

Social Security isn't a ponzi scheme. It's not bankrupting us. It's not an outrage. It's working.
--Rachel Maddow

    Social Security catches a lot of flak as an entitlement program. If the fund had a dollar for every time someone called for it to be repealed or reformed, solvency would not be an issue. The truth is Social Security is a subject that should be discussed apart from the other entitlement programs it has been fused together with. Social Security and Medicare receive most of the heated rhetoric because of all the programs they are the largest. These two programs make up more than a third of federal mandatory spending. By definition of the word: entitle, these are programs that you have as a legal right, but Social Security goes deeper than the other programs classified as entitlements.

    The Free Dictionary defines a retirement program as a plan for setting aside money to be spent after retirement. That sounds very much like Social Security. General wisdom says if it looks like a duck, walks like a duck and quacks like a duck, it's a duck. In an article in the *Los Angeles Times* (March 8, 2013), Michael Hiltzik clarified the description when he said that the very word "entitlement" is a lie, "*Social Security and Medicare got that name because workers became 'entitled' to benefits by paying into the system. In recent years, however, the term has become distorted to signify benefits people are entitled to without earning them.*"

    Economic security was becoming a concern in the early years of the 20th century as the life expectancy of the population increased and the country became more industrialized. Social insurance would be the means to assure income for those workers who had become too old or too ill to work, and to prevent the surviving members of the breadwinner from becoming destitute. Although this concept of social insurance already existed in quite a few European nations, it became a pressing problem under Franklin D. Roosevelt's administration during the Depression. The Committee for Economic Security, a special panel formed by President

Roosevelt, was assigned the task of designing a social insurance program that would tackle the concern of economic security for the country with the directive that it be self-supporting.

It was first instituted in America in 1935 and was called the Social Security Act. The theory was individuals would contribute to a government managed fund that would be used to provide income to workers when they were no longer able to be employed. None of the general government revenues would be used. All of the funds would come from payroll taxes on the wages of workers that would be held in a large designated reserve or trust fund. As Roosevelt put it, *"We put those payroll contributions there as to give the contributors a legal, moral, and political right to collect their pensions and unemployment benefits. With those taxes in there, no damn politician can ever scrap my social security program."* The programs created are noted in the following table.

Table 1. Programs in the Social Security Act of 1935

Title	Program	Description
I	Old-Age Assistance	Federal financial support and oversight of state-based welfare programs for the elderly
II	Federal Old-Age Benefits	The Social Security program
III	Unemployment Insurance	National unemployment insurance, with federal funding and state administration
IV	Aid to Dependent Children	State-based welfare for needy children (what would come to be called AFDC)
V	Grants to States for Maternal and Child Welfare	Federal funding of state programs for expectant mothers and newborns
VI	Public Health Work	Federal funding of state public health programs
X	Aid to the Blind	Federal funding of state programs to aid the blind

SOURCE: http://www.socialsecurity.gov/history/35actinx.html.

The Social Security Act was amended in 1956 adding Disability Insurance with its own trust fund. It was created to provide disability benefits to employees who have been determined to be medically impaired and unable to work for at least 12 months or with a condition that could result in their death. Initially it covered those who were age 50 or older and disabled children who were disabled before age eighteen. This benefit is an earned right, recipients must have worked and been covered by Social Security for a specific amount of time to be eligible. Benefits for dependents and disabled spouses were added later and the age requirements were eliminated.

The lack of adequate healthcare for the elderly was the major gap among the social insurance programs. Health cost increase as we get older just as our income is going lower. The cost for private health insurance for retirees or those over age 65 on a fixed income was more than most could afford, just over 50 percent had any type of hospital insurance, surgeries and out-patient visits were rarely covered. In some instances private policies were canceled as older persons moved to the high risk category. Neither federal nor state programs were sufficiently meeting the needs of the elderly. This was not only a problem for the poor; with the high costs of healthcare anyone who had considerable income or savings could be totally wiped out in the event of a serious illness. The solution was a federal program to provide a health insurance plan for senior citizens and the disabled. The program to complement Social Security was Medicare, signed into law by President Lyndon Johnson in 1965.

The Federal Insurance Contributions Act (FICA) is the law that mandates the payroll deductions from our paychecks to finance Social Security and Medicare. They are identified on the pay stub as Social Security, Medicare, or FICA. The employer and the employee both pay 6.2 percent of earnings into Social Security and another 1.45 percent into Medicare. That means 15.3 percent of your paycheck amount is contributed into these funds. Each of these programs has its own separate trust fund. These Social Security and FICA taxes are restricted or limited. For 2016, the threshold is $118,500, meaning any earnings above this amount are not subject to taxes. From the establishment of Social Security, 96 percent of all the income to the program have come from payroll taxes. In order to keep the reserve funds intact and free from speculating they can only be invested in government securities or "only in interest-bearing obligations of the United States, in obligations guaranteed as to both principal and interest by the United States."

The foundation principle for Social Security was that the benefit should be "adequate and equitable," meaning they should be sufficient enough to provide economic security to the recipients and that the benefits should correlate to the level of the contributions that have been made to the system by the recipient. Benefits are based on the earning from your lifetime of working. For the 35 years that you earned the most, a formula will be applied to your average indexed monthly income to determine your benefit. Higher contributions over the years should generate higher benefits.

More Americans are aided by Social Security than any other federal program. According to the trustee's report at the end of 2014, 59 million Americans were receiving retirement, survivor's benefits, or disability from Social Security. The total cost of these benefits was $848.5 billion with 166 million people paying into the trusts. In 2015, payroll taxes paid jointly by workers and employers were $1.07 trillion, equaling 34 percent of all tax revenues.

So what's the problem?

The consensus is that the Social Security trust fund is being depleted and at the present rate is expected to run out in 2034. That means that the program will be paying out more money than it takes in. Payroll receipts will cover about 77 percent of expenditures. This situation is happening now because of several reasons. The main reason is income inequality. If the majority of workers' wages are stagnant, then the amount of payroll taxes remains stagnant as well. As mentioned before, wage gains have been going to the top of earners since the 1980s. With the ceiling cap on payroll deductions at $118,500, none of the gains are subject to deductions for the trust fund. If they want higher revenue from payroll deductions then paychecks have to increase (a shameless plug for raising the minimum wage). Another reason is that the U.S. population is growing older. By the time the trust fund is expected to be depleted, 20 percent of the country will be age 65 or older. That means less workers will be contributing for beneficiaries.

In the article, "Social Security: The National Disgrace," published in the *U.S. News and World Report* by Andrew Soergel (August 2015), he said that Social Security was a Ponzi scheme. "Each generation takes from the next, steals from the next. It's generational theft. It's immoral. It's bankrupting our children. This is the time to recognize the thing as a national disgrace as currently constructed and financed." That was pretty harsh criticism for a program that each generation has contributed to, and has helped so many elderly with economic security and health care. Others say that Social Security is broke and they mean that financially and figuratively, that it has created a massive unmanageable federal bureaucracy. What's the truth?

At the end of 2014, Social Security had a 2.8 trillion surplus. Contrary to the propaganda that's spread about, the administrative cost of Social Security and the other entitlement programs are less than 10 percent of their total spending, compared to 17 percent of revenues spent on administration and investors by private insurers. As far as bankrupting the country when tax receipts fall short, that's what the Treasury bonds in the trust fund are for. They are redeemed by the government to cover the income gap. Let's not forget the money borrowed from the fund by the federal government to pay for two wars, bailouts, stimulus programs, and income tax cuts for the wealthy by George W. Bush. It's another example of the little man paying the bills for big business.

Fairness is a question that seems to be muted or at the very least kept to a small volume when we talk about Social Security taxes and income taxes. The original contribution to Social Security was 1 percent of wages and matched by employers. The rate increased to 2.5 percent in 1950 with gradual increases that reached 5 percent by 1978. Currently the tax rate is 6.2 percent, in effect since 1990. With the tax rate cap at $118,500, lower incomes bear more of the tax burden than those with higher incomes. FICA payroll taxes are extremely regressive. Data from the non-partisan Tax Policy Center show that the lowest incomes pay 7.3 percent of their incomes while the top 1 percent earners pay only 2 percent, and the top 0.1

percent pays a mere 0.9 percent of their income. That means the poorest of workers pays a rate 8.1 times as high as the rate of the top 0.1 percent of earners. So while the average worker has had to pay more of their income in Social Security taxes, personal income taxes from the top earners and corporate taxes have dropped. The tax burden has shifted onto those who are less able to pay it.

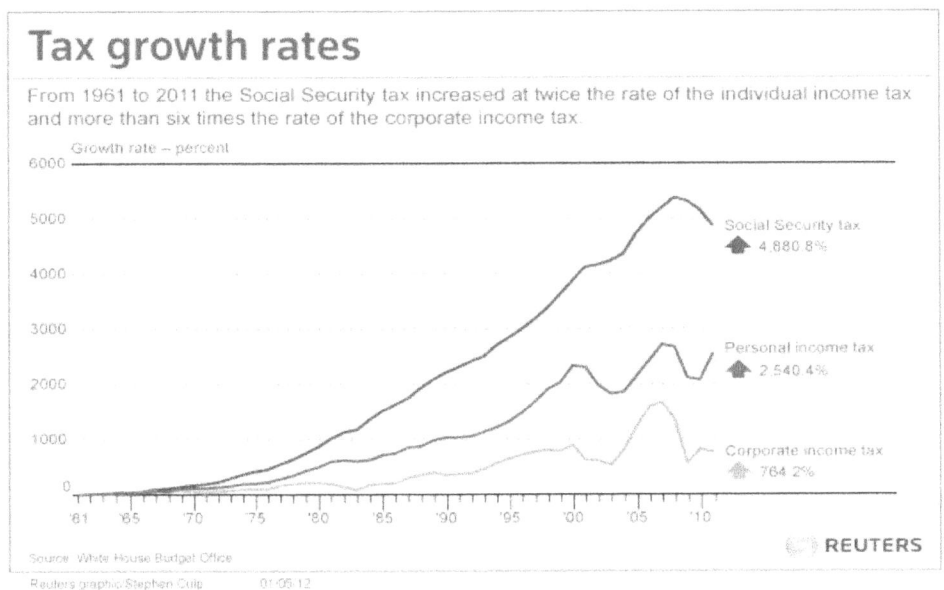

The federal budget is comprised of income taxes from individuals, payroll taxes from workers and employers, and corporate taxes. During the 1980s, Ronald Reagan increased Social Security taxes to where they collected more than it paid in benefits with the notion that the large number of 'Baby Boomers' could prepay part of their retirement benefit. This was supposed to create a huge surplus and balance the federal budget. It didn't work out that way because raising the taxes on the average worker while lowering the tax rate on the top earners from 70 percent to 28 percent and corporations from 50 percent to 35 percent only served to deepen the deficits. Tax increases on those barely making it to finance tax cuts to those living the high life won't get us where we need to be. In the profound words of rapper DJ Quik, "*If it don't make dollars, it don't make sense.*" Make no mistake, Social Security taxes bring in a ton of money, $1.02 trillion in 2014.

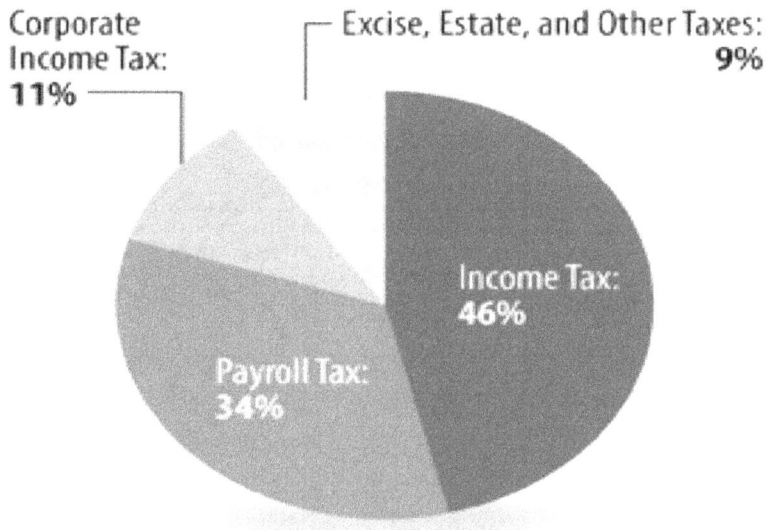

Something is wrong, the numbers don't add up. The money is pouring in but it's draining out like a sieve. What's at the bottom of the incessant suction? The major sources from my perspective are the Disability Insurance Fund and Medicare. Most of us are not aware of it but the Social Security payroll tax for the Old-Age Survivor's Insurance trust fund is actually 5.3 percent, the additional 0.9 percent tax goes into the disability fund. It's kept quiet compared to the other noise but the Social Security trustees have reported that the disability trust fund will run out of money at the end of 2016. At that point the amount taken in will only cover about 80 percent of the payout. The decision to be made is whether benefits will be cut or the payroll tax will be raised.

The numbers of disability beneficiaries has increased over the years with more working-age applicants. There were 10.9 million recipients in 2014, and that total is expected to grow much higher in the coming decades. When you look at the statistics they show that during hard economic times when decent jobs are hard to find more people apply for disability benefits. It has become a long term solution to the short term unemployment benefit.

The similar problem with Medicare is that the payout amounts are proportionately higher than what is taken in. For Medicare the payroll tax is 1.45 percent for incomes up to $200,000 for a single person or $250,000 if married, then it increases by 0.9 percent on all income above this level. However, this particular benefit is the one we can least control. What we should be talking about in this instance is health care costs, specifically doctor and hospital fees. The exorbitant charges for medical treatment are more of a drain on the program than the growing number of recipients and no one seems to want to have that discussion.

Federal law requires that Medicare reimbursement rates be adjusted each year based on a sustainable growth rate tied to the strength of the economy. This law established in 1997 was designed to contain Medicare costs by cutting payments to doctors if they went up too fast. The cuts have never happened because Congress has suspended them each year. Fear that doctors would stop seeing Medicare patients was the reason for acquiescing. Congress reached an agreement in April 2015 that would get rid of the cuts for physicians and create a new system of payment that gives financial incentives for doctors to bill Medicare patients for overall care instead of individual office visits. To help pay for the costs, premiums for higher income seniors would be raised.

What can we do about it?

Reform is the word on lips of the conservatives, strengthen is the word spoken by the liberals. Basically there have been four solutions proposed to end the "crisis" within the three trust funds of the Social Security system or at least extend their solvency. The first and most logical solution would be to eliminate the ceiling on income subject to the Social Security tax. A consequence of the growing income inequality is that the portion of income above the earnings cap has risen. According to the Congressional Budget office, this is the answer to the financial crisis of the trust funds. I've strained my brain and I can't think of one reason why this income level should not be subject to the payroll tax.

The second solution is to change how Social Security funds are invested. Presently the trust funds are only allowed to invest in special U.S. Treasury bonds. With interest rates held at zero for a decade, the returns on that investment have been meager. There is also the criticism that if the government defaults on its debt the $2.7 trillion trust funds would be lost and benefits couldn't be paid. Supposedly if we put the trust funds in a diversified portfolio of stocks and bonds outside of the government bonds the money would be safer. The added bonus to being more secure is that it would raise the return on the funds' investments, making it possible to continue paying benefits without having to increase taxes or raise income limits. This sounds like a recipe for massive corruption and underhanded deals. Chosen companies would benefit from the windfall of revenues and others would suffer. The stock market would be even more artificially lifted than it is now creating instability for the conventional investor and the government as well. Downturns are a fact in financial markets, it's not a constant ride up in value. Emotionally, I don't think most of us could deal with the fund going through the fluctuations of the market.

The third solution being banded around is raising the retirement age up to 70 years old. This idea isn't new or original. Initially, the Social Security amendment had added early retirement provisions, first to women in 1956, and then men in 1961. Presently, the earliest age you can receive Social Security retirement benefits is 62 years. Amendments made in 1983 to the Social Security Act phased in gradual increases in age for collecting full retirement benefits from 65 years to 67 years. The rationale was that the health of senior citizens has improved along with life expectancy. Benefits are reduced for each month for receiving benefits before age 65.

The reality is that a large part of the work force is employed in blue collar industries like construction, factories, and farming. It's hard to envision older workers toiling up to 70 years old in physically demanding jobs without it taking some toll on their health. These workers would most likely opt for early retirement benefits. Let's tell the truth, jobs are harder to find and harder to keep as we get older. Raising the retirement age doesn't guarantee that seniors will be able to maintain steady employment.

The fourth solution would be changing the method used to determine the cost-of-living-adjustment. This wolf disguised in sheep's clothing is just a means of cutting off payment increases due to inflation. Social Security benefits are indexed for inflation to protect the purchasing power of beneficiaries as prices continue to rise. The argument is that some people feel that the Bureau of Labor Statistics Consumer Price Index for Urban Wage Earners and Clerical Workers doesn't given an accurate reflection of the rate of inflation. Some feel that inflation is larger than it reflects and others feel it is overestimated. I don't want to bore you with the numbers from calculating the COLA using several methods because from what I could gather we are only talking about 1 percent difference, plus or minus, to the present method. The average monthly Social Security benefit was $1,341 for the month of January (2016). That's not a lot of money where we need to haggle over a cost-of-living-adjustment. I'm sure it's always needed.

Then there is the popular solution of Republicans and hedge fund managers; privatize it, throw that baby out with the bath water and let the business community with their unique expertise get their greedy hands on it. There are no limits to the outstretched hands looking for ways to increase their fortunes by taking care of it. Sucking at the government's breast is a never-ending source of nourishment.

Analyses of all these solutions have been done. Teresa Ghilarducci, a professor of economic policy analysis, affirmed this in an article for *The Atlantic* (Ghilarducci, 2105). Data shows that raising the retirement age from 67 to 68 would only remove 12 percent of the Social Security deficit. "Getting rid of this cap (income limit) would reduce 70 percent of the expected deficit 75 years from now." Attempts to reduce the cost-of living-adjustment isn't practical, it will only cause other problems in the long run. As for the second option, I've always heard that you don't gamble with money you can't afford to lose, so investing in the stock market is slightly risky for my taste. Eliminating the income ceiling is the most effective and most fair solution.

Social Security is not the great cure-all for what ails us, it's insurance. Some people won't live long enough to benefit, for some their children will benefit, some will have to collect disability benefits, some will die after a short time of receiving benefits, and some will collect more benefits than they ever paid in. As the richest country in the world, it is our responsibility to ensure that every American can retire, not impoverished, but with adequate income and quality health care. At some point we have to stop looking at the poorest and most vulnerable of our society to suffer when we come up short. It's time to shift the burden back to those better positioned to handle it.

txking / Shutterstock.com

Affordable Healthcare

"When we look back, five years from now, 10 years from now, or 20 years from now, we'll be better off because we had the courage to pass this law and keep moving forward."

---President Barack Obama

Affordable Health Care

Finally! The United States now has a plan to offer health care coverage to the 55 million Americans without health insurance, and improved coverage for those who are underinsured. We have finally taken a step towards the rest of the world's industrialized nations with universal healthcare for their citizens. Most people would think this is something to celebrate, a milestone that has taken almost a century to accomplish. Except that's not how this landmark program was received. Republican conservatives have been bombarding President Obama with criticism and hurling rhetoric at the rest of us, opposing the Patient Protection and Affordable Care Act (ACA) from the day of its inception. This legislation is vital to deal with the high cost of medical insurance and prevent the premature deaths of so many who have no means to seek expensive medical treatment. Health care should not be a luxury that a significant number of our population cannot afford. When you have government leaders who are supposed to be for the people, fight national healthcare for the people, then you know something is wrong.

With all the protest and threats to repeal the ACA and the intense lobbying by insurance companies against any health care reform in the past, I was wondering why this legislation was able to move through Congress after other futile attempts made over the decades. There is a simple answer. In the words of Bill Clinton's campaign strategist, James Carville, "It's the economy, stupid." Even before the Great Recession more businesses were decreasing employer sponsored health insurance coverage for workers by limiting them to part-time hours. Then there were those who got laid-off and downsized. The number of people without health insurance was rising. The higher number of people unable to pay means that those of us who can pay are going to have to pay more. All the while the price of health care kept rising as well.

Of all the rights that we profess to have in this country, the right to health care is not one of them, unless it's emergency medical treatment. Following countless tragedies of people being turned away by hospitals for the lack of health insurance a federal mandate was placed on hospitals to provide care for anyone in need of care. That means patients in urgent need or life threatening situations. Hospitals were required to evaluate and stabilize all emergencies. Uninsured patients could not be turned away from emergency rooms regardless of their ability to pay the bill. Nearly 20 percent of those coming into emergency rooms were uninsured. For the twenty-five years before the ACA became law those unpaid bills were passed on to the fortunate employed and insured as higher taxes and insurance premiums.

What is the Patient Protection and Affordable Care Act?

The new health insurance reform signed into law on March 23, 2010 is also called the Affordable Care Act, or more commonly, Obamacare. This legislation is the first meaningful change to the U.S. health care system since the implementation of Medicare and Medicaid in 1965. It's a combination of the Affordable Health Care for America Act, the Patient Protection Act, and the health care sections of the Health Care and Education Reconciliation Act and includes the Student Aid and Fiscal Responsibility Act. A part of what it does is expand Medicaid to cover millions of low-income Americans, and improves Medicaid and the Children's Health Insurance Program (CHIP).

On January 1, 2014, with few exceptions, all Americans were required to have health insurance. Under the mandate, those not covered by some form of health insurance will have to pay a penalty. The ACA doesn't sell health insurance. It created a marketplace where you can buy regulated, subsidized, private insurance. Cost assistance is based on income. If your employer provides an affordable insurance plan you are not eligible for subsidies. Guidelines are a part of the law to protect patients from subpar insurance. The purpose of the ACA was not only to reduce the number of uninsured but to heighten the quality of and affordability of health insurance and health care for all Americans. The key objectives are to lower the number of uninsured persons with more public and private insurance options, and reduce the costs of health care for patients and the government. Insurance companies are held accountable with new minimum standards and the requirement that the premiums be the same regardless of a pre-existing condition or gender.

Affordable health insurance exchanges were created for individuals, families, and small businesses in all states where they can compare policies and purchase insurance during open enrollment. After the open enrollment of 2015, 20 million people have been covered under the Affordable Care Act. Of this number, some registered for private health insurance on exchanges, some were eligible for Medicaid under the state expansions, and others were young adults who were able to remain in their parent's insurance coverage until they turn 26 years old.

What does it cost? What does it save?

The Obama Administration has touted the ACA as a self-funded program but for most of us that's a little hard to believe knowing what medical care costs. Self-funded is not quite accurate, it will be paid for by taxes, penalties, spending cuts, and reforms to the health care industry. The point is those funds were already being used to cover the medical bills of the uninsured already. It's no secret that people who didn't have insurance prior to Obamacare used the most expensive place to receive health care: the emergency room. Common sense tells you that if they couldn't afford health insurance they certainly cannot afford the massive bill for walking into the emergency room. The federal and state governments have been reimbursing hospitals for their care of uninsured patients. The idea is that instead of funding hospitals for the care after the fact, the money would be shifted to pay for insurance premiums before the fact. If the insurance leads to more preventive care then the costs in the long run should be less or even pay for themselves.

The Congressional Budget Office's updated estimates project that the net cost of the Affordable Care Act's coverage provisions will be $1.207 trillion from 2016 to 2025. The money will be spent on "subsidies for insurance obtained through the exchanges and related spending and revenues, for Medicaid and CHIP, and for tax credits for small employers." The amount spent on the 16 million that will be getting subsidies and the 13 million added to Medicaid/CHIP will be close to $5000 per person. Gerald Kominski, the director of the UCLA Center for Health Policy Research, emphasized that while the costs associated with the ACA are substantial, they are only a small portion of the total national health expenditures in the U.S. The amount spent on national health in one year, during 2013, was $2.9 trillion or $9255 per person.

The PPACA gives states 100 percent federal funding for the first three years of those newly eligible for Medicaid under the expansion starting on January 1, 2015 to December 31, 2016. On January 1, 2017, the funding will be lowered to 95, decreasing by another 1 percent on the following years until 2020 when the funding will be down to 90 percent. Qualifications are: American citizen, under 65 years of age, and below 133 percent of the poverty limit.

Assistance is available for low- and middle-income families on the Health Insurance Marketplace. For those families with incomes up to 400 percent of the federal poverty level ($47,080 for an individual and 97,000 for a family of four) that are not eligible for Medicaid, have no employer-sponsored health insurance, or any other type of acceptable coverage, there are subsidies or tax credits available to obtain coverage on the Health Insurance Exchanges. The tax credit is calculated on a sliding scale, the health insurance will cost from 2 percent to 9.5 percent of their income after the credit. Small businesses are also eligible for the tax credit.

There are four tiers of insurance coverage, the bronze, silver, gold, and platinum plans. They all offer the same essential health benefits. The differences in the plans are the premium price and the out-of-pocket expenses. The bronze plans will have the lowest premiums and the highest out-of-pocket costs, the platinum plans will have the highest premiums and the lowest out-of-pocket costs. The average premium for a plan purchased on a marketplace exchange during the first open enrollment period of the ACA was $82 after the subsidy. In 2015, 87 percent of those purchasing a plan on the exchange received financial assistance. For those returning to the exchange in 2016, 80 percent of them can get a plan for $100 or less.

What are the benefits?

Health care isn't something you can pay for out of your pocket, and medical expenses can balloon so quick that the average person couldn't pay them off in a lifetime. The good news is that millions of this country's uninsured now have affordable health insurance. One out of the three previously uninsured now has health coverage, and nine out of ten of them were eligible for subsidies. The enrollment in employer-sponsored insurance plans has grown also. More people have access to a personal physician and can get the care and medicines that they need. Debt from medical treatment and hospitalization is the leading cause for bankruptcy in this country. Hopefully this program will go a long way in reducing the number of people who lose everything they have when they or a family member become ill.

The Affordable Care Act is a great start in addressing the racial and income disparities that have been associated with overall health. Insurance companies on the health insurance exchange are held accountable. Only approved insurance plans with "essential health benefits" are available on the exchanges. That means the low quality plans that offered virtually no significant coverage are not available on the exchange, only those that meet certain standards are allowed, and insurers are not permitted to deny consumers based on pre-existing conditions or drop policyholders who become ill. Price regulations are in place to prevent insurance companies from pricing out the poor and the sick. Any increase in premiums above 10 percent must be justified and approved before the rate can be changed.

The ACA has had a positive effect on health care costs. In 2015, spending grew at the slowest rate since 1960 and the inflation on health care prices is at the lowest rate in five decades. The quality of health care should improve with the standards set by the "essential health benefits, and they have no lifetime caps or annual limits." The essential health benefits include outpatient services, hospitalization, obstetrics and newborn care, mental health and substance abuse treatment, rehabilitative services, laboratory services, preventive and wellness check-ups, pediatric care, dental care, vision care, and prescription drugs. Unlike typical plans, these benefits also include "habilitative" services for those who have long-term disabilities like Lou Gehrig's disease or Multiple Sclerosis.

Where many health insurance plans had prescription drug coverage as an option with additional cost, under the ACA, all individual plans and small group plans cover at least one drug in every category and class listed in Pharmacopeia, the official publication of approved medications in the U.S. Medicare has also been strengthened by the ACA: there are prescription discounts for seniors, a wellness check-up, and a number of preventive services. Services under preventive care are not subject to deductible, co-pays, or co-insurance. Prior to this health reform, insurers were cutting benefits and raising deductibles in order to offer competitive premiums. Insurance that doesn't cover the basics is worthless.

Most importantly, lives will be saved. A publication by Families USA reported that in 2010 the number of uninsured reached a record high, close to 50 million Americans because of unemployment and the high cost of health care. Their study also showed that 26,100 people died prematurely that year as a result of not having health insurance. That number comes out to 2,175 dead each month, 502 each week, 72 every day, and three each hour. Those numbers should begin to decrease with Obamacare.

Arguments Against It

The resistance against the proposed health care bill by conservative Republicans was so vehement and zealous that threats were thrown about towards members of Congress. To calm the fervor of the polarized joint session of Congress, Obama quoted from the late Ted Kennedy's letter that urged them to reform, *"What we face is above all a moral issue; that at stake are not just the details of policy, but the fundamental principles of social justice and the character of our country."* When it was all said and done the bill passed in the Senate by the skin of its teeth, 219-212, with 34 Democrats and 178 Republicans voting against it. The very next day after President Obama signed the ACA into law, the Republicans introduced legislation to repeal.

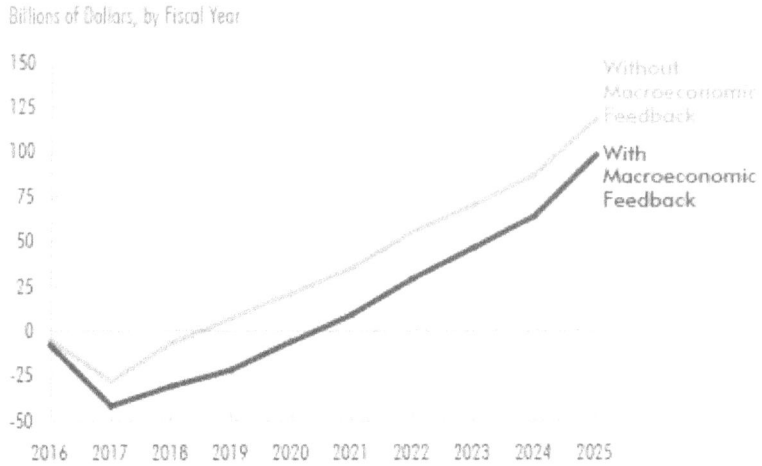

Estimated Effects on Deficits of Repealing the Affordable Care Act

We hear so much about how the ACA is going to bankrupt the country with deficits that have no limits. It must be another scare tactic for the people because the Congressional Budget Office reported in June that the repeal of the ACA would increase the deficit between $137 billion and $353 billion over 2016-2025. Contrary to what we are told the ACA actually reduces the deficit. The areas where the deficit reduction would come from are from higher Medicare fees on the wealthy, annual fees on health insurance providers, fees on manufacturers of brand name drugs and certain medical devices, limits on tax deductions of medical deductions and flexible spending accounts, and from mandate penalty payments.

Quite a few states argued against the costs they would incur and took it to the courts. The Supreme Court decided that states could not be forced to participate in the expansion of Medicaid by the ACA. As of January 2016, there are 19 states that have still declined to expand Medicaid funding in protest of the ACA. The sad thing is that these States are among the poorest in the nation with over half the uninsured population living in them. These Republican governors insist that the 10 percent they would pay in the expansion is more than they can afford. The truth is studies have shown that their resistance to the expansion is costing them more without the reimbursement of emergency medical care and the additional federal funding.

One of the major complaints is the individual mandate which requires persons not covered by an employer sponsored plan, Medicare, Medicaid, or any other public insurance program to purchase an approved private insurance policy or pay a penalty. The irony of this objection is that the individual mandate was one of the key elements of the law that Obama was initially against. Even so, Obamacare does include subsidies for those individuals with low incomes. There are some people who may be exempt because of financial hardship or their membership in a recognized religious sect.

The other argument is the employer mandate that requires businesses with more than 50 employees to offer a health insurance plan to their full-time employees or pay a tax penalty. Complaints have been that the mandate is going to kill so many small businesses who can't afford to offer health insurance to their employees. This in turn will have an adverse effect on the national economy with the loss of jobs or companies limiting workers to part-time hours. There is also an issue of fairness, large employers are not presently required to have the essential health benefits in the plans they offer their employees.

Republicans in Congress protest that the mandate is "unconstitutional." However, the mandate is necessary; otherwise most healthy people would put off buying insurance until they were sick. That would mean that the only people paying premiums are the same people reaping benefits. You have to have a large number of people paying in to have revenues for payouts. Most of us don't like to be forced into buying something whether it's good for us or not. Money is so tight these days that we don't want to buy something until we need it. I have my complaints about the auto insurance that is the law in most states but I must admit that I need it and would hate to be in an accident with somebody who doesn't have any. The upside is if you don't need it, then be thankful. It's there to help you maintain your good health.

For those on the liberal side of the aisle with complaints, please remember that all the gains in getting this health care legislation were gotten under intense opposition. There was no way the Medicare (single payer for all) was going to pass. Sometimes when you ask for too much you wind up with nothing. Let's be thankful for the bill that we have. Instead of listening to those ranting to repeal why not propose measures to improve it.

There is also the complaint that some insurers are terminating insurance plans. The reason being is that those plans that don't meet the standards set by the ACA must be canceled. Most of the blame and anger has been focused on President Obama's statement, "if you like your health care plan, you'll be able to keep your health care plan." Possibly they should have taken offense with the insurer who opted not to bring the coverage up to the required criteria. Quality and coverage of the insurance policy does matter.

Economic consequences

There are still millions of people who are not enrolled in Medicaid that are eligible for the benefit. Then there are other citizens who have opted to pay the penalty instead of purchasing insurance. There are those who signed up and then didn't pay their premiums. There are people who live in states that have not expanded Medicaid and are ineligible for subsidies. There are millions of illegals who are uninsured and not subject to the penalty that continue to use emergency rooms for access to health care. There are fewer avenues to reimburse the costs that hospitals incur treating these groups. All of these people continue to be a drag on hospitals that have to care for them under the 1986 Emergency Medical Treatment and Active Labor Act.

Rising insurance costs are one of the excuses from employers for stagnating salaries. These stagnating salaries become a problem for consumers who have a problem paying their premiums. That's why the subsidies in the law are so important. The Supreme Court 6-3 ruling of King v. Burwell on June 25, 2015 rescued this key feature of affordability for the Affordable Care Act. The court ruled that the ACA federal subsidies to help individuals pay for their health insurance premiums are available in all states, not only in the ones that have set up state exchanges.

As far as being the ACA being a "job killer" that would lead to the loss of 650,000 jobs, the Center for Economic Policy Research hasn't seen any evidence that companies are reducing hours for their workers to avoid providing health insurance. In fact, the implementation of the ACA has brought new customers to insurance companies, new patients to doctors and hospitals, and new prescriptions to be filled for the pharmaceutical industry. More competition among insurance companies should lower prices as more companies enter the market. Hospitals in states that have opted not to expand Medicaid are suffering from the cuts in Medicare payments from the law. Those states forfeited hundreds of millions of federal dollars that could have offset the cuts.

Large companies paying for the benefits of their employees is the norm for the time being. Most companies will continue to offer health care benefit to their employees but changes are bound to come as they make adjustments to follow the new ACA mandated provisions. Some are already considering other options such as a defined contribution plan where they give their employees money to purchase health insurance on a private exchange. According to reports by the Kaiser Family Foundation, expensive health care plan costs have already begun to be shifted onto the employee through rising premiums and higher deductibles, and only 25 percent of the firms thought they would be offering any insurance plans ten years from now.

Speaking to an audience in Milwaukee in February 2016, President Obama announced that the enrollment in health insurance under the Affordable Care Act had reached 20 million, a new high. He characterized the law as an overwhelming success in the city and around the nation despite the opposition. "Congressional Republicans have tried and failed to repeal Obamacare about 60 times," President Obama expressed to the audience, "They have told you what they would replace it with about zero times." I'm beginning to wonder if the Republicans are incensed about the ACA or just the fact that President Obama was able to pass it.

By all appearances the Affordable Care Act seems to be a great health care plan. It's not cheap and for some a huge burden to carry but what are the alternatives. There are some kinks to work out on the exchanges, balancing premiums with payouts, and doctor network issues, but at least we have something to improve upon. Subsidizing health insurance for the uninsured citizens of this country is the right thing to do. Certainly for all those who say this country has to lead; on the issue of national health care we're trailing the pack. Instead of trying to reverse the progress why don't we focus on how we can pull ahead? For the group that shouts about their values and being Christian remember the quote by John Bradford, the English church reformer who said, *"There, but for the grace of God, go I.*

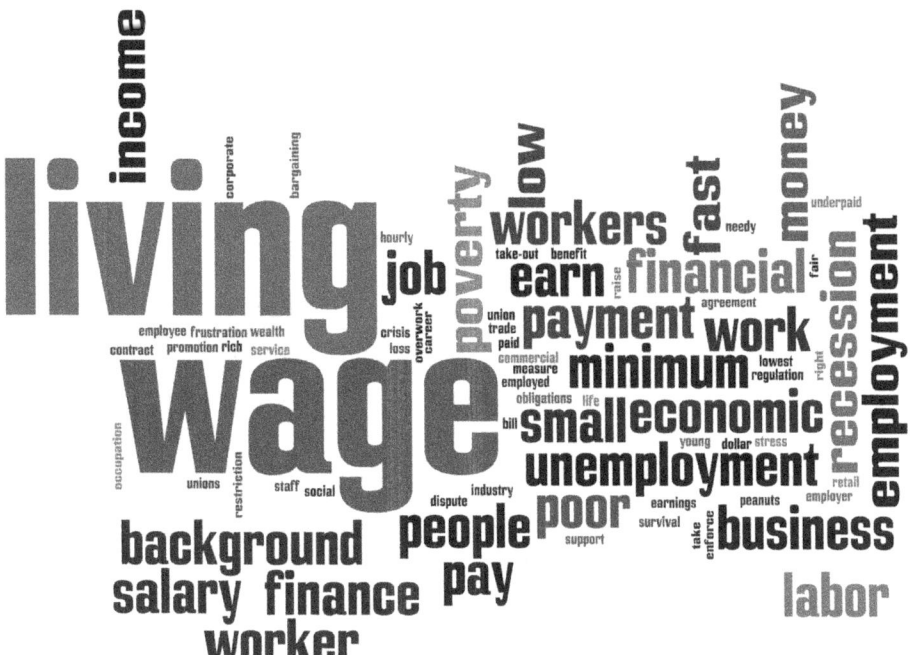

Wages vs. Inflation

"Every economist knows that minimum wages either do nothing or cause inflation and unemployment. That's not a statement, it's a definition."
--Milton Friedman

Wages vs. Inflation

There are few matters that have moved steadily in opposite directions from each other as wages and inflation. The perception is that they are very closely related, perhaps parallel entities, moving in tandem, urging each other along. In a perfect world they would be two soldiers locked in step. Yet the truth is this pair has grown so far apart there are doubts to whether the relationship can be saved. Except it has to be saved, wages and inflation have got to come back together, or life, liberty, and the pursuit of happiness in American as we have known it is doomed. The notion that we can move on, regain a robust economy with increased tax revenues without reeling in inflation and increasing wages is just more insanity.

This is more than likely common knowledge but in the interest of being thorough, wages are by definition monetary compensation paid by an employer to an employee in exchange for work done. The payment of wages can be calculated as a fixed amount for each task completed or at an hourly or daily rate. Activists who want to raise wages emphasize that a wage is more than compensation for work done; it's a means of maintaining a living. Higher wages help the worker so they can live a better life, they help the employer reduce employee turnover, and with an improved economy they help our society. Nevertheless, wages are the thorn in capitalism's side. If they could be completely eliminated it would create the perfect business model, except slavery was abolished more than 150 years ago. The bottom line is that wages cut into profits. Never mind that it's hard to manufacture goods, harvest crops, or provide services without workers.

The rubber hit the road as we arrived in the new millennium. Inflation or the rise in the cost of things has left most of us in the dust. The average worker can't keep up and is priced out. This is the result of stagnant wages for more than three decades. In a still sluggish economy, we've discussed them, complained about them, and even compared them, but nothing has been done to raise them. It's time to get serious about wages. If we continue to pretend that wages don't matter as much as profits, this out of balance vehicle we call our economy is headed for a crash.

Some Wage History

Before the Great Depression, which seems to have been a catalyst for quite a few changes, there was no national minimum wage in the United States. Without this regulation I'm sure you can imagine, or then again maybe not, the exploitation of tens of thousands of workers. Most of us have heard the horror stories of factories, sweatshops, child labor, long hours, and the dreadful conditions people were forced to work under for mere pennies. Efforts to establish a minimum wage were ruled unconstitutional by the U.S. Supreme Court on the grounds they violated the Due Process Clause and interfered with a person's right to freely contract labor.

The 1920s were a period of escalation in terms of wealth and capitalism. Nonetheless, the English proverb still applies, *"The more you get the more you want."* All the money flowing only made businesses greedy. Instead of sharing the wealth they cut wages and went about busting unions. When the stock market crashed and the demand for work intensified they used it to justify cutting wages even further until they hit rock bottom. Anybody who complained or tried to organize labor was labeled a communist. Those workers who were bold enough to march in protest were met with guns and sticks to beat them into submission but it only strengthened their resolve, after all what choice did they have. The violence got so bad in some cities that the police and even the National Guard were ordered to fire on marchers and strikers.

The level of poverty brought on by the Depression reached crisis proportions and couldn't be ignored. Franklin D. Roosevelt pushed the Nation Labor Relations Act through Congress which gave workers the freedom to organize and choose their own representatives for negotiating the terms and conditions of their employment, and made it illegal for employers to refuse to bargain with unions. In his re-election campaign of

1936, he promised protection for workers through child labor provisions, minimum wages, and maximum hour standards. He won the election in a landslide victory. Speaking about his inaugural address he said:

> "I laid down the simple proposition that nobody is going to starve in this country. It seems to me to be equally plain that no business which depends for existence on paying less than living wages to its workers has any right to continue in this country. By "business" I mean the whole of commerce as well as the whole of industry; by workers I mean all workers, the white collar class as well as the men in overalls; and by living wages I mean more than a bare subsistence level—I mean the wages of decent living. Throughout industry, the change from starvation wages and starvation employment to living wages and sustained employment can, in large part, be made by an industrial covenant to which all employers shall subscribe. It is greatly to their interest to do this because decent living, widely spread among our 125,000,000 people, eventually means the opening up to industry of the richest market which the world has known.
>
> No employer and no group of less than all employers in a single trade could do this alone and continue to live in business competition. But if all employers in each trade now band themselves faithfully in these modern guilds--without exception-and agree to act together and at once, none will be hurt and millions of workers, so long deprived of the right to earn their bread in the sweat of their labor, can raise their heads again. The challenge of this law is whether we can sink selfish interest and present a solid front against a common peril."

In FDR's letter to Congress on May 24, 1937 he said, "*The overwhelming majority of our population earns its daily bread either in agriculture or in industry. One-third of our population, the overwhelming majority of which is in agriculture or industry, is ill-nourished, ill-clad and ill-housed.*" The Fair Labor Standards Act was signed into law in 1938. Among its across-the-board regulations to protect American workers it established a federal minimum wage of 25 cents an hour. This amount was determined to be sufficient to maintain, "A minimum standard of living necessary for health, efficiency and general well-being, without curtailing unemployment." This may sound miniscule but at the time 25 percent of workers earned only a fraction of that per hour. It was certainly enough to bring the ire and ferocious opposition from employers and fiscal conservatives who swore it would bring an end to the free market. Looking back, they seemed to muddle through just fine.

Minimum Wage vs. Living Wage

The purpose of the minimum wage was to ensure that workers' pay kept up with rising prices. It has been raised 22 times since 1938; the last time was in 2009 when it was raised to $7.25. The problem is that we have had a long extended period of inflation rising without any adjustment to the minimum wage. The Great Recession is supposedly over but wages haven't recovered and the purchasing power of a dollar has shrunk. A 2013 Gallup poll showed 76 percent of Americans would vote to raise the minimum wage up to $9 per hour.

Similar to the period in the 1920s, companies have spent decades fighting and weakening the unions to erase the collective bargaining power

Psst: Somebody Speak the Truth

they'd gained. Workers' pay has suffered with wages they can't afford to live on. Protests and marches to increase the minimum wage are picking up steam all across the country. On November 10, 2015, a national walk-out and rallies in 1000 cities were scheduled to protest low wages and to "Fight for $15." The 64 million low-wage workers across the United States are poised to wield their political power in the next election and make their voices heard.

Similar to the reaction in the 1930s, the argument against raising the minimum wage is the harm it will do to the economy and how it will kill job growth. The irony is that the greatest opposition that minimum- and low-wage workers face is not only from employers, conservative Republicans, but from a large part of their fellow workers. Many skilled and professional workers whose wages haven't risen much either feel some resentment about fast-food workers and others earning low pay suddenly making close to the salary they're earning. They're not able to see how we'll all benefit in the long run.

a katz / Shutterstock.com

To keep the discussion from getting too complicated let's go back to the purpose of the minimum wage. From the beginning it was to change starvation wages to living wages. So what is the difference between a minimum wage and a living wage? The living wage is usually higher than the minimum wage. The living wage is the minimum income required for a worker to meet their basic needs, a "fair and decent wage." This is not merely food on the table and a roof over your head, but nutritious food, safe drinking water, suitable housing, and other necessities such as utilities, transportation, clothing, and other social needs. In other countries like the United Kingdom this definition includes healthcare, childcare, education, savings for emergencies and long term purchases, and recreation for a person working 40 hours a week with no additional income.

The living wage is sometimes defined as income equal at the poverty line for a family of four with two adults working full-time supporting two children. The expectation in our present economy is that there are two breadwinners in the household, yet some standards say the living wage should assume only one wage earner for the family. However, D. Caradog Jones, editor of The Social Survey of Merseyside in England, made a distinction between the poverty standard of living appropriate for a family on public assistance and the standard of living appropriate for a working and self-supporting family (Jones, 1941). Still, there is no consensus on the living wage; it depends on who you ask, when you ask, and the location where you ask. Some have defined the living wage in some U.S. cities between $8 and $10 while other groups place it in the $16 to $19 range. The National Priorities Project and Jobs with Justice estimates the living wage for one worker in the U.S. to be $31,616 annually.

The minimum wage also differs from the living wage in that it is set by law. The minimum wage does not necessarily meet the requirements of "fair and decent." In most cases, families earning the minimum wage must rely on the government for additional income or resources just to supply their basic needs. Reliance on government assistance by working families makes it obvious that the minimum wage is not a living wage. When the first minimum wage was created it was meant to be a living wage, now critics who want to re-write history say it was never supposed to be a living wage, but instead an entry-level wage for unskilled workers.

Increasing poverty of workers and their families in the U.S. over the last 30 years has led community initiatives to launch living wage campaigns. There are several cities in the United States that have raised their minimum wages to meet the living wage standard for their region; they include Santa Fe and Albuquerque, New Mexico, San Francisco, California, and Washington, D.C. Maryland passed ordinances that set its minimum wage to meet the living wage in its region. Workers there earn $3 - $7 more than the federal minimum wage. In 2006, Chicago, Illinois passed a living wage ordinance but it was vetoed by Mayor Daley.

Charting the Path of Wages

The rise in income inequality is largely a result of the continuing lack of significant wage growth. In spite of GDP growth of 149 percent over the last 35 years, net productivity of 64 percent, and corporate profits up 20 percent which could have afforded broad-based wage growth, there was none. Incomes of the vast majority of American workers have been flat or declining irrespective of whether the economy was adding jobs or not. The income gains that have been made have gone to the higher-income earners. Reduction in the collective and individual bargaining power of workers explains most of this phenomenon but there are other contributing factors. Businesses stress that employer-provided health insurance restrains employers ability to raise wages. The decline in better-paying jobs and the growth in the low-wage service industry have also shifted the direction of wages.

Raising wages for all workers is key to stimulating the sluggish economy. Looking at the chart below, it's plain to see that 80 percent of households in this country have not seen significant gains in income over the last 50 years.

Wages vs. Inflation

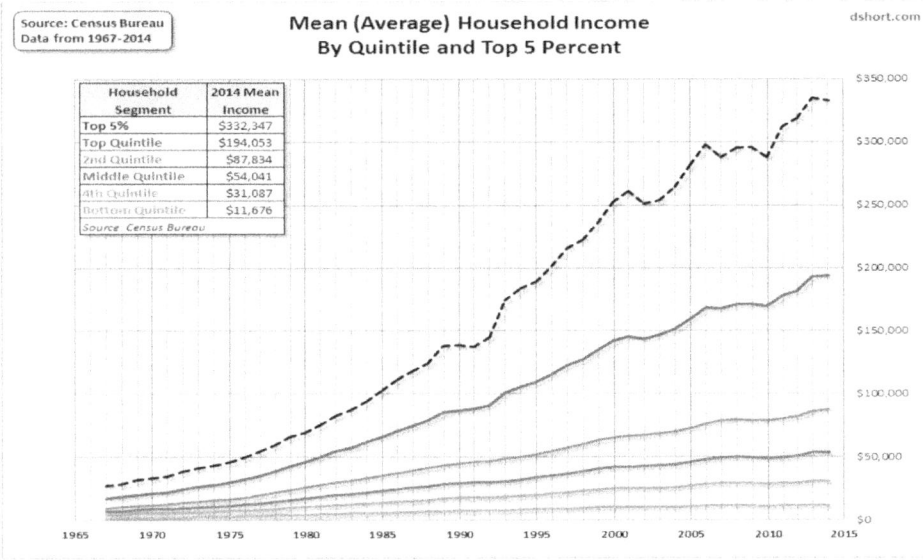

Arguments against Higher Wages

I have never seen a more eloquent and illogical speech on why we should hold wages down than by James Sherk, Senior Policy Analyst in Labor Economics at The Heritage Foundation during his testimony before the Health, Education, Labor, and Pensions Committee of United States Senate June 25, 2013.

> "Supporters of the minimum wage intend it to lift low-income families out of poverty. Unfortunately, despite these good intentions, the minimum wage has proved ineffective at doing so. Indeed, it often holds back many of the workers its proponents want to help. Higher minimum wages both reduce overall employment and encourage relatively affluent workers to enter the labor force. Minimum wage increases often lead to employers replacing disadvantaged adults who need a job with suburban teenagers who do not.
>
> This can have long-term consequences. Minimum wage positions are typically learning wage positions—they enable workers to gain the skills necessary to become more productive

on the job. As workers become more productive they command higher pay and move up their career ladder. Two-thirds of minimum wage workers earn a raise within a year. Raising the minimum wage makes such entry-level positions less available, in effect sawing off the bottom rung of many workers' career ladders. This hurts these workers' career prospects.

Even if minimum wage workers do not lose their job, the overlapping and uncoordinated design of U.S. welfare programs prevents those in need from benefitting from higher wages. As their income rises they lose federal tax credits and assistance. These benefit losses offset most of the wage increase. A single mother with one child faces an effective marginal tax rate of 91 percent when her pay rises from $7.25 to $10.10 an hour. Studies also find higher minimum wages do not reduce poverty rates. Despite the best of intentions, the minimum wage has proved an ineffective—and often counterproductive—policy in the war on poverty (Sherk, 2013)."

I'll give Mr. Sherk the benefit of doubt that he means well but the reason that the minimum wage has not lifted low-income families out of poverty is because it is in fact too low. Higher minimum wages in the past have not reduced employment. Rises in unemployment are due to a slowing economy. Since 70 percent of the U.S. economy is based on consumer spending, it would stand to reason that the lack of disposable income to spend would be the problem. I also seriously doubt that raising the minimum wage to $10 0r even $15 would inspire affluent people to enter the workforce.

I would like to believe that minimum wage positions are learning or training wage positions, except that would not explain why wages have been basically flat for decades. Employers are not concerned with raising wages; they are concerned with turning a profit. The lagging economy has been used as an excuse to hold wages down while profits have soared. I'm not aware of a career ladder where you can advance in unskilled and blue collar jobs. Where you start is pretty much where you'll end up.

Wages vs. Inflation

This is the first time I've heard qualifying for welfare benefits as a reason for holding wages down. It sounds like he's advocating low wages to keep poor people eligible for government benefits. Given the choice I'm sure workers would rather have a job that pays them a living wage with benefits versus working for a menial income where they still qualify for food stamps, Medicaid, and earned income credit.

More arguments are that most workers earning the minimum wage are under 25 years of age and live in household that don't rely on their paycheck. Sixty-two percent of these workers are usually students working part-time with limited education and experience, and only 22 percent of them live at or below the poverty line. None of this data explains why anyone working shouldn't receive a "fair and decent" wage for their labor.

If the truth is that less than 2.9 percent of workers earn $7.25 an hour, then raising it shouldn't have a dire effect on employers. Advocates for raising the minimum wage say it wil help low-income single parents support their children. The response is that there aren't many single parents working full-time for minimum wage jobs. The key word was full-time. Most jobs paying minimum wage are part-time jobs. If they don't want to pay you a decent wage they certainly are not going to pay you benefits as a full-time employee.

Let's not forget those who are temporary workers. According to the U.S. Bureau of Labor Statistics, temporary workers make up 19 percent of all new jobs in the U.S. It's another option corporations use to hold wages down and avoid paying benefits. The BLS data also shows that 54 percent of all the jobs created after the 2008 recession are contigent positions, and that number contines to grow. Research done by Ardent Partners, a suppy management firm, found contingent workers, including independent contractors, statement-of-work-based labor and freelancers, will account for nearly 45 percent of the world's total workforce by 2017.

President Roosevelt said it best in a fireside chat before he signed the Fair Labor Standards Act:

> "Do not let any calamity-howling executive with an income of $1,000 a day, who has been turning his employees

over to the Government relief rolls in order to preserve his company's undistributed reserves, tell you—using his stockholder's money to pay the postage for his personal opinions-/that a wage of $11 a week is going to have a disastrous effect on all American industry."

Inflation

Inflation is defined as the rate at which prices for goods and services rises and the decline in the purchasing value of money over a period of time. There are four reasons for rises in inflation, increases in demand, decreases in supply, higher labor costs passed on in higher prices, and simple greed. High rates of inflation cause problems for the overall economy as the purchasing power for individuals and companies drops, it discourages saving and investment. For most people it lowers the standard of living that they can afford.

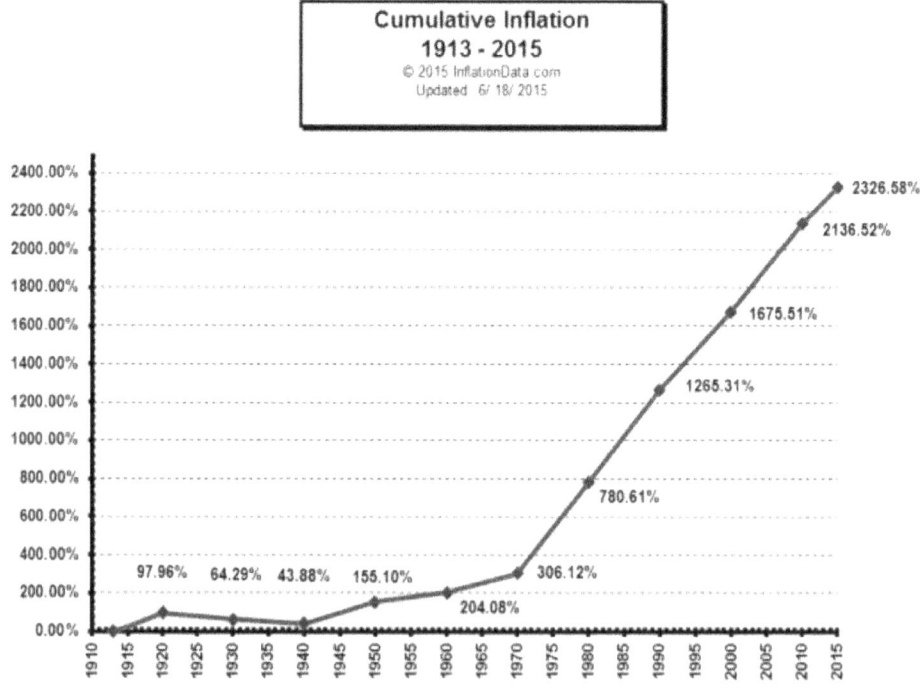

Wages vs. Inflation

Monetary policy is directed by the central bank or the "government's bank." Controlling inflation and keeping prices stable is one of their principal priorities. The central bank interjects more money into the market or absorbs it to affect the level of inflation. Another tool used is the manipulation of the interest rate. Inflation and the interest rate are said to move in opposite directions, meaning a rise in the interest rate should lower inflation. As borrowing becomes more expensive it discourages buying and investing causing higher prices and inflation to retreat.

The measure of the change in purchasing power and the rate of inflation is called the Consumer Price Index (CPI). The CPI is determined by taking price changes in a basket of goods and services from the same period in a previous year. Each month the Bureau of Labor Statistics releases the latest CPI. The CPI is used as an economic indicator and a means for adjusting wages and income payments. Getting a clear picture of whether wages are keeping up with inflation you can't simply follow the rise in wages over the years, the cost of living continues to change. Inflation and the rise in prices has to be taken into account.

After adjusting for inflation, the current hourly wage has about the same purchasing power that it did in 1979. The average wage peaked over forty years ago. The hourly rate recorded in January 1973 of $4.03 had the same purchasing power as $22.41 would have today. The current minimum wage of $7.25 has lost 8.1 percent of its purchasing power to inflation. That would apply to "near minimum wage" workers, those who make more than $7.25 but less than $10.10. Even if the data shows that only 2.9 percent actually earn the minimum wage the Current Population Survey estimates that 20 million people, 30 percent of all hourly, non-self-employed workers, eighteen years and older, are "near minimum wage workers."

The protests of "Occupy Wall Street" and "Fight for $15" are evidence of the frustration and growing desperation caused by income inequality, stagnating wages, and growing poverty. Contention between employer and employee over compensation is not new but at least now it's less violent. The only difference is big business has the politicians to fight its battles instead of the police. It's much more civilized.

Outsourcing and Offshoring

Outsourcing and Offshoring

The mystery of the "disappearing middleclass" can be explained as a result of outsourcing and offshoring. Outsourcing is defined as the use of outside resources to perform tasks traditionally completed by internal staff, basically contracting out a business process to another party or firm. It sometimes involves the transfer of employees or assets. It can be the shift from public services to a private corporation. Outsourcing can be offshore or global sourcing where jobs are transplanted to another city or another country. For most people it means our job just left the building. This business strategy which advocates taking advantage of the "specialization and division of labor across global markets" was summed up in the early 1990s by the words of Peter Drucker and Tom Peters, management consultants, "Do what you do best and outsource the rest." The impetus was to cut costs and save money, code words for eliminating staff.

Very few industries are immune to outsourcing. Cheaper labor is enticing and intoxicating and has created long-term unemployment for American workers. The truth is that every job going across the border or overseas is a job lost in the United States. Global competition for foreign imports in the auto industry in the 1970s was the catalyst. Then came the greed of the 1980s with public companies demanding higher profits and share prices. No industry has remained unscathed from automobiles to food service, customer service, shipping, clothing, and manufacturing.

It began innocently enough with companies outsourcing or contracting out services to be done in-house for more budget control and flexibility. It was about being efficient. Management could prune and cut corners to maximize profits. They only pay for the services they need when they need them. It reduces capital operating expenses without having to hire and train specialized staff. Then outsourcing expanded with plant closings or divisions of one company dissolved and the work transferred to another company, from American companies to other American companies, and gradually moving offshore. New companies were created with their business being the relocation of jobs out of the U.S. to low wage countries.

Outsourcing and Offshoring

The reasons given for off-shoring sound noble, "it's to preserve jobs and create jobs." Shoes and clothing firms say they outsource their entire manufacturing units so they can concentrate on design and marketing, but more likely it's to avoid union interference. Other incentives for companies to outsource jobs include relief from government regulations but most are tied to boosting their bottom-line. Employee-related costs apart from labor are the mandated benefits of Social Security and Medicare. Additional business expenses eliminated are corporate taxes, high energy costs, and production costs.

Outsourcing wasn't a huge issue impacting the U.S. economy until after the North American Free Trade Agreement (NAFTA) was implemented on January 1, 1994. It was first proposed by Ronald Reagan in 1979, called the "North American Accord," George H. Bush negotiated the final agreement, and Bill Clinton, surrounded by economic advisers from Wall Street pushed it through Congress, (Faux, 2013). NAFTA was put to together to eliminate the trade barriers between the U.S., Canada, and Mexico, even though these countries had been trading with each other for hundreds of years. The new thing was tariffs were eliminated on more than 50 percent of Mexico's export to the U.S. This was a sweet deal for corporations; they could relocate their plants to Mexico and send goods back home without taxes. Then in 2000, they got an even sweeter deal when Bill Clinton signed a bill granting "permanent normal trade relations" with China guaranteeing them low-tariff access to U.S. markets for their goods. China was accepted into the World Trade Organization in the following year.

Outsourcing and Offshoring is a national concern without a doubt. The United States has lost more than 5 million manufacturing jobs. Research by the McKinsey Global Institute reported that 31 percent of workers that lost their jobs due to outsourcing never found employment, and 80 percent suffered pay cuts. It has given us much to debate about, whether it's necessary to hold prices down, or whether it's American corporations playing us all for fools just to make an extra buck or billion.

Jobs Crossing the Border

NAFTA was supposed to created jobs. It was supposed to be a win-win-win for Canada, Mexico, and the United States with expanded access to the goods and services of all countries. Once again, "the best laid plans of men often go awry." NAFTA created economic instability and job losses in the United States, Mexico, and Canada. Whether it was because of miscalculation or deception, it depends on who you ask. None of the workers, in either of the countries has much good to say about it. It seems corporations were the winners again.

Depending on which data you reference, NAFTA caused the loss of 700,000 to 1 million jobs, with most of them high-paying manufacturing jobs coming from California, Texas, Michigan, Ohio, Pennsylvania, and Indiana. Workers in manufacturing traded down to jobs in the service industry. Between 1993 and 2013, the U.S. trade deficit with Canada and Mexico ballooned from $17 billion to $181 billon as imports from Mexico swelled. This agreement was more of a scheme by corporations to take advantage of Mexico's lower wages and more lenient environmental standards.

In November of 1993, before the agreement was approved, *NAFTA We Need It* was released by the National Association of Manufacturers. It contained narrations from over 250 companies describing how they would create more U.S. jobs if Congress passed NAFTA. The result played out like a bad marriage, promises were made, trust was given, the dotted line was signed, promises weren't kept, and then you ran off and left me. The safety net for American workers was the Trade Adjustment Assistance program. Worker and unions were able to apply for assistance to help transition to a new career, find another job, and supplement their lost income. Over 850,000 U.S. workers in the manufacturing sector who lost their jobs due to imports have qualified for TAA since NAFTA.

Research by the Public Citizen organization in 1997, stated that Allied Signal, Chrysler, Caterpillar, General Electric, Johnson and Johnson, Kimberly-Clark, Lucent Technologies (formerly AT&T), Mattel, Proctor and Gamble, Siemens, Whirlpool, Xerox, and Zenith all made promises to create or maintain jobs in the U.S., and all have laid off workers and moved operations to Mexico as certified by the U.S. Department of Labor's NAFTA Trade Adjustment Assistance program. In their study they did not focus on the workers from more than 1400 companies in 48 states who have filed petitions under one narrow NAFTA assistance program for having lost their jobs because of NAFTA.

Bill Clinton said, "*NAFTA means jobs. American jobs, and good paying jobs. If I didn't believe that, I wouldn't support this agreement.*" Technically he wasn't wrong. There were new jobs created during the Clinton Administration and they were high-paying jobs but they were not in the industries that would benefit those who lost jobs to Mexico. They were in the information technology sector and business and finance sectors where the bubble later busted. In 2012, the Angus Reid Public Opinion poll showed that 53 percent of Americans feel the U.S. should "renegotiate" or "leave" NAFTA.

Twenty years later, NAFTA is still costing U.S. jobs. A *USA Today* article written by Aamer Madhani reported that executives of Mondelez, the parent company of RJR Nabisco, announced in January 2016 that they were shifting production from Chicago to a more efficient factory line in Mexico where they have invested $130 million in a new cookie and cracker plant. The company generated over $30 billion in revenue in 2015 but say the move will save them $46 million annually. I presume that a respectable amount has passed from the time they accepted the $90 million from the city of Chicago in the early 1990s to remain there. "This is about putting more money into the CEO's pocket," LaDonna DeGoyler, a fork lift operator at the plant said, choking back tears as she spoke, "It is straight up greed" (Madhani, 2016). Personally, I've enjoyed eating Oreos, Chips Ahoys, and Nilla Wafers cookies all my life but this leaves a bad taste in my mouth.

Jobs Sailing Overseas

The job market for U.S. workers took another hit when China entered the World Trade Organization. According to the Economic Policy Institute, between 2001 and 2013, 3.2 million jobs floated away to China, and 75 percent of them were in manufacturing. The insult to injury is the fact that the low-wages in China and other Asian countries drive down the wages for those who still happen to have a job in the U.S.

Free trade in China was supposed to be a boon for the United States with the opening of a huge market. So far it hasn't worked to our benefit. Instead of exporting tons of goods into the Chinese market we import tons of goods from China. We've gone from an $83 billion trade deficit in 2000 to over $240 billion in 2013. In 2014, China became the largest recipient of foreign direct investment with $129 billion inflows, and Hong Kong in second with $103 billion inflows. This is a continuation of the growth of thousands of manufacturing plants that export back to the U.S.

Every one of the fifty states have experienced job losses because of offshoring, including D.C. and Puerto Rico. California alone lost 560,000 jobs. Thirty-nine percent of the job losses were concentrated in the manufacturing of computers and electronics and accounted for half of the trade deficit between 2001 and 2011. The recession in 2008 accelerated the trek of jobs overseas as more companies sought to cut labor costs. According to a study by The Hackett Group, a total of 2.3 million jobs in business services such as human resources, finance and purchasing, including 1.1 million information technology jobs will be offshored to Asian countries by 2016.

Not only are manufacturing and technical jobs leaving the country but the offshoring of service jobs is growing also. India is the top-rated country for outsourcing because of its huge workforce of nearly 1.5 billion. It also had the largest offshoring center for service jobs but they have also gone to China, Eastern Europe, Mexico, and the Philippines. The Hackett Group estimates that a third of the U.S. jobs in these industries will have moved offshore by 2016. Once service jobs are offshored it's unlikely they'll return back to the U.S.

Just in case you think that the health care industry is safe from offshoring, an article in the Los Angeles Time by Don Lee reported that some healthcare companies who had outsource their data-processing and accounting work overseas have begun to shift clinical services such as reading X-rays and other diagnostic tests (Lee, 2012). Pre-service nursing jobs where nurses at insurance firms assess patient needs and make decisions on medical care are being outsourced overseas to health professionals in India and the Philippines.

Benefits to Offshoring

Most of the benefits of offshoring go to the corporations; however, offshore outsourcing has been a boon in Asia, South America, and Eastern Europe. It has given millions of the poor in developing countries jobs and opportunities to improve their lives. The hope is American markets will benefit from their economic growth and that will boost higher employment for us here at home.

Not only does offshore outsourcing reduce costs for businesses, it benefits them with increased access to global talent, being more efficient with cutting technology, and generating higher profits. These higher profits make the company stronger and should translate into more opportunities for the American worker. Cheaper labor also enables companies to provide us with cheaper goods. This helps lower-income Americans purchase goods at lower prices.

The Affordable Healthcare Act limits the amount of the premium that can be spent on administrative expenses. Offshore outsourcing enables insurers to move jobs to cheaper-wage countries where they can save 30 percent in labor costs.

Executives and CEOs can demand even higher salaries for the money they save with offshoring. It seems that executive and managerial positions are rarely outsourced to cut costs. Executives in the United States earned 400 times the salary of the average worker in 2007. The tax break from being offshore doesn't hurt either, twenty-six of the largest U.S. corporations paid more money to their CEOs than they did in federal taxes.

Consequences of Offshoring

Outsourcing and Offshoring

The biggest consequence of offshoring took place back in the 1970s when companies began outsourcing the production of electronic products to Japan. Manufacturers took the technology, upgraded it, and put a number of American companies out of business. It opened up a whole can of worms we now call competition. U.S. corporations insist that offshoring gains them entry into emerging Asian markets. The Hira brothers, authors of *Outsourcing America*, beg to differ, "There is no evidence that American companies will be able to outcompete local Chinese and Indian companies, who are rapidly assimilating the technology and know-how from the local U.S. plants."

Companies complain about how this competition is making it hard for them to make a profit. Unions are the problem and cheaper labor is the answer. Local and state governments were effectively extorted by corporations threatening to move to Mexico if they didn't get tax deductions and other subsidies. Workers were also coerced by threats if they didn't accept lower wages and benefits. The bargaining power of unions was severely compromised. Who needs to come to the table and negotiate higher wages they have no desire to pay at home when they can get cheaper labor at somebody else's house.

Union busting or outsourcing? It's a question of which came first, the chicken or the egg. Membership is the strength of unions. When jobs are sent over the border or overseas union membership is diminished and weakened. With unions at a disadvantage, workers lose their bargaining power, making it easier for corporations to lay them off and outsource their jobs. More than 5 million manufacturing jobs were lost in the U.S. between 1997 and 2014, and most of those were good-paying jobs. Those jobs won't be coming back to this country and may not exist in the future as automation increases and corporation can get along with fewer workers.

The middleclass in American has diminished with every job sent overseas. U.S. workers who lost their jobs as a result of offshoring have lost a total of $37 billion in wages. According to the U.S. Bureau of Labor Statistics, two out of three workers who lost their jobs and were rehired in 2012 suffered wage reductions. Employment options are limited to low-skilled positions such as hospitality and food service. Despite the 188 percent rise in food imports from Mexico and Canada under NAFTA the nominal prices of food have risen 65 percent. Cheaper goods imported are not enough to offset the decline in wages. So end's the idea of wages keeping up with the cost of living and the growing income gap. If we are ever to lift our economy out of the doldrums we have to have jobs that pay middleclass salaries.

Shipping jobs across the border or overseas deprives the U.S. out of tax resources that are greatly needed to run this country. Corporations that outsource abroad avoid paying their "fair share" of taxes. American tax policy allows companies to postpone paying taxes until they bring those profits into the country. Some choose to leave those funds in offshore banks. A study by the Citizens for Tax Justice and the U.S. Public Interest Research Group Education Group based on an analysis of company filings to the IRS and the Securities and Exchange Commission found that the largest 500 U.S. companies would owe an estimated $620 billion in U.S. taxes on the $2.1 trillion held in offshore tax havens at the end of 2014. Of the top three, Apple had 181.1 billion, General Electric had 119 billion, and Microsoft had 108.3 billion in offshore bank accounts not subject to U.S. taxes.

Paul Craig Roberts explained it perfectly in an article for *The Washington Times*, "Corporate America's short-term mentality, stemming from bonuses tied to quarterly results, causes U.S. companies to lose not only their best employees –their human capital—but also the consumers who buy their products. Employees displaced by foreigners and left unemployed or in lower-paid work have reduced power in the consumer market. They provide fewer retirement savings for new investment (Roberts, 2005)."

American Workers, Hopeful or Hopeless

Back at home the unemployment rate in the U.S. is a nightmare that won't end. Despite the unemployment rate being reported at 4.9 percent, the lowest point since the Great Recession, the labor participation rate is also nearing a 38-year low. The unemployment rate is calculated by dividing the number of unemployed persons by all of the persons currently in the labor force. The reported measurement of the unemployment rate reflects the number of people who looked for a job in the last four weeks; the "real unemployment rate" which includes long-term discouraged workers, and those working part-time who would prefer a full-time job is 9.7 percent. According to the Bureau of Labor Statistics only 62.7 percent of adult Americans are working.

The largest employer in the country is Wal-Mart with 1.2 million employees. One third of those workers work less than 28 hours per week and don't qualify for company benefits. The average pay for part-time workers is $10.58. According to the Economic Policy Institute, Wal-Mart's Chinese imports have contributed to the loss of about 400,000 jobs. They also estimate that Wal-Mart sold $49 billion of Chinese-made products in the U.S. between 2001 and 2013, making them a big contributor to the expanding trade gap with China.

Meanwhile the Obama Administration is hoping to negotiate a new trade agreement called the Trans-Pacific Partnership (TPP). Once again the White House says this deal will *"help increase Made-in America exports, grow the American economy, support well-paying jobs, and strengthen the American middle class."* We've fallen for this 'pie in sky' twice before, but this time it's supposed to be different. This TPP agreement would renegotiate NAFTA with fundamental labor rights at its core, making those rights enforceable, and including the option to impose trade sanctions.

> These rights include freedom of association, the right to collective bargaining, prohibitions on and effective elimination of child and forced labor, and protection against employment discrimination. And for the first time in a trade agreement, TPP requires countries to adopt laws on minimum wages, hours of work, and occupational safety and health. TPP will make it easier for American entrepreneurs, farmers, and small business owners to sell Made-In-America products abroad by eliminating **more than 18,000 taxes** & other trade barriers on American

products across the 11 other countries in the TPP—barriers that put American products at an unfair disadvantage today.

I'd love to be optimistic, especially with Barack Obama proposing this, but corporations have yet to "Do the right thing" and this treaty is unlikely to make them see the light. This TPP proposal provides $450 million for displaced worker training in the Trade Adjustment Assistance program, so it anticipates workers losing jobs. Data from the Economic Policy Institute show the TAA program having helped more than 2.2 million workers who lost their jobs to international competition and trade, but even this is only half the number who lost jobs. Robert Reich, former Secretary of Labor for the Clinton Administration, says of the TPP, "That deal would give giant corporations even more patent protection overseas. And it would allow them to challenge any nation's health, safety, ad environmental laws that stand in the way of their profits –including our own."

Yes, global competitiveness is an issue. To maximize greater profits jobs are outsourced, workers are laid-off, or wages are held down. The stockholders are rewarded and the CEOS and upper-management are richly rewarded. The growing dilemma is that there are less of us working who can afford to purchase the product. To make up the difference the price is increased, the box shrinks, or the amenities are lessened. To keep making the profits, the process must be repeated. The reality is still supply and demand. In order for there to be a demand for the supply there has to be cash to buy the supply. If you don't want to supply workers with adequate wages you cut off the demand for another company. Believe me when I tell you, what goes around comes around.

This is becoming a moral question of what obligations corporations who sell their goods and services to the public have to employ the public. Corporations would rather employ a robot that doesn't need a salary, belong to union, or want healthcare or a pension before they put a human being to work (Leo, 2014). This has not been addressed by our elected representatives. It has been a gradual process but we now have a government that is for business, fools the people, and deceives them for their support and money. To our legislators who insist this is a

Christian nation, Matthew 6:24, "*No one can serve two masters. For you will hate one and love the other; you will be devoted to one and despise the other. You cannot serve God and money.*" Bruce Watson in Daily Finance summed it up, "The conflict may come down to a choice of either increasing the economic growth of America's companies or increasing the economic security of its citizens."

Education, the Economy, and Who Should Pay

"Education is the most powerful weapon which you can use to change the world."

~Nelson Mandela

Education, the Economy, and Who Should Pay

Most American companies engaged in offshore outsourcing claim that a shortage of skilled domestic employees, not cost cutting, is the primary reason they shift some of their job functions to foreign countries. Sorry to say, that doesn't mean jobs for the less educated are anymore plentiful. We are officially into the knowledge economy. If your job isn't already outsourced, replaced by some sort of software, a self-serve checkout system, or being done by a robot, then you're one of the fortunate ones. For the time being we haven't created a machine that can think or drive a vehicle but they're working on it. None of this bodes well for the American worker.

Technology is the catalyst that has revolutionized the skills needed from the workforce. One hundred years ago it was the manufacturing assembly line, in the new millennium it's computers and the internet. The world is being re-shaped by the knowledge-based and an ever expanding global economy which requires a more educated worker. Global competitiveness and the interdependent nature of the world require that America must make postsecondary education more accessible to greater numbers of people than ever before. The proportion of college graduates in the U.S. has grown at one of the slowest rates among developed countries. Twenty years ago, the U.S. ranked second in the world in the rate of college graduations, we've now fallen down to 12th. This new reality has led to an awakening for business, economic, and political leaders to the crisis of education in America.

Other countries have expanded their educational systems and the advantage the U.S. once had has narrowed. Robert Reich, former Secretary of Labor, warned us about this predicament in his book, *The Work of Nations: Preparing Ourselves for the 21st Century* when he said, "Each nation's primary assets will be its citizens' skills and insights. Each nation's primary political task will be to cope with the centrifugal forces of the global economy which tear at the ties binding citizen's together—bestowing ever greater wealth on the most skilled and insightful, while consigning the less skilled to a declining standard of living."

The United States ranks 5th among the most educated countries with 43 percent of our population having a college degree. Russia has the highest population of post-secondary with 53.5 percent followed by Canada, Japan, and Israel. The majority of countries who lead in education tend to have higher levels of advanced skills and perform higher in literacy and math proficiency exams. The U.S. breaks the trend, scoring worst than most of the developed nations in reading and high-level math skills. This explains why Americans don't have the necessary skills to compete in the global job market.

"Foregoing college is not what we should aspire to," said Joe Minarik, of the Washington-based Committee for Economic Development, "Right now you can look around the world and you can see a lot of high-tech, high-value high-productivity jobs that we are not doing in this country, in part because this country does not have the requisite skills." Caterpillar is just one company that says they have hundreds of unfilled job openings for machine operators, sales representatives, and a long list of other positions they can't find qualified people to fill.

A college education is no longer a privilege, it's a necessity. Opportunities for postsecondary education will need to be expanded to increase participation and build an educated workforce. The earning level of high school graduates hasn't changed in 35 years while the earnings of those with a bachelor's degree have doubled. Unless the issue of education is seriously addressed the growing gap in income inequality will widen even more and the national economy will suffer. A Manpower survey of 1,300 employers found the hardest positions to fill include skilled trades, engineers, and sales representatives.

Anthony P. Carnevale and Stephen J. Rose, authors of *The Undereducated American*, say that the U.S. has been under-producing college-educated workers since 1980. They recommend that we add an additional 20 million post-secondary workers to the economy by 2025 to meet our efficiency and equity goals for the economy and to reverse the growth of income inequality. To reach this challenge it requires greater productivity from our educational system on all levels.

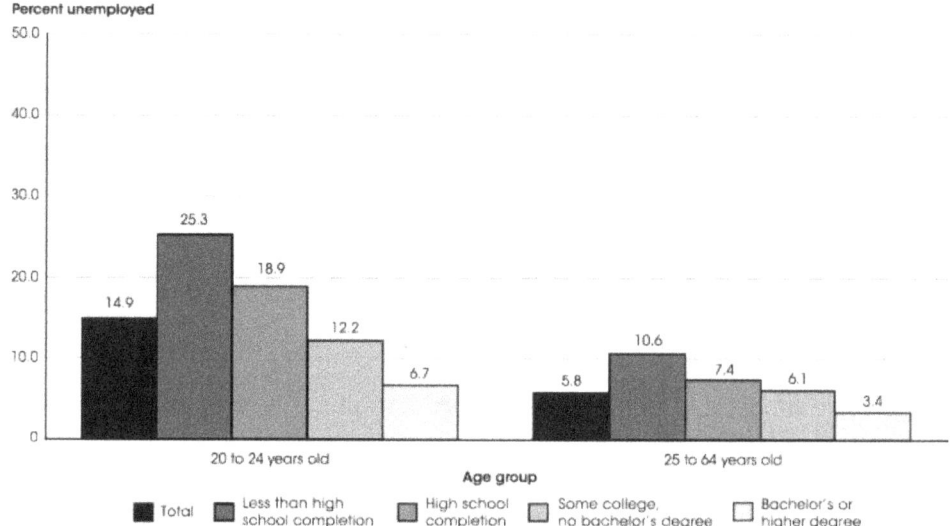

Figure 4. Unemployment rates, by age group and educational attainment: 2014

. High school completion includes equivalency credentials, such as the General Educational Development (GED) credential.
SOURCE: U.S. Department of Labor, Bureau of Labor Statistics, Office of Employment and Unemployment Statistics, unpublished annual average data from the Current Population Survey (CPS), 2014. See *Digest of Education Statistics 2014*, table 501.80.

Educating more Americans

The United States Constitution, through the tenth amendment, designated power to the States giving them the duty to provide an adequate education to all of its citizens (Alexander and Alexander, 2005). In the decision of the Claremont School District v. Governor, Chief Justice Brock stated, *"A constitutionally adequate public education is not a static concept removed from the demands of an evolving world. It is not the needs of the few but the critical requirement of the many that it must address"* (Alexander and Alexander, 2005). If the needs for an adequate education have changed, then the state's obligation has also changed.

The struggle of the national economy and the shrinking tax base are precursors of limited funds for higher education due to the discretionary nature of some state appropriations (Schmidt, 2008). Globalization dictates that the United States must continue to contribute to new innovations, attract new businesses, and compete for higher paying jobs. Policymakers recognize that changes are necessary in the immediate future to increase the education and training of their constituents.

Higher education is an investment in human capital, and our society views higher education as a public benefit. Economists agree that higher levels of education are critical to economic growth for the country, every state, and each individual household. Nonetheless, the higher education industry is not immune to the economic issues that are presently challenging our society. Escalating tuitions and a contracting national economy have sharpened the focus on the economics or finance of postsecondary education.

Tuition and fees at colleges and Universities in the U.S., both public and private, have gone up like a runaway hot air balloon over the past 20 years and are now out of sight. Financing a post-secondary education is akin to buying a house and for some is the impossible dream. According to the U.S. News Best College rankings from 1995 to 2015, the average tuition at private universities went up 179 percent, out-of-state tuition and fees at public universities jumped 226 percent, and in-state tuition and fees at public universities skyrocketed 296 percent. Even with the largest price increase, in-state public colleges and universities are still the most affordable.

Financing College Educations

Now that we're on the same page with the realization that we need to educate and train the American workforce, the question is: How do we pay for it? If someone is unemployed or underemployed they obviously don't have the means to afford college tuition. The $165 billion that the federal government spends on higher education grants, student loans, and tax credits to make college more affordable seem to be having the opposite effect. The more money that they provide the more colleges and universities increase their costs. It's like chasing a locomotive on foot, you'll never catch it.

The Pell Grant, federal financial aid that doesn't have to be paid back, used to cover 75 percent of tuition at the average four-year public college or university; presently it barely covers 33 percent. For the 2016-2017 award year; the maximum Pell grant is $5,815. The U.S. Department of Education uses a standard formula to determine financial need based on information reported on the Free Application for Federal Student Aid (FAFSA). The amount awarded depends on your estimated family contribution, cost of attendance, whether you're a full-time part-time student, and whether you plan to attend for a full academic year or less. In 2014, more than half of the recipients of Pell grants had family incomes under $20,000.

The Pell grant provides an opportunity for low-income students to attend college. For the very wealthy, money is no object in educating their family. It's the middle-class family that lacks options. The average middle-class family with income between $37,000 and $75,000 isn't eligible for federal or state assistance, yet paying $7,500 college tuition at a public four-year university is basically unaffordable. In the 2014-2015 academic year, private institutions charged an average $31,000 for tuition and fees, and many cost well over $50,000. Without an academic or athletic scholarship there is only one choice, getting a loan. Most have borrowed student loans from private and publicly-funded programs to cover tuition and fees to the tune of $100 billion each year. That brings with it a whole new set of problems. Americans now owe over $1.3 trillion in student loan debt; this is four times the amount owed just ten years ago.

Believe it or not, back in 1862 when the first Morrill Act established public universities through federal land grant, going to college was practically free. States opted to charge little or no tuition. This ended in the 1960s when campuses were becoming more populated and more diverse. Bernie Sanders in his presidential bid has proposed making public college and universities tuition-free again. He says it can be paid for by a new federal tax on financial transactions, including stock, bond and derivative trades.

Public colleges and universities are tuition-free in Denmark, Finland, Iceland, Ireland, Mexico, Norway, and Sweden. These countries understand the importance of investing in the education of their people. Post-secondary education is also free in Germany, not only for Germans and Europeans but for international students as well. In 2015, BBC News reported there were more than 4,600 U.S. students enrolled in German universities to take advantage of the free education. A nominal fee of less than $200 per year, rent, mandatory health insurance and living expenses are the charges to earn a degree from a premier university.

In January 2015, President Obama proposed *America's College Promise*, a plan to make tuition free at two-year community colleges. The California-based non-profit, Campaign for Free College Tuition, says we need more, "calling for a full college scholarship to every academically qualified student whose family makes less than $160,000 a year.

Changing Demographics and Education

The face of the U.S. workforce is changing. The millennial generation, defined as those from age 18 to 34, has taken over the baby boomers and is now the largest generation. According to the Pew Research Center, millennials will make up 46 percent of the workers in this country by 2020. Director of Georgetown University's Center of Education, Anthony Carnevale says, "Millennials are going to dominate all the numbers, employment and unemployment, from here on out." The demographic changes in the population also predict that a larger portion of the future workforce in this country will come from ethnic minority and low-income groups. In 2020, the white working-age population is projected to decline to 63 percent while the minority workforce is projected to double to 37 percent.

Given the changing demographics and the current educational disparities among racial/ethnic groups, the overall education level of the workforce is projected to decline. Those with lower levels of education are entering the workforce as those with higher levels are retiring. If this continues you have a workforce undereducated for high-skilled jobs necessary for our knowledge economy. This in turn will have the bulk of Americans relegated to menial and service jobs and result in further decreases in personal income per capita for workers. In order to grow the national economy this population must be prepared to be full participants. The educational underachievement of minorities in the United States will have serious implications in maintaining a competitive global workforce.

Looking back over the history of this country, postsecondary education has been one of the safest and beneficial investments that we've made that contributes to the economic success of the nation. Educated workers are more productive, they earn more, and they pay more in taxes. Federal funding for education must be increased to make a significant effort to raise the educational level of U.S. workers. There's no reason why a high school graduate in this country, regardless of their family's income, who wants to go to college and further their education should not be able to do so without drowning themselves in debt.

Are the Jobs Really Out There?

Now that the case has been made for educating our uneducated workforce to stay competitive in the global economy, what is the reality on the job market? Are the college graduates we already have being utilized to their full potential? Data from the Economic Policy Institute show that the unemployment rate for young college graduates is currently 7.2 percent and their underemployment rated is 14.9 percent. For high school graduates, the unemployment rate is 19.5 percent and their underemployment rate is 37 percent.

Underemployment is as serious an issue for college graduates as unemployment, particularly for those who are burdened with heavy loan debt. Fourteen percent end up defaulting on their loans after three years because they don't make enough to keep up with the payments working as waiters, bartenders, and retail clerks. Underemployment or people working below their skill level became a problem for new graduates and professionals who were laid-off during the 2001 recession; it got worse in the 2008 Great Recession.

According to the New York Federal Reserve, 34 percent of recent college graduates in 2001 were underemployed; in 2010 the number was 45 percent. In that same year, a study done by the Center for College Affordability and Productivity showed that 25 percent of retail clerks, 15 percent of taxi drivers, and 115,520 janitors had bachelor's degrees. Contrary to what offshore outsourcing corporations have claimed, Richard Vedder, founder of the study said, "The problem is the stock of college graduates (41 Million) in the workforce was larger than the number of jobs requiring a college degree (28.6 Million).

U.S. Census Bureau statistics show that from 2002 to 2012, the number of Americans earning an associate's degree increased 31 percent; the number earning a bachelor's degree grew 25, and the number of those earning a master's or doctorate degree rose by 45 percent and 43 percent respectively. These graduates have an average of $33,000 in student loan debt. The difficulty in obtaining a job in their chosen field that pays the bills has many wondering if the rewards are worth the effort or the costs. Forty-one percent of college graduates in 2013 and 2014 earn less than $25,000.

Rising costs for college tuition and the tepid job market emphasize the need for government intervention to ensure Americans are educated without crippling debt. College graduates have unemployment rates that are half of those without post-secondary education and training. Students can increase their odds for employment by choosing an area of study that is in demand for a viable degree. Less than 45 percent of recent college graduates who majored in business, communications, liberal arts, and social sciences were employed in jobs that required a degree. Results show that students who major in technical fields like engineering, math, or computer science fare better in the job market. Fields such as education and health have the lowest unemployment rates of all the majors, these areas are always expanding as our population continues to grow.

An article by Bill Gates discussed ways to improve the number of college graduates in the U.S. He said, "By 2025, two-thirds of all jobs in the US will require education beyond high school. At the current rate that the U.S. is producing college graduates, however, the country is expected to face a shortfall of 11 million skilled workers to fill those roles over the next 10 years." There are politicians, analysts, and critics who say that we don't need to increase the education of the U.S. workforce, that there are already too many college graduates, and that it doesn't make sense to spend more money on post-secondary education with so many unemployed and underemployed. Underemployment is certainly an issue for college graduates but it is even more of a problem for less educated workers. It seems yet again, we are damned if we do and damned if we don't.

Affirmative Action

Affirmative Action

"In matters of truth and justice, there is no difference between large and small problems, for issues concerning the treatment of people are all the same." ~Albert Einstein

Lawmakers and leaders in a number of states have pushed for a ban on affirmative action policies. These protests assert that affirmative action is not needed and causes whites to suffer discrimination. The truth is that the circumstances and reasons that required affirmative action policies haven't gone anywhere. NAACP President Benjamin Todd Jealous stated, "The only question about affirmative action isn't whether or not we need the hammer. The question is whether the hammer is big enough."

The affirmative action debate is back in the forefront with the U.S. Supreme Court decision on the Fisher v. University of Texas at Austin case. A white female applicant sued the University after she was denied admission. She contended that the reason for her rejection was the use of race in the admissions process violating the Equal Protection Clause of the 14th Amendment. This is the most commonly used and most often litigated portion of the amendment.

Texas law offers automatic admission to eligible freshman applicants in the top 10 percent of their high school class to public colleges and universities. The University of Texas at Austin uses two factors in determining admission for students, the academic index and the Personal Achievement Index (PAI). The PAI score measures leadership qualities and work experience, extra-curricular activities, community service and other specific circumstances of a student's background. In 2004, the student's race was included as a component of the PAI score. The petitioner applied for admission in 2008, 1 of 29,501 applicants. Of this group 12,843 were admitted, 6,715 accepted and enrolled. The current student body is 52 percent women, 46 percent white, 22 percent Latino/Hispanic, 19 percent Asian, 5 percent international, and 4 percent black.

It may seem to some white applicants who see blacks attend college and universities where they have been denied admission that it must be due to some affirmative action. How could this student possibly be more desirable than they are? The petitioner was obviously not in the top 10 percent or she would have been automatically accepted. The University of Texas at Austin is a very competitive institution with a large number of applicants. There were probably quite a few white students who scored higher than she did. Why would she assume that the reason she was denied admission was due to discrimination based on her race or an African American student taking her slot. When African American students are denied admission it's not a federal case.

What is Affirmative Action?

Affirmative action is defined by Merriam-Webster as the practice of improving the educational and employment opportunities of members of groups that have not been treated fairly in the past because of their race, sex, etc. The term "affirmative action" was first used in an executive order issued by President John F. Kennedy. It was Executive Order 10925, signed on March 6, 1961. The subject of this executive order was equal opportunity employment. "The contractor will take affirmative action to ensure that applicants are employed, and that employees are treated during employment, without regard to their race, creed, color, or national origin."

The affirmative action policy statement presented by college admission offices and most employers says: Affirmative Action is a program of positive action, undertaken with conviction and effort to overcome the present effects of past practices, policies, or barriers to equal employment opportunity and to achieve the full and fair participation of women, minorities and individuals with disabilities found to be underutilized in the workforce or affected by policies and practices having an adverse impact.

The purpose of affirmative action is to balance out the effects of discrimination, overt and institutional racism by establishing fair access to education and employment opportunities. Discrimination is defined as the treatment or consideration of, or making a distinction in favor or against, a person or thing based on the group, class, or category to which that person or thing belongs rather than on individual merit. Discrimination is as much a fact of life as growing old and just as persistent in our diverse society. We base our choices on our inclination or preference and in certain situations it may be unfair and prejudiced. Affirmative action policies and programs are tools through which additional efforts are made to hire and promote qualified minorities, women, and individuals with disabilities.

Racism is the Reason

The nature of the United States and its diversity lends itself to discrimination, prejudices, and racism. Some of it is driven by the human instinct to thrive but most of the behavior is learned. Racism comes in a variety of forms, individual racism, institutional racism, and structural racism. Jim Wallis characterized it as *"America's Original Sin"* in his book about racism in this country. Structural racism or systemic racism is defined as "the normalization and legitimization of an array of dynamics—historical, cultural, institutional, and interpersonal—that routinely advantage whites while producing cumulative and chronic adverse outcomes for people of color" (Lawrence and Keleher, 2004).

Structural racism is the mother of all forms of racism. The foundation on which the United States was built is structural racism. We don't like to talk about and would like to think we have grown and moved past it but unfortunately that is not our truth. It is inherited, not transferred through our DNA, but passed down by generation just as effectively. It is impregnated in every aspect of our society, our history, education, politics, economics, and culture. It perpetuates a system of white supremacy and racial group inequities.

Institutional racism, the term coined by Stokely Carmichael (later known as Kwame Ture) in the late 1960s, is the discrimination that occurs within and across institutions based on race, where one race is favored or another group is disadvantaged. An institution is representative of its history, culture, and the people that govern it, along with their personal bias. In a free society it's impossible to control the hearts and minds that direct racist behavior within individuals; however, we can make allowances to limit the effects of institutional racism. The first step was to admit that segregation was discrimination. More than half a century later, the after effects of segregation and its structure remain intact. It's not a wrong that will gradually right itself with equality growing and spreading naturally. Activism is necessary to counter the generations of inequities and balance opportunities. That's why we still need affirmative action.

President Lyndon Johnson sufficiently clarified the basis for affirmative action in his June 4, 1965 commencement address at Howard University.

> Freedom is the right to share, share fully and equally, in American society--to vote, to hold a job, to enter a public place, to go to school. It is the right to be treated in every part of our national life as a person equal in dignity and promise to all others. But freedom is not enough. You do not wipe away the scars of centuries by saying: Now you are free to go where you want, and do as you desire, and choose the leaders you please.
>
> You do not take a person who, for years, has been hobbled by chains and liberate him,bring him up to the starting line of a race and then say, "You are free to compete with all the others," and still justly believe that you have been completely fair. Thus it is not enough just to open the gates of opportunity. All our citizens must have the ability to walk through those gates. This is the next and the more profound stage of the battle for civil rights. We seek not just freedom but opportunity.

The impetus was ensuring opportunity, an attempt to level the playing field and add a degree of fairness. There are individual and institutional barriers that block equal opportunities and discriminate, subtle and covert, or we would not have the underrepresentation of minorities, women, and those with disabilities in colleges and universities and in the workforce.

History of Affirmative Action

This is not the first time that the need for affirmative action was recognized and proposed. It is not a new or unique concept. The necessity to respond to the effects of discrimination with legal action goes far back into our history. The first attempt of affirmative action in the United States took place after 4 million African American slaves were freed after the Civil War during Reconstruction. Congress created the Freedmen's Bureau to combat measures from the South that were designed to keep black people inferior and perpetuate the supply of cheap labor. Southern state legislators resistant to the 13th Amendment and the end of slavery enacted a number of laws during 1865 and 1866 referred to as the "black codes" to limit the freedoms of blacks. These laws varied from state to state.

There were vagrancy laws that declared a black to be vagrant if they were unemployed and without a permanent residence; they could be arrested, fined, or bonded out for labor if they couldn't pay the fine (Meier and Rudwick, 1976). Blacks were denied fair wages for work. Apprentice laws granted the hiring out of orphans or children of "unfit parents" to serve those who were often times their former owners. In some states the type of property blacks could own was limited, and in others they were excluded from skilled trades and certain businesses. Former slaves were forbidden to carry firearms or testify in court, except in matters relating to other blacks. Interracial marriage was illegal.

Then were the bloody race riots of Memphis and New Orleans in 1866 with attacks on blacks by the KKK, race supremacy organizations, and the police force. The violence and the killings were an affront to the efforts to re-unite the country. The necessary reaction from the North, the affirmative action, to deal with the injustice against former slaves was known as Radical Reconstruction. In rejection of the racist black codes, Congress passed the Freedmen's Bill and the Civil Rights Act of 1866, the first federal law to define citizenship and affirm that all citizens are equal under the law. It was also the first major presidential vetoed piece of legislation overturned in history.

> That all persons born in the United States and not subject to any foreign power, excluding Indians not taxed, are hereby declared to be citizens of the United States; and such citizens, of every race and color, without regard to any previous condition of slavery or involuntary servitude, except as a punishment for crime whereof the party shall have been duly convicted, shall have the same right, in every State and Territory in the United States, to make and enforce contracts, to sue, be parties, and give evidence, to inherit, purchase, lease, sell, hold, and convey real and personal property, and to full and equal benefit of all laws and proceedings for the security of person and property, as is enjoyed by white citizens, and shall be subject to like punishment, pains, and penalties, and to none other, any law, statute, ordinance, regulation, or custom, to the contrary notwithstanding.

Radical Reconstruction

Radical Republicans pushed the Radical Reconstruction believing that the emancipated blacks should have opportunities to compete in the free-labor market. In 1867 they passed the 14th Amendment.

> All persons born or naturalized in the United States, and subject to the jurisdiction thereof, are citizens of the United States and of the State wherein they reside. No State shall make or enforce any law which shall abridge the privileges or immunities of citizens of the United States; nor shall any State deprive any person of life, liberty, or property, without due process of law; nor deny to any person within its jurisdiction the equal protection of the laws.

Because of reconstruction laws in the south, enfranchised black males had a voice in the government and were allowed to vote in 11 Southern states that were controlled by the Republican reconstruction leadership, also known as carpetbaggers and scalawags. Incredibly or maybe not, the North was not thrilled about blacks voting in elections and denied them the right. The 15th Amendment was ratified on February 2, 1870 stating: "The right of citizens of the United States to vote shall not be denied or abridged by the United States or by any State on account of race, color, or previous condition of servitude."

African Americans were being elected to political offices, sixteen sat in Congress from 1867-1877, and 600 served as legislators on the local level. They filled schools to educate themselves, integrated juries, became sheriffs and judges, and held positions on city councils and school boards. Racial discrimination in public places, in restaurants, on streetcars, and train stations was illegal. Some African Americans were able to accumulate some wealth but most lived as sharecroppers, another form of slavery.

Support for Reconstruction diminished with time during an economic depression and later a stagnated economy. Racism, fueled by frustration and resentment in the impoverished South, became a powerful violent force to take away the gains achieved by blacks. White Supremacy groups like the Ku Klux Klan, the Knights of the White Camelia, and the White Brotherhood were formed, murdering, lynching, raping, pillaging, and intimidating black people who dared to exercise their rights. After a decade, Reconstructions was over. "Jim Crow" laws would soon disenfranchise and segregate black people in every aspect. It would be almost a century before "Reconstruction" would be revived in the Civil Rights struggle for political, economic, and social equality.

Brown v. Board of Education of Topeka (1954)

In 1896, the Supreme Court case of Plessy v. Ferguson challenged the "separate but equal" statute. Homer Plessy, a 30 year old shoemaker, was arrested on June 7, 1892 for sitting in the 'white' car of the East Louisiana Railroad. His lawyer argued that his Thirteenth and Fourteenth Amendment rights had been violated by the Separate Car Act. The Supreme Court decision held that segregated facilities were legal as long as they were equal to each other. Justice Henry Brown wrote: "The object of the Fourteenth Amendment was undoubtedly to enforce the absolute equality of the two races before the law, but in the nature of things it could not have been intended to abolish distinctions based upon color, or to enforce social, as distinguished from political equality, or a commingling of the two races upon terms unsatisfactory to either."

Justice John Harlan, the lone dissenter, and able to foresee the dreadful consequences wrote: "The present decision, it may well be apprehended, will not only stimulate aggressions, more or less brutal and irritating, upon the admitted rights of colored citizens, but will encourage the belief that it is possible by means of state enactments to defeat the beneficent purposed which the people of the United States had in view when they adopted the recent amendments of the Constitution." The separate but equal doctrine expanded to cover almost every area of public life, restaurants, restrooms, public schools and theaters despite the fact that they were never equal.

More than 50 years later, the Brown v. Board of Education challenged the "separate but equal" doctrine. Brown claimed that the racial segregation in Topeka's schools violated the "equal protection" clause of the Fourteenth Amendment, charging that the city's black and whites were not equal and never could be. The Supreme Court ruling in the Brown case overturned the Plessy v. Ferguson decision and was one of the most significant decisions of the 20th century. In a unanimous decision the court held that racial segregation in public schools violated the equal protection clause of the Fourteenth Amendment. This landmark case was a huge victory for the Civil Rights movement setting a precedent and supplying the legal means for challenging segregation in every area of American society.

Implementation of Affirmative Action

The longest-standing affirmative action program was instigated by A. Philip Randolph and Bayard Rustin, activists prior to the Civil Rights Movement, after they organized a 1941 march on Washington, D.C. to protest and pressure the U.S. government into desegregating the armed forces and providing fair working opportunities for African Americans. President Franklin Roosevelt, hoping to avert the march, issued Executive

Order 8802 which barred discrimination in the federal government and against blacks by defense contractors, and established the first Fair Employment Practices Committee (Lucander, 2014).

Two decades later, in light of the increasing federal dollars going into construction projects during the 1960s, the NAACP and the Urban League protested the lack of an African American presence on construction crews. In 1969, responding to the pressure, the Nixon administration initiated the "Philadelphia Order," the most definitive plan of affirmative action thus far to guarantee fair hiring practices in construction jobs. It was designed to rectify institutional discrimination by building trade unions. Assistant Secretary of Labor, Arthur Fletcher, explained why Philadelphia was chosen as a test case. "The craft unions and the construction industry are among the most egregious offenders against equal opportunity laws . . . openly hostile toward letting blacks into their closed circle." The order required government contractors to hire African American workers with certain hiring goals and specific dates.

Nixon then signed Executive Order 11478, which expanded affirmative action in all government hiring. The positive impact was seen immediately as large numbers of African Americans were added to the federal payroll. In just a few years, 57 percent of black male college graduates and 72 percent of black female college graduates were working in government jobs. President Nixon emphasized, "We would not impose quotas, but would require federal contractors to show 'affirmative action' to meet the goals of increasing minority employment." The plan was promptly extended to other cities.

Nevertheless, there are always roundabout paths to get you to the place you want to be, particularly if you are trying to skirt an issue. Companies got creative to avoid fairness in hiring and promotion. Duke Power Company, with a long history of discrimination against blacks, established new standards for employment and transfer that required a high school diploma and the passing of an intelligence test. Black employees of Duke brought action against them challenging that the requirements discriminated against black employees, noting that white employees who did not fulfill the requirement were able to perform the job satisfactorily.

The Griggs v. Duke Power Company went all the way to the Supreme Court. The 1971 landmark decision was in favor of the complainants. The Supreme Court held that under title VII of the Civil Rights Act, not only is overt discrimination prohibited but also "practices that are in form fair but discriminatory in operation." The ruling was based on what we now know as the "disparate impact theory," meaning a policy may be considered discriminatory if it has a disproportionate "adverse impact" against any group based on race, ethnicity, religion, gender, or disability. Testing requirements are allowed for hiring and promotion as long as they measure the suitability of the person for the job and are not used to exclude African Americans or other minorities from the job. The court found Duke had violated the Act.

Disparate impact was evident again in the Texas v. Inclusive Communities Project case where low-income housing tax credits were disproportionately granted within minority neighborhoods and denied within white neighborhoods. This led to the concentration of low-income housing in minority neighborhoods which perpetuates segregation and is in violation of the Fair Housing Act. In a 5-4 decision, the Supreme Court ruled that disparate impact claims are clearly identified under the Fair Housing Act. This is a clear example of why we need affirmative action. There are subtle instances of discrimination or prejudice without deliberate intent. Without the policy, business will be conducted as usual without a measure to guide outcomes toward a more integrated path.

In 1972, the Equal Employment Opportunity Act was passed, cementing the legal foundation for affirmative action. For the rest of the decade, data from the Bureau of Labor Statistics shows the large employment gains for blacks in white-collar positions. The number of black women professionals and clerical workers also rose higher. Black representation in skilled trade and craft grew as well. Although the largest percentage of black workers was still concentrated in laborer and low-skilled job categories, the affirmative action policy did open doors that under ordinary conditions would have remained closed.

Challenges to Affirmative Action

"Goals and timetables" applied to higher education institutions to increase underrepresented minority students. One remedy was to reserve a certain number of slots for African American and Latino applicants. The Regents of the University of California v. Bakke case challenged this process. The plaintiff argued that he had been twice denied admission to the medical school even though his MCAT scores and grades were higher than those of some minority students who had been admitted. Bakke sued, charging that the admission process violated Title VI of the Civil Rights Act and the Equal Protection Clause of the Fourteenth Amendment. The California Supreme Court found that the quota system used discriminated against other racial groups and that no applicant could be rejected based on race in favor of another who is less qualified. The medical school appealed to the Supreme Court.

The Regents of the University of California v. Bakke was reviewed by the Supreme Court in 1978. In a 5-4 decision, the court ruled that the use of quotas violated the equal protection clause and discriminated against whites by excluding them from 16 out of 100 spots because of race. The court also upheld that diversity in higher education as a "compelling interest" and race could be used as a factor in admissions decisions. Affirmative action programs to accept more minority students are constitutional when used along with other factors.

Removing race as factor in admissions was revisited in the Hopwood v. Texas case where a white female was denied admission to law school in favor of less qualified applicants. In 1996, the Fifth Circuit Court of Appeals ruling barred the use of racial preferences in university admissions. When the U.S. Supreme Court declined to hear the case, the Fifth Circuit decision became constitutional law in their jurisdiction, which included universities in Texas, Louisiana, and Mississippi. It was after this decision that Texas adopted the "10 percent Plan" where anyone who graduated in the top 10 percent of a Texas high school was entitled to automatic admission to any Texas state university as a means to increasing diversity. This enabled Texas to raise the number of minority students enrolled without violating the constitution.

The Hopwood v. Texas decision was overturned by the Supreme Court in 2003 in the Grutter v. Bollinger case where a white female alleged that she had been denied admission based on her race. The 5-4 decision upheld the affirmative action policies of the University of Michigan Law School. The Court found that the non-determinative weight of race among other factors was "neutral" enough, that they did not have a quota system, and their interest in a diverse student body was compelling enough to meet the constitutional standard of equality. In the Gratz v. Bollinger case, decided on the same day, the Supreme Court found that the University of Michigan undergraduate admissions policy, with its automatic distribution of 20 points to all qualified applicants who are African America, Hispanic, and Native American, violates both the Equal Protection Clause and the Title VI of the Civil Rights Act. Despite the argument that diversity is a compelling state interest, the use of racial preferences was not narrowly tailored and not individually based.

Ten years later in 2013, another challenge to race as a factor in admissions policy caused the debate to re-heat in Fisher v. University of Texas at Austin where a white female charged that her rejection was based on race. During oral arguments in response to African-Americans being underrepresented Justice Scalia stated, "I'm just not impressed by the fact that the University of Texas may have fewer. Maybe it ought to have fewer." Justice Ruth Bader Ginsburg wrote in a dissenting opinion that the University's policy uses race as only one factor in the overall decision and was permissible by previous judicial precedent and that the Equal Protection Clause does not require that public universities ignore the history of overt discrimination.

Affirmative action policies adopted by colleges and universities in admission increased the number of African American and Latino students enrolled but not sufficiently enough to close the gap between white and minority students. Yet the use of race as a factor in the college admission process is still controversial. In 2014, the Supreme Court upheld the

Michigan constitution amendment that banned affirmative action in the admissions to state public universities. This ruling will probably lead to more states banning the use of racial preferences to increase diversity. The fact remains that those states that have banned affirmative action in higher education have seen significant drops in the enrollment of Black and Latino students at selective colleges and universities.

Pros and Cons of Affirmative Action

Backlash against the Civil Rights Movement and the Feminist Movement caused a shift in policies that ushered the country away from the progressive 1970s towards the "conservative" 1980s of Ronald Reagan. The government itself was considered to be the problem. The conservative belief is that affirmative action is unconstitutional under the Equal Protection Clause of the Fourteenth Amendment. Proponents of conservatism feel the role of government should be limited to necessities like national defense. They feel the more control the government has over our lives the less liberty we have. Affirmative action is seen as undue interference by the government.

Conservatives argue against any preferential treatment saying that affirmative action is merely "reverse discrimination" and that it actually feeds more racism by dividing society by race, ethnicity, and gender. Race preferences in the workplace were removed and policies for affirmative action were weakened. The impetus being opportunities for promotion and higher education should be based on merit alone. Affirmative action sends a bad message to minorities, that they are not good enough to make it on their own qualifications. Critics of the policy say that it lowers standards and students are less accountable. Others feel the policy is outdated and no longer necessary. The playing field has become leveled. They admit some persons maybe racist but the total society is not.

Some critics argue that affirmative action doesn't do enough, that it doesn't work. It only gives the illusion that things are moving toward equality. Blacks still have double the unemployment of whites. That may be true but without it there wouldn't have been the small amount of progress that we've seen. It's also said that those who've benefited from affirmative action are burdened by the stigma of it. Not true, the lack of opportunity is the greatest burden that one can carry. Until a better plan is put forth we have to strengthen and enforce the one we have.

Affirmative action has contributed greatly to the diversity within higher education and the workplace. The resources available make a tremendous difference in what an individual can accomplish. Graduates who have benefited from affirmative action say they received better jobs and led better lives because of the opportunity afforded them. The reality was and still is that the hiring or admittance of person in the workplace or at an educational institution is highly based on someone's discretion or possible discrimination. Race and gender will be taken into account before qualifications with or without affirmative action. Ralph Waldo Emerson explained, "Nothing can resist states; everything gravitates; like will to like..." There has to be a system or a formula to interject a degree of impartiality or fairness when those in the position of choosing are mostly white male. When the use of race and affirmative action are eliminated, the degree of diversity nosedives.

Affirmative Action is viewed in an over-simplistic manner, that a minority is taking a position that should rightfully belong to a white. The point is inclusion for those who have historically been excluded. This is about who Americans ultimately want to be. Are we going to be a nation separate and unequal? The fourteenth amendment is still about segregation as well as equal rights. Without affirmative action segregation will creep back into our society from the places where it still reigns supreme. The separation has widened with the economic and educational gap between races and the poor and wealthy. There has to be some method or means to compensate for or alleviate the effects of centuries of racial, social, and economical oppression.

Aspen Photo / Shutterstock.com

College Athletes, Pay or No Pay

College Athletics Pay or No Pay

Sports are the embodiment of America. They represent everything that we envision as great within ourselves: strength, competitiveness, and invincibility. It is our best self. We hold our athletes in high esteem much like our soldiers, for they too lay their bodies on the line for honor. At least the amateurs do, and that's the way we want to keep it. They should remain pure and unsullied. Except, the truth is that it isn't all clean fun. There are plenty dirty hands at the table. How could there not be with so much money being generated. Honestly, there's absolutely nothing wrong with a profitable enterprise. As usual the crime comes in the choice not to share the wealth with those that generate the financial windfall. In this case that's the college athlete.

Once upon a time college sports were played for the love of the game and the thrill of competition. What was more awesome than hitting a homerun, running in a touchdown, swimming the fastest time, or jumping above the rim and making the basket? It was all about the glory of it, the cheers from the stands. That was then. Now it's all about the Benjamins. College athletics is big business, really big. Revenue for the NCAA in 2014 came in just under $1 billion, 90 percent from television and marketing rights fees, mostly from March Madness.

Whenever there's a ton of money being made there's always controversy swirling around it. As coaching salaries for college football and basketball have soared more support is growing for compensating the athletes. After all, they're the ones drawing the crowds and risking their lives and limbs on the field and on the courts. The opposition says they're already rewarded with college scholarships. The National College Athletic Association reports, "The NCAA and our member colleges and universities together award $2.7 billion in athletic scholarships every year to more than 150,000 student athletes."

It's past time for taking a candid look at the business of college athletics and determining if the athletes are getting a fair deal or being taken advantage of. Investment bankers are paid millions to make money for Wall Street and nobody has a problem with it. Why do we have a problem with paying college athletes who make millions of dollars for the NCAA and their colleges? The arguments against doing so are starting to sound very familiar, much like filthy-rich CEOs complaining about having to pay workers higher wages. It's a long list of what they're already giving you, how you should be grateful, and how they can't afford to give you another penny. It may be a complicated issue on paying athletes for their talent but athlete directors and coaches have no problem paying themselves.

The simple truth is young talented athletes are being exploited. Not all high school athletes have a desire to go to college and get an education. Honestly, many of them just want to play ball. Except the NFL won't allow players to be drafted until three years after high school, and the NBA insists that players wait one year until they're eligible for the draft. Those who have the skills and gifts to possibly be professional athletes are forced to go to college and pay their dues to the NCAA before they can consider a NFL or NBA career. It's a high-risk when you think about all the athletes who had career ending injuries playing college sports.

There is also a racial equity issue to consider with the majority of student-athletes generating the revenues being African American. They basically support the NCAA and their governance costs. These players risk their bodies on the field and court, all the while wearing corporate logos and are rewarded with scholarships that have a litany of restrictions and no promise of an education. The NCAA started with good intentions and then like so many other ventures was corrupted by money. Dale Brown, the former LSU coach said, "Look at the money we make off predominately poor black kids. We're the whoremasters.

History of College Sports

The beginning of collegiate sports as we now know them sprouted from the humble beginnings of purely recreational sports for student physical activity. Rivalries among student clubs, associations, and organizations, encouraged intramural competition. Between the 1840s and the end of the nineteenth century administrators of colleges and universities began to lend financial support to athletics other than physical education and intramural sports. Yale University created a boat club which became the first organized sports team. When Harvard followed suit, that opened the door for the first intercollegiate sporting event between the two rowing teams in 1852. The crew competition sparked the formation of a variety of college athletic organizations. There was baseball, football, gymnastics, ice hockey, rugby, soccer, tennis, and track and field.

    The excitement and spirit of the games attracted spectators among the students, faculty, administrators, and alumni. Open to the community, the exhibitions attracted attention from newspapers and magazines and drew support from local businesses. The more popular the matches became the greater the stakes became in winning. Academic pursuits became secondary to training and competition for student athletes. Issues of cheating and unfair advantages clouded the competitions. As a remedy more control was shifted from the students to faculty. The more prominent schools designated funds for athletic budgets to organize teams and leagues and established rules and regulations for the sanctioned matches. As a result, intercollegiate sports expanded and audiences grew larger loving the thrill of competition. The desire for status and money played a huge part in the games. Student athletes accepted compensation for competing. Professional Coaches were hired, some eager and pressured to win hired professional athletes to compete on the teams with students, and gamblers attempted to fix games by paying players to not win.

    Academics objected to the fervor surrounding college athletics. In the Harvard president's 1892-93 report to the Board of Overseer's, Charles W. Eliot wrote:

> "From the college or university point of view, athletics sports are to be promoted either as wholesome pleasures which do not interfere with work, or as means of maintaining healthy and vigorous bodies…With athletes considered as an end to themselves, pursued either for pecuniary profit or for popular applause, a college has nothing to do. Neither is it an appropriate function for a

college or university to provide periodic entertainments during term-time for multitudes of people who are not students."

He also said that no sport which requires more than two hours a day from players during term-time is fit for college uses. Eliot's stance may be a little hard to swallow but it clearly articulated the argument for colleges' obligation for educating versus entertaining. Aware of the impact of commercialization of intercollegiate competition he was concerned that *"lofty gate receipts from college athletics had turned amateur contests into major commercial spectacles."* Massachusetts Institute of Technology (MIT) president, Walker remarked, *"If the movement shall continue at the same rate, it will soon be fairly a question whether the letters B.A. stand more for Bachelor of Arts or Bachelor of Athletics."*

It's hard to stand in the way of progress or the opportunity to make money. As the years went on collegiate sport events became more successful. The intensity of the games and the fierce competition yielded serious injuries, even deaths playing football, and students were being exploited. It was time to regulate intercollegiate sports, particularly football, or get rid of them all together. In 1906, for the protection of student athletes from the complications and abuses of power in intercollegiate competition, a group of faculty athletics representatives from 68 colleges met in New York and formed the Intercollegiate Athletic Association of the United States (IAAUS). Four years later they changed their name to the National Collegiate Athletic Association (NCAA).

Initially, eight athletic conferences or athletic associations were formed to shift away from faculty oversight. Only universities where the faculty had complete control of athletic programs were allowed to be members. Faculty athletic representatives could not be employed by or be connected to the athletic department in any way. These representatives represented the NCAA and were responsible for assisting both members of the faculty and athletic department in the understanding of NCAA and determining the eligibility of student athletes.

College athletics was divided into two tiers. The first tier was comprised of sports that were sanctioned by one of the collegiate sport governing bodies and athletes that have been selected for participation. The top sanctioning organizations are the NCAA, the National Association of Intercollegiate Athletics (NAIA), and the National Junior College Athletic Association (NJCAA). The second tier included the intramural and recreational sports clubs and was open to the greater portion of the student body. Individual sports were governed by their own organization.

The NCAA

Al Sermeno Photography / Shutterstock.com

Intercollegiate athletics is governed for the most part by the NCAA. For that reason it's important to understand their function in college sports. The NCAA was formed to protect the welfare of student athletes and to foster college competition in sports events and draw up the eligibility rules for football and additional intercollegiate sports. Its first national championship event was the National College Track and Field Championship in 1921. Over time the NCAA expanded its authority to include intercollegiate competition in other sports and their conferences. The organization implemented guidelines for colleges and universities in the recruitment of student athletes, and monitored the scholarships and financial aid available to them. They also established regional and national championships for twenty team sports.

After World War II, with the presence of radio and arrival of television in the majority of homes, the NCAA began regulating and controlling live televised coverage and broadcasts rights of football and basketball games. In the 1952 season, the NCAA negotiated its first contract with NBC for $1,144,000, just the beginning of even more lucrative television deals to come. Hopes for big contracts got more balls rolling. Existing athletic programs were expanded and more college and universities started new programs to benefit from the growing interest in intercollegiate sports.

The increasing number of intercollegiate programs in the early 1970s prompted the members of the NCAA to create three divisions where schools would be categorized according to their different level of competition. Division I schools offer full athletic scholarships, Division II schools offer partial sports scholarships, and Division III schools don't offer any athletic scholarships. Each college was allowed to choose the division where they would belong. The NCAA applied standards for amateurism, standards for academic eligibility, regulations for recruitment of athletes, and rules governing the size of teams and coaching staff. Services and representation for women's athletic programs were approved and encouraged.

The resistance from colleges and universities came when the NCAA was given additional authority to enforce the rules by penalizing schools directly, and consequently, athletes, coaches, and administrators indirectly. College presidents continued to criticize the NCAA's enforcement authority for more than a decade determined to take more active roles in the governance of the NCAA. In 1984, they formed the Presidents

Commission at the NCAA Convention. They were able to push through initiatives that restricted the size of coaching staffs, limited the amount of time student-athletes could spend on their sport, and set higher academic standards for Divisions I and II. The involvement of college presidents grew to the point where they changed the governance structure of the NCAA by adding an Executive Committee and a Board of Directors for each of the divisions.

The challenges to the extended power of the NCAA reached all the way to the Supreme Court in 1981. The NCAA wanted to limit the number of televised football games because they impacted attendance at the stadiums. The NCAA would hold all the agreements for broadcasting with ABC and CBS networks. The College Football Association (CFA) believing they should have more of a voice in forming football television policy than they received by the NCAA, negotiated a deal with the NBC network to increase their revenues. The NCAA threatened disciplinary action and the CFA took it to the courts. In the case of the NCAA v. Board of Regents, the United States Supreme Court ruled that the NCAA had violated antitrust laws with price fixing and the elimination of competition from other broadcasters. The decision opened the door for schools to directly reap profits from televising their football games.

Going into the new millennium the NCAA membership included more than 1083 colleges and universities. The growth and commercialization of intercollegiate athletics as a result of televising and the revenue it generates has strained educational institutions and the NCAA. Providing a balanced playing field and a working enforcement process takes a great deal of effort as costs incurred by non-revenue producing sports rise, costs related to Title IX and gender equity requirements increase, along with the need for new facilities.

How much money is made in College Sports?

The Chronicle of Higher Education has estimated the cost of college athletics to be in the area of $10 billion. That's not surprising with the numerous broadcasting contracts, ticket sales, merchandising, alumni contributions, and NCAA distributions for athletic programs throughout the

United States. Then there are student fees for athletics, direct and indirect institutional support, and government appropriations. The amount varies according to how successful the team. Though it may be hard to believe, sports for most colleges and universities are a money-losing proposition.

Football is the big money maker. Their advantage over basketball is the large stadiums for ticket sales versus a small arena. Stadiums of powerhouse teams hold 100,000-plus paying customers, and secure seven-figure donations from boosters to enjoy luxury suites. The top two most profitable college conferences are the Southeastern Conference (SEC) and the Big Ten, both earning in the billion dollar range. The most valuable program of all is the University of Texas' football program with forbes.com estimating $133 million generated in the last season.

Men's college basketball is the only other sport that generates meaningful income for schools. The University of Louisville's Cardinals are the most valuable basketball team, worth $38.3 million in the last season. Still, even the most successful program produces less than half of the amount of football. Division I schools make the biggest profits. For most schools, football and basketball revenues fund the whole athletic department. Playing in conferences is where schools can get huge bonuses. Millions are paid out by the NCAA to schools that advance in the tournaments; even the coaches get a piece of the pie.

The NCAA seems to be the big winner earning $989 million in 2014 from television, advertising, and licensing with a net surplus of $80.5 million. Included with the $665 million in unrestricted net assets is an endowment fund of $385 million which increased by $59 million at the end of the year. Even with all the revenues generated, the NCAA is considered to be a nonprofit association. Only 4 percent of the funds are retained, the rest are given to member conferences and schools or spent on championships and other programs that benefit student athletes.

The base revenue for each of the "Power Five" conferences, the Southeastern, the Atlantic Coast, the Pacific-12, the Big 12, and the Big 10, will increase to $50 million this year. Money earned from conferences is divided among teams according to the number of games that are played. Administrators are not left out of the equation. Mark Emmert, NCAA president, makes more than $1 million a year, and Larry Scott, commissioner of the Pas-12 Conference, makes $3.5 million.

The networks broadcasting college sports make a killing. The NCAA basketball tournaments better known as "March Madness" are hugely successful. In a Forbes article, Chris Smith noted, "CBS and Turner Broadcasting make in excess of a $1 billion from the games. Ad rates for the Final Four were $700,000 for a 30-second spot. The College Football Playoff for the FBS national championship signed a 12-year contract for $7 billion with ESPN.

Benefits to Schools

The contributions and costs of athletic programs to colleges and universities are a hotly debated topic in higher education. In all fairness, there are both tangible and intangible benefits from athletic programs for higher education institutions. There is no argument that sports on campuses promotes healthy lifestyles and provides extracurricular activities. Intercollegiate competition unites college students and the community. The more successful the athletic program the more exposure they garner and the more students are attracted to the schools. There is also no argument that collegiate athletic programs generate big dollars. The question is how many of these dollars are a benefit to the schools.

A report from the NCAA revealed that out of the 1083 college athletic programs under the NCAA only 20 made money. An article by Nancy Madsen schools noted there are 346 Division I schools, of those, 123 are top tiers in sports competition and are classified as members of the Football Bowl Subdivision. A report from the NCAA revealed that only 20 of those school programs made money and the median profit was $8.4 million. Of the 103 programs that lost money, the median deficit was $14.9 million.

We already know that large amounts of revenue are being made; one athletic department was reported to have made $169.7 million. The quandary is how the money is being spent. One athletic department reported expenses of $146.8 million. The NCAA 2013 report shows that athletic departments are making record amounts of money every year from television contracts and endorsements. So where is the leak? Why are so many schools losing so much money? The answer lies with the athletic directors as they play a high stakes game of "Keeping up with the Joneses." That's the core of the debate. What is the rationale for siphoning off funds from academic programs and increasing student fees to pay coaches millions of dollars and upgrade facilities when the overall purpose of colleges and universities it to educate versus entertain.

Benefits to Coaches

When the highest paid public employee is the state university's head football or basketball coach then that pretty much explains how well college coaches are doing financially. Universities are spending a great deal of money on coaches and athletic directors. Division I football and basketball coaches and athletic directors receive multimillion dollar salaries yearly. In 2014, Duke University's Mike Krzyzewski was the highest paid coach in the NCAA, making $9,682,032, and the University of Alabama's Nick Saban was the highest paid football coach, making $,7,160,187.

The average compensation for head football coaches at public universities has escalated 750 percent over the last 30 years, now above $2 million. That doesn't include the up to a half million dollar bonuses, endorsements, private planes for recruiting, and possibly a percentage of ticket sales. Assistant coaches filed an antitrust suit in 1999 when the NCAA attempted to cap their salaries. They now earn about $200,000, with top assistants in the SEC averaging $700,000.

Benefits to Athletes

College athletic programs have provided opportunities for millions of student athletes to attend and earn degrees at higher education institutions that they otherwise would not have been able to attend. For recruited athletes, you get the economic benefit of a scholarship, training, competitive experience, exposure, and the possibility of signing a professional contract. The drawbacks are an athletic scholarship is offered one year at a time, renewal depending on the decisions of the coaches, and there's the risk of career-ending injuries in practice and competition. There is also an issue with the chosen majors of athletes and whether they graduate with the necessary skills to get a well-paying job.

Contemplating the huge amount of money that is being made in college football, the fact that it's all because of student athletes, maybe this is not such a good trade off after all. Why shouldn't college athletes share in some of the wealth they create? If they do everything that professional athletes do, then they should be paid. As employees of the schools they would be able to join labor unions and collectively bargain, according to the National Labor Relations Act.

Support for Paying Athletes

Benefiting from the labor and talents of someone without adequate compensating them for their efforts is pure and simple exploitation. Student athletes contribute not only to the prestige of the school but to the finances as well. The NCAA says its amateurism rule of students not receiving salaries is to ensure that the students' priority remains on obtaining a quality education and that all student athletes are competing equally. This sounds good but with the terms and conditions of a one-year scholarship somebody isn't putting their money where their mouth is. Still, the scholarship may cover tuition cost but so many athletes are living below the poverty line. Barring athletes from receiving pay also eliminates any workman's compensation benefits if they are incapacitated by injuries.

An article in USA Today by Steve Wieberg stated, "Players in the NCAA's top tier Division I bowl subdivision say they devote more than 43 hours a week to the sport during the season... and baseball and men's basketball approach that commitment, an NCAA study shows." As far as my knowledge goes, that's a full-time job. With that demanding schedule these athletes don't have time to work or earn pocket money doing anything else for personal expenses. Some have suggested that the Olympic definition of amateurism be used, permitting athletes to secure endorsement deals, get paid for signing autographs, work jobs, have control over their image and likeness, and have access to the commercial free market. It would remove the temptation to violate NCAA rules and increase incentives for students to complete their degrees instead of leaving early for the pros.

College athletes playing football and basketball are in sports where they can't go pro when they have the inclination, unlike baseball, hockey, soccer, tennis, and golf where athletes can skip college and go pro at age eighteen or younger. Truly they are entertainers and like any other performer should be paid for exhibiting their talents. Several have suggested lifting the ban on receiving gifts. Other students are allowed to benefit from their personal talents as amateur musicians and actors.

A report called, "The Price of Poverty in Big Time College Sport," presented by a national college athlete advocacy group and a sports management professor calculated the value of some college athletes. Based on the revenues for the Football Bowl Subdivision, the average player would be worth $121,000 per year, and the average basketball player on that level would be worth $265,000. Players at the top programs are worth even more, Texas' football players are worth around $513,000 each, and Duke's basketball players rate the highest at about $1 million each. NerdWallet, a personal finance website, calculated Duke's freshman Jahlil Okafor's worth to be $2.6 million alone.

Critics Against Paying Athletes

Advocates against paying college athletes argue they are students not professionals, playing college sports is not a career. They say student athletes are attending college primarily for a post-secondary education and it isn't mandatory that they play on sports teams. They also say those students earn scholarships through their participation in sports, and student athletes can easily be replaced. The cost of a college education is not cheap, and after four years many student-athletes can earn a degree free of charge. It's a great point if you don't mention that several of the top schools competing in Division I earning the big dollars, including the University of Connecticut, Syracuse University, and Kansas State University, are among the bottom ranks in terms of graduation rates.

Paying male athletes would be unfair to female athletes and possibly a violation of Title IX, which requires that institutions that accept federal funds must offer equal opportunities to men and women. Some opponents protest the commercialism and corporate interference in the culture of college sports and advocate returning back to the 'good old days' where student athletes were educated and prepared to be members of society, not trained to be members of professional ball clubs. As Tulane University President Scott Cowen stated in an article: *"It is not too late for those of us in leadership positions to recapture the original philosophy of intercollegiate athletics and return it to its appropriate place as a supporter and participant in the educational goals, mission, and values of the university."* Unfortunately for them the genie is out of the bottle and we can't turn back time.

Despite all of the money changing hands, the majority of colleges and universities cannot afford to pay student athletes. Most schools operate their athletic programs in the red. It would give an unfair advantage to big-time colleges. There are others who claim that paying some player would create conflicts among players on teams even though it isn't an issue in professional leagues. Most of us in the working world accept that we are not all going to be paid the same money for the same job. The coaches seem to manage very well with that aspect.

It may be just a coincidence but those that complain the loudest about athletes being paid are the ones benefiting the most from student-athletes: coaches and athletic directors. University of Louisville Coach Rick Pitino insists that athletes should not be paid, "They are being paid," he said, referring to room and board, books, and tuition. That's easy for him to say making $3.9 million a year with a $425,000 bonus for winning the national title.

Options for Paying Athletes

In 2013, Steve Spurrier, head football coach at the University of South Carolina, announced that it was unanimous among all 28 men's football and basketball coaches in the SEC; athletes should be paid. The group suggested $300 per game for football players and slightly less for basketball players. It would cost the SEC around $280,000 a year. That would amount to about $3600 for each player per season, allowing them to have pocket money and help cover travel expenses for family members to attend games. Jay Bilas, ESPN college basketball analyst, advocates the free-market approach where athletes can receive whatever the market will bear. Progress is slow but Val Ackerman, Big East commissioner, has said that the NCAA is considering letting student athletes receive endorsements without losing their eligibility.

College athletes who've come up against opposition to compensating them for their efforts are taking the contests to court. Former U.C.LA. basketball player, Ed O'Bannon, filed a class action antitrust lawsuit on behalf of Division I football and basketball players against the NCAA challenging their unwillingness to share revenue from the use of players' likeness and images for commercial purposes. Federal Judge Claudia Wilken ruled in his favor stating that the NCAA practice of barring payments to players was in violation of the antitrust laws. She also ruled that the players should receive the full cost of attendance, including cost-of living expenses in their scholarships. An additional $5000 would be held in trust for athletes for each year of eligibility. The judgement was appealed and the appellate court has issued a stay on the ruling.

Northwestern University football players, backed by the College Athletes Players Association and led by quarterback Kain Colter, filed a petition with the Regions Labor Relations Board for the right to unionize and bargain collectively. The regional director ruled in their favor, deeming the football players are employees of Northwestern. However, the National Labor Relations Board declined to assert jurisdiction and dismissed the petition.

Joe Nocera wrote an article in the New York Times called, *A Way to Start Paying College Athletes.* He proposed that every Division I men's basketball and football team would have a salary cap, $650,000 for basketball and $3 million for football. This amount would no doubt be affordable compared to the figures doled out for head coaches. He recommended dropping the number of scholarships for football down to 60 from 85 in the top tier. A minimum salary of $25,000 per player in each sport was suggested, enough to live like most college students. For the other half of the cap, the free market aspect comes into play. These funds would be used as a recruiting tool where star players could be offered additional money to attend a particular school.

The United States is the only country with huge sports programs conjoined with institutions of higher learning. Yet we extol the purity and integrity of the academic halls of our colleges and universities and denounce paying our athletes for their performance on teams. How can college sports retain its "amateur" status in football and basketball when billions of dollars are being made? Not paying college athletes goes against our American philosophy of free enterprise when you say an individual can't benefit from their own talent, skills, and fame. If we can't create a system where student athletes can receive salaries, then it's unreasonable to block them from receiving money from other sources.

Support for a presidential commission on college sports is growing in Congress. There is speculation that the federal government might offer the NCAA a partial antitrust exemption whereby they could begin the long overdue reforms. It would also allow them to cap the salaries of coaches and athletic directors who profit heavily off of student athletes. Hopefully some of the money generated will be passed on to those who actually do the work.

Victims of the Legal System and Police Brutality

"Justice will not be served until those who are unaffected are as outraged as those who are."

~Benjamin Franklin

Victims of the Legal System and Police Brutality

The United States is considered to be the leader in the free world but it also holds the distinction of having more of its citizens locked up in jails or prisons. The U.S. comprises 5 percent of the world's population with 25 percent of the world's inmates. In 2015, the Department of Justice reported that 2.3 million people were incarcerated and 4.5 million are on probation or parole. This means one out of 35 people in this country have been imprisoned at one time. Ironically, this number has continued to grow even as the crime rate has fallen. These numbers are troubling at first glance but when you look closer they're even more disturbing given the history of this nation. People of color make up 60 percent of the people behind bars while comprising only 30 percent of the overall population.

My first inclination is to think of it as some sort of covert conspiracy but it is too blatant, unyielding, an unashamed. The truth is simple; the poor are victims of the U.S judicial system. The words "equal justice under law," taken from a clause in the Fourteenth Amendment and engraved on the United States Supreme Court building in Washington DC, are a nice concept but more accurately they are a fantasy, specifically for the underprivileged in this country. The criminal justice system is anything but equal. Let's just tell some more of the truth, the poor and black are targeted by the police in America from sea to shining sea. African Americans are more likely to be stopped by police, searched, arrested, charged with a crime, found guilty, and sentenced harsher than whites.

Nationwide there were 11,205,833 arrests for all offenses in 2014. During 1973, before the declaration of the war on drugs, there were 328,670 arrests for drug offenses out of 9,027,700 total arrests nationwide. Presently, the single most common reasons leading to arrest are drug offenses. According to the FBI Uniform Crime 2014 report, there were 1,561,231 drug related arrests, 83.1 percent were for the possession of a controlled substance, and only 16.9 percent were for the sale or manufacturing of a drug. About half of the drug related arrests were related to marijuana. This may be one of the reasons why most states are reluctant to legalize marijuana, there is so much money being generated by policing it.

The surge in prisoners is a result of the "War on Drugs." The fact that it was and still is waged in poor Black and Latino communities exacerbates the racial disparities within the criminal justice system. The oppressiveness of these policies has had and will continue to have long-term ramifications for people of color. Aside from significant numbers of those disenfranchised because of a felony conviction and the difficulty in obtaining employment due to a felony conviction, there is the price in dollars and cents. Inarguably this is another instance of depriving minorities of their basic civil rights.

Certainly there are things money can't buy but justice isn't one of them. Legal representation, bail, fines, and fees are above and beyond what the most-likely of us to be arrested: the poor, uneducated, African American or Latino, can afford to pay. I'm not sure when the tables turned or if they had ever been situated properly, however, instead of the justice system protecting and serving the people; the people are protecting and serving the justice system. The burden is falling on those least able to support it: the poorest citizens of the United States. It's a vicious circle, a horrible merry-go-round: born into poverty, petty crime to make some money, drink or drug to forget, arrested for a misdemeanor, unable to make bail, penalized with fines and charged fees, re-arrested for nonpayment of fines and fees, and trapped in the system with no way out.

NPR's Nick Shapiro conducted a yearlong investigation in the fees leveed on the poor by the criminal justice system. He found that defendants and offenders are paying the cost of their trials, sentencing, and jail time. In Washington State, defendants are charged $125 for a 6-person jury; a 12-person jury costs $250. Forty-nine states charge for the use of electronic monitoring, 44 states charge fees for probation and drug testing, 43 states charge for the use of a public defender, and 41 states charge for room and board. If you are poor and can't pay the fees then you have to suffer more jail time.

The criminal justice system has turned into a loan shark for those hard on their luck; the difference is instead of threatening the debtors with broken knee caps they are blackmailed with the threat of incarceration. On any given day 25 percent of the people at the courthouse are there for not paying fees. If they can't get blood from a stone then they lock you up. The charges continue to run up as more fees are charged on top of other fees. These are the penalties that a defendant with money wouldn't have to face.

In defense of the system some judges say if it were not for the criminals there would be no need for the criminal justice system, so why shouldn't they pay the cost they create. The problem with that rationale is there are some innocent people, who through no fault of their own, have been punished with harsh penalties and jail time. At the bottom of the controversy is that federal funding has declined and states are struggling with budget deficits. The tax payers are stressed and can't stand higher taxes. The solution of state legislators was to shift the costs to the defendants who are disproportionately poor and minority.

The History of the Criminal Justice System

Back in the colonial days of the United States there was no legal system, criminal codes varied from colony to colony, many times unfair and unjust, and the people were subject to the rules and laws of the British. Initially, confinement was rare, public humiliation was the prevailing punishment. Over the years as the country matured, dozens of prisoners would be incarcerated together in one room in atrocious conditions. William Penn, a Quaker and first prison reformer, promoted criminal justice reform to make it more humane. Penn helped to organize a justice system to protect and defend the equal rights of its citizens. In what was called his "Great Experiment" in the 1680s, he introduced what were considered to be radical reforms starting with the separation of prisoners.

Penn abolished the death penalty for all crimes except pre-meditated murder, preferring the confinement of criminals. Before the reforms,

Victims of the Legal System and Police Brutality

prisoners had to pay for their food and all services, including the unlocking of their chains so they could appear in court. Penn said prisons should be workhouses; bail should be allowed for minor offenses, and all fees, food and lodging, should be free in prison. The Quaker faith believes that all people are equal and can always change. Penn provided rehabilitation for prisoners where they could learn a trade to earn an honest living when they were released. The 'experiment' lasted for a while but soon reverted back to the status quo.

After the American Revolution and newfound independence, the U.S. Constitution was written, guaranteeing the rights and freedoms of the people, and assuring protections for the innocent. In 1787, the first prison reform organization was created, called the Philadelphia Society for Alleviating the Miseries of Public Prisons. The Society preferred rehabilitation over physical punishment and all prisoner were supplied a Bible to help treat their problems. In the early 1800s, other states began to eliminate whipping, branding, and mutilation as forms of punishment as more penitentiaries or state prisons were built.

Basically, there were two types of prison systems, one based on the New York model called the Auburn plan where inmates worked in groups during the day and were locked in separate cells at night. There wasn't a lot of money to maintain the new prisons; some thought the answer was to make prisons self-sufficient by having inmates produce goods to be sold. During the Civil War, the prison inmates were used to produce uniforms, shoes, and other clothing. The Pennsylvania plan was more expensive and thought to be more cruel. Inmates were kept in solitary confinement around the clock, and not allowed to make money for the prison. The Auburn plan was more widely used at the time but the business community objected, considering it unfair competition.

Gradually the criminal justice system evolved to include a collection of public agencies that set guidelines for crimes, legal procedures, and punishment. There began the professional policing for apprehending criminals, courts to determine guilt and impose sentences, and prisons and prison officials to supervise correctional facilities and rehabilitation at the federal and state levels. The number of cases grew as urban areas expanded rapidly. The courts multiplied and fragmented to handle particular types of cases.

Criminal Justice in the 20th Century

At the beginning of the 20th century, public concern over increasing crime and complaints of the inefficient and ineffective criminal justice policies were escalating. Political corruption by criminal elements decimated the trust in the legal system. This caused a shift from rehabilitation to efforts to control criminal behavior. This brought about nation-wide prohibition of alcohol, which over a decade proved to be a failure at curbing crime.

Racial discrimination was entrenched in the Southern judicial system in the early decades. There were lynchings, harsh sentencing, and chain-gang style penal practices orchestrated against African Americans. The police were instrumental in race riots by actively participating, instigating hostility, or failing to restrain mobs. The Civil Rights Movement exposed the unjust legal system through the progress of obtaining equal treatment under the law for all citizens. Gains were made in a number of areas with a critical exception – criminal justice. Instead of moving forward, racial equality in this area slipped backward. Criminal laws were enforced in a racially biased manner.

A new era of law enforcement began in 1965 when President Lyndon B. Johnson called for a "War on Crime." Then there were the mandatory minimum sentences for drugs in the 1980s and the "3-Strikes" law in the 1990s. These criminal justice policies precipitated a flood of mass arrest and incarceration that has disproportionately affected poor blacks and Latinos. The century ended much like it began, with the public police beating of a black man.

The Lack of Criminal Justice in the 21st Century

In the wake of new technologies, namely the cellphone and bodycam we have had to look at policing through a different lens. Similar to the reaction people had when the Birmingham police attacked and hosed down peaceful demonstrators during the Civil Rights Movement, we don't like what we see. It's heavy-handed, unjust, and directed towards African Americans and other minorities. Granted there are lawbreakers who should be apprehended and punished, the concern is that we don't sacrifice their rights and everyone else's in the process. The history of this country creates a challenge in that aspect. It was only a couple of years ago when we celebrated the 50th birthday of The Civil Rights Act. There are still quite a few Americans around who were born and bred to believe that Black people are second-class citizens.

The criminal justice system is guilty of the unequal treatment of blacks and other minorities throughout every stage of the process: disproportionate targeting and arrest by police, skewed charges and plea bargaining during pretrial and prosecution, unfair adjudication and sentencing by judges; and in corrections. Racial disparities victimize innocent minorities who are detained much more often than whites. Despite the fact that the majority of crimes are not committed by minorities (FBI, 2011), more minority arrests convince us otherwise, which further perpetuates racial profiling and targeting.

The truth is between 70 and 100 million Americans have some type of criminal record according to a 2012 Department of Justice survey, that's about one-third of us. Usually it's a misdemeanor or an arrest without conviction. However, even a minor criminal record can have adverse effects on your life and economic security. The internet supplies easy access for background checks and information about a criminal record. It can hamper your opportunities for employment, education, and housing. This means millions of individuals are held back from being productive members of society.

There are several criminal justice practices that are unlawful or probably violate a person's right to due process: jailing someone because they can't pay fines, requiring payment of fines for a judicial hearing, and using bail practices that leave the poor in jail because they can't afford to pay. These policies lead to defendants coming out of the system deep in debt. For some, their paychecks are garnished, others have liens placed on their homes. In some cases, the denial of a driver's license is imposed. There are countless instances where poor defendants have lost jobs or homes serving time in jail for victimless violations.

Budget Cuts and Making up the Shortfall

The recession, federal budget cuts, and lower income taxes and corporate taxes have affected States' revenue all across the nation. At the same time, the United States was incarcerating record numbers of prisoners in the penal system. The result was skyrocketing costs for correctional facilities. To make up the shortfall, the whole of the criminal justice system has resorted to increased fines, charges, and fees to make up the difference. The practice is common and widespread but we never knew how prevalent and profitable it was until the riots in Ferguson, Missouri after the Michael Brown shooting.

The Civil Rights Division of the U.S. Department of Justice Department's 2014 investigation of the Ferguson Police Department and Municipal Court found that the city relied on municipal court fines to make up 20 percent of its $12 million operating budget in fiscal year 2013. They determined that the Ferguson Police Department's motivation was focused more on revenue generation than it was on public safety, that they used unconstitutional racial biases to write traffic tickets and imposed excessive fines, arrested low-income residents when they failed to pay the exorbitant fines, used unlawful bail practices, and jailed people unnecessarily. President Obama responded to the report saying, *"What we saw was that the Ferguson Police Department, in conjunction with the municipality, saw traffic stops, arrests, and tickets as a revenue generator, as opposed to serving the community, and that it systematically was biased against African Americans."*

Who knew that traffic tickets, parole fees, ankle bracelet fees, and criminal bonds would be big business? Cities and states are generating revenue through frivolous misdemeanors and traffic violation fines by the police. In metropolitan Detroit, suffering from an ailing economy and struggling to balance its budget, officials have been using law enforcement to produce revenue since 2002. There the police have issued 50 percent more moving violations in 18 communities, 11 of which have seen a 90 percent jump in tickets written. In Los Angeles the amount of revenue from fines has gone up 50 percent since 2013, it's expected to reach 180 million by 2018.

Getting legal representation for low-income defendants can be another "Catch 22" situation. Around 80 percent of those arrested and charged with a crime are unable to afford a lawyer. Then there are the working-poor who have been denied court-appointed attorneys because they don't qualify based on their income or those who failed to convince the judge they lacked sufficient funds. In more cases poor defendants have to pay for public defenders. It's a similar situation if you can't afford to make bail, county jails in jurisdictions all across the country charge prisoners for room and board, work release, and other services. Some jails charge for clothing and toilet paper. Inmates are also billed for health treatment including physicals, nurse sick calls, dental work, and prescriptions. If you're released, an ankle-monitoring bracelet can cost up to $300 per month.

For those who can least afford them, the fees are added to the fines and compound until they are, double, triple, or 10 times the initial costs. It's basically a tax on poor citizens in urban communities. This process not only generates revenue for municipalities, it serves the whole justice system from the bail bondsman to attorneys to courts to correctional facilities. After the Department of Justice report on the city of Ferguson, Representative Emanuel Cleaver of Missouri introduced a new bill stating that unjust "policing for profit" tactics should be considered violation of federal civil liberty. He stated:

> "The time has come to end the practice of using law enforcement as a cash register, a practice that has impacted too many Americans and has disproportionately affected minority and low income communities. No American should have to face arbitrary police enforcement whose sole purpose is to raise revenue for a town, city, or state."

The Justice Department finally put out guidelines to state and municipal court systems to prevent destitute defendants from being jailed because of

their inability to pay fines for minor infractions.
- Court systems shouldn't jail people for nonpayment of fees and fines without first establishing that nonpayment is willful and not just the result of indigence.
- Courts must consider alternatives to incarceration for indigent defendants who can't pay fines.
- Arrest warrants and license suspensions shouldn't be used routinely as a way to coerce payment of court debt.

Bail and bonds regulations shouldn't cause poor defendants to remain in jail solely because they can't afford to pay for release.

Mass Incarceration and Privatizing

Greta Gabaglio / Shutterstock.com

According to Amnesty International, the U.S. prison population had quadrupled since 1980. More than 2 million people are locked in penitentiaries and jails throughout the nation. Around another 5 million are under federal or state supervision on parole or probation. These greater numbers were driven by the "get tough on crime" mentality and harsher penalties for non-violent offenses. A massive amount of money has been spent on building prisons and jails, 1000 have been built in the last 20 years, and now this country spends more than $80 billion running them. Federal, state, and local governments spend between $20 thousand and $50 thousand each year to incarcerate one individual. These high costs are causing some states to shift the weight of the costs burden onto defendants and cut funding for rehabilitation and education.

Federal sentencing laws related to the 'War on Drugs' have contributed to the rise in America's prison population but the fact is the real mass incarceration has taken place on the state level. According to Prison Policy Initiative data, 57 percent of U.S. inmates are in state prisons. Louisiana holds the distinction of being the world's prison capital with 1341 inmates for every 100,000 people. Mississippi runs a close second. Still, all the states have booming prison populations with 30 percent of inmates in local jails for violating state laws.

Believe it or not, FBI crime data on 2014 show that the rate of violent crime is continuing to decline. If that's true, why are we still building jails so fast, and why do we still have a problem with overcrowding? Who benefits from all of these federal penitentiaries, state corrections facilities, and local jails? Some call it the prison industrial complex. An *Atlantic* article by Eric Schlosser described it as "a set of bureaucratic, political, and economic interests that encourage increased spending on imprisonment, regardless of the actual need." The prison industrial complex is the driving force behind all of the prison construction. The bigger it gets the more support it has from poor rural communities who have come to depend on the prisons as employers.

Private prison companies and the additional companies that profit with contracts through them have a thriving and lucrative business in the corrections industry. Presently, twenty-seven states have private prisons. Nevertheless, I'm not one who believes that public services should be privatized. The government may be inefficient and wasteful at times but at least there's not a greedy CEO profiting off the misery of others. The more people who are arrested and locked up the more money they make. They are probably very content now that prisons are more overcrowded than they have ever been. With so much money to be made housing prisoners, nonviolent crimes that would have been punished with drug treatment, community service, and fines in other countries now lead to a prison term in the United States.

Police Policy and Over-policing

The "War on Drugs" was supposed to be meant figuratively, however for those in low-income urban areas of color, it is most definitely literal. Beginning in 1997 as part of the 1033 Program, the federal government began transferring excess military equipment to civilian police forces. As of 2014, $5.1 billion worth of military hardware has been transferred from the Department of Defense to law enforcement agencies, one-third of the equipment is new, and the most common item is ammunition. There are no directives on how to use these resources and as a result lead to dangerous over-policing and mass incarceration.

The American Civil Liberties Union (ACLU) has been voicing concerns about the militarization of state and local police forces without public discussions or oversight stating, "Neighborhoods are not warzones." The practice of sending heavily armed officers for regular police work escalates peaceful situations into violence. SWAT teams, usually reserved for extreme emergency circumstances, are being used more for drug searches than for anything else. In their report the ACLU said, "It's time for American police to remember that they are supposed to protect and serve our communities, not wage war on the people who live in them."

The issue gained full media coverage during the community protest in Ferguson, Missouri over the police shooting of Michael Brown. The police seemed overaggressive with helmets, riding in tanks, wearing full military riot gear, and carrying military-grade weapons. President Obama assembled the Task Force of 21st Century Policing to examine current police policies and strengthen public trust. The task force reported a nationwide pattern of police militarization, finding local police departments were using armed vehicles, explosives, flashbang hand grenades, and riot gear.

Following the report, President Obama announce the federal government would no longer provide local law enforcement agencies with certain military equipment, including, armored tanks, weaponized aircraft or vehicles, high-caliber weapons, bayonets or camouflaged uniforms. In a visit to the Camden, New Jersey Police Department, Obama said, *"We've seen how militarized gear can sometimes give people a feeling like they're (police) an occupying force, as opposed to a force that's part of the community that's protecting and serving them."*

Police Shootings and Brutality

a katz / Shutterstock.com

In the wake of the Michael Brown shooting the debate on police officers shooting to kill has been revived. Many have contended that law enforcement protocol and training in terms of deadly force must be re-evaluated. Presently, members of law enforcement are permitted to use deadly force if they have reason to believe that a suspect poses a physical threat to him or to others. However, there are far too many instances of fatal police shootings of unarmed and nonviolent suspects.

The 1985 Supreme Court ruling in the Tennessee v. Garner case should have clarified any confusion about using deadly force but it seems we still are grappling with the issue. A lawsuit was filed by the father of a 15-year old boy who was shot by two policemen while running from a home he was suspected of robbing. The boy had stolen a purse containing $10 from the house. The officers used deadly force even though they were "reasonably sure" the suspect was unarmed. The Supreme Court found that the Tennessee statute authorizing the use of deadly force against a non-dangerous fleeing suspect is unconstitutional.

> Apprehension by the use of deadly force is a seizure subject to the Fourth Amendment's reasonableness requirement. To determine whether such a seizure is reasonable, the extent of the intrusion on the suspect's rights under that Amendment must be balanced against the governmental interests in effective law enforcement. This balancing process demonstrates that, notwithstanding probable cause to seize a suspect, an officer may not always do so by killing him. The use of deadly force to prevent the escape of all felony suspects, whatever the circumstances, is constitutionally unreasonable.

The use of deadly force by law enforcement in the United States has not ebbed; cell phones and body cams bear witness to that fact. The Washington Post in answer to the Michael Brown shooting controversy launched a comprehensive project to research all of the on-duty shooting by police in 2015. The results showed that 990 people were shot and killed by the police. In more than 25 percent of the cases police were chasing someone on foot or by car. A number of police chiefs and training experts in the report said more restrictive rules on when officers should give chase could prevent unnecessary shootings. In the words of Benjamin Franklin, *"That it is better 100 guilty Persons should escape than that one innocent Person should suffer, is a Maxim that has been long and generally approved."*

On average two black men are killed every week by white policemen every year. It's difficult to argue that race has no place in this matter given these statistics. The Washington Post reported that 40 percent of the unarmed men shot to death in 2015 were black men, while making up a mere 6 percent of the U.S. population. A number of studies have noted that excessive force by police officers is more likely to be used against black men than any other race. This is the source of the anger and indignation of the Black Lives Matter movement which organizes protests and campaigns against racial profiling, police brutality, killings by members of law enforcement, and the racial inequality in the criminal justice system.

The country is being distressed and divided by the killings and injuries of hundreds of unarmed people at the hands of law enforcement. Protests and demands for justice and a shift in policing policies are heard after each incident, yet nothing changes. Our local Police Commissioners and their departments serve at the pleasure of the Mayor. It's time to use our votes at our pleasure if we truly want to see changes.

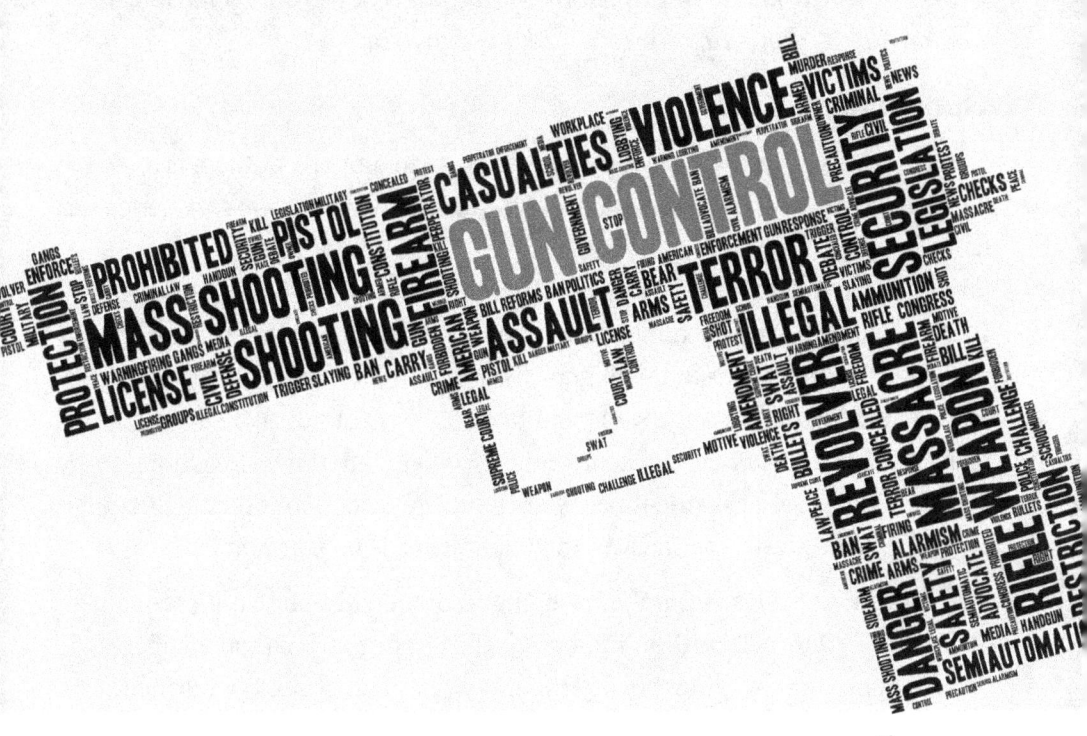

Gun Control or Not

"The world will not be destroyed by those who do evil, but by those who watch without doing anything." ~ Albert Einstein

Gun Control or Not

Of all the wonders of the world created by man, not one of them is a weapon. So why all the fascination and infatuation with firearms? America has had a long standing love affair with the gun. Quite a few Americans equate guns to our freedom and our security. From the time of the Declaration of Independence to the new millennium guns have become more efficient and more deadly. Our obsession with guns feeds the desire for bigger firearms and gun manufacturers supersize them like combo meals at McDonalds. Gun sales have increased in recent years, especially after mass shootings and consequently during the times when there are discussions relating to gun control. Paradoxically, our answer to gun violence is to get more guns.

The United States is number one in gun ownership per capita with an estimated 270 to 300 million firearms in this country. That means there are enough guns for almost every man, woman, and child to be armed. Congressional Research Service data shows there were almost double the numbers of guns in the U.S. in 2015 than there were in 1968. About one-third of all households have one or more firearms in the home, down from 50 percent in the late 1970s and early 1980s. This means more guns are being concentrated in fewer households.

Guns and the right to carry them are the objects of a much impassioned debate that has been fired up with the seeming epidemic of mass murders in this country. The fever ebbs until there is another high-profile incident and then the controversy is reheated. The horror of unsuspecting children and adults being shot down in the midst of their everyday activities by crazed gunmen generates two divergent responses. One, to reduce and restrict the number of guns in the public, the other, to increase the number of guns and the number of people armed to defend themselves. The arguments continue without a compromise and so does the gun violence.

The FBI defines a mass killing as having more than four victims. Over the last decade, from 2006 to 2016, there have been 201 mass killings in the United States. In most of these killings, hand guns were used, with the majority of them being obtained legally. Mass killings receive a great deal of attention by the media but the truth is they are only a small representation of gun deaths. Based on tracking data from the Gun Violence Archive, there have been more than 50,000 incidents of gun violence in the United States in 2015. Firearms are involved in more than 30,000 deaths in the U.S. annually.

After another mass shooting in San Bernardino on December of 2015, President Obama was prompted to issue a series of executive orders aimed at reducing gun violence. The orders contained new restrictions on gun sellers. If you sell firearms you must obtain a license and conduct background checks on potential buyers. Another provision requires that any firearm lost in transit between a manufacturer and a seller should be reported to federal authorities.

On June 16, 2016, 102 people were shot in a mass shooting in an Orlando gay nightclub. It was the deadliest mass shooting in U.S. history, 49 of the victims were killed. It was labeled a terrorist attack, called a hate crime, and by others, yet another tragedy caused by mental illness. President Obama said gun violence was preventable and too common, "It's unconscionable that we allow easy access to weapons of war in these places." He urged Congress to "Do the Right thing." Our legislators responded with four bills relating to gun restrictions, two from Democrats and two from Republicans. All four measures proposed were voted down in the Senate in spite of polls by the American people favoring more gun control. Democratic lawmakers, led by Rep. John Lewis, held a 25-hour sit-in in the floor of the House Chamber to no avail, the gridlock remained unabated. The NRA presence in the room was undeniable when Paul Ryan shut down the House and ended the debate.

What Does the Constitution Say?

The Second Amendment of the Constitution reads: "A well regulated Militia, being necessary to the security of a free State, the right of the people to keep and bear Arms, shall not be infringed." The first four words of the phrase, in my understanding, clearly state to whom the right was deemed for, a well regulated Militia. The reason for the amendment was to allow the states to form militias to protect themselves from any possible federal oppression. The founding fathers clearly had no qualms about regulating gun ownership as they refused guns for slaves, free blacks, and those loyal to the British after the American Revolution.

Since those latter years of the 18th century, the interpretation of the Second Amendment has varied. The NRA (National Rifle Associatio), along with a multitude of gun owners, feels the above phrase establishes the individual constitutional right for citizens of the United States to possess firearms. Another interpretation of this phrase is the "collective rights theory" which say that citizens don't have an individual right to possess guns and that local, state, and federal law makers have the authority to regulate firearms without compromising any constitutional right.

In the 1875 case, *United States v. Cruikshank*, the Supreme Court ruled that the Second Amendment does not bar state regulation of firearms; the amendment has no other directive than to restrict the powers of the federal government. This was reiterated in the 1886 case, *Presser v. Illinois*, and then again in the 1939 case, United States v. Miller, concluding that, "in the absence of any evidence tending to show that the possession or use of a sawed-off shotgun…has some reasonable relationship to the preservation or efficiency of a well-regulated militia, we cannot say that the Second Amendment guarantees the right to bear such an instrument."

In 1976, in an effort to protect the citizens of the District of Columbia from death, injury, and the loss property, Mayor Walter Washington signed the Firearms Control Regulations Act of 1975. The new law to control the availability of guns in the city prohibited the purchase of handguns, automatic guns, and high-capacity semi-automatic firearms other than by members of law enforcement or the military. The exception was for D.C. residents who had registered their firearms within the last 60 days. Additionally, all lawfully owned firearms contained in the home must be kept unloaded, have a trigger lock, or be disassembled.

The Firearms Control Regulations Act precipitated the next U.S. Supreme Court ruling on the Second Amendment in 2008. In the *District of Columbia v. Heller*, the case involved the purchase of a handgun to keep in the home. The Court ruled that the Second Amendment does give the right to an individual

Gun Control or Not

to possess a firearm for traditional lawful purposes such as self-defense. The decision further said that two of the District of Columbia provisions violated the right also, (1) the ban on handguns, and (2) the requirement that lawful firearms be unloaded, trigger-locked, or disassembled.

This shift in interpretation of the Second Amendment has been used to support anti-gun control campaigns by the NRA and gun lobbyists. They refer back to the days of the 'old West' where everybody had a gun without question. There is no doubt that the early settlers of American did have guns. Living in the wilderness there wasn't a plethora of grocery stores to choose from. A gun was necessary for hunting and protection from wildlife and angry natives. Most of us don't have to contend with these issues in the 21st century. The difficulty we're having is trying to apply a rule that was instituted during the days of the musket and apply it to this era of semi-automatic weapons.

Was it the Wild, Wild West?

I've seen my share of western TV shows with cowboys riding around with guns on their belts and shootouts between the good guys and the bad guys. That was the way Hollywood portrayed it, but was it an honest account? Research based on actual history shows the Old West was not as violent as we believe, guns were allowed at home for self-defense but there were laws that prohibited folks from carrying their guns in public. Eugene Hollon, author of *Frontier Violence –Another look,* wrote that life on the western frontier *"was a far more civilized, more peaceful and safer place than American society today."*

The wildest and most wicked cow towns in the Old West were Dodge City, Kansas, Deadwood, South Dakota, and Tombstone, Arizona, the home of the most legendary gunfight in American history. It didn't take much provocation for someone to be gunned down; the loss of a card game was reason enough. Eventually, the leaders in these frontier towns realized that too many guns causes too much trouble and they were weary of all the gun violence. The answer was gun control laws. Carrying a deadly weapon in city limits was banned. Signs went up at the entrance of cities that said, "The Carrying of Firearms Strictly Prohibited."

Sheriffs and marshals strictly enforced the gun control laws; the common reason for arrest was for illegally carrying a firearm. Bob Boze Bell, executive editor of True West Magazine said, "You could wear your gun into town, but you had to check it at the sheriff's office or the Grand Hotel, and you couldn't pick it up until you were leaving town."

According to Adam Winkler, author of *Gunfight: The Battle over the Right to Bear Arms in America,* almost every state has a provision in its constitution giving citizens the right to keep and bear arms that has reference to militia service. He also noted that gun control laws in the early history of America were more restrictive than today's statutes, "gun rights and gun control are not only compatible; they have lived together since the birth of America."

The Business of Guns

Gun and ammunition manufacturers profit from our fears: fear of being a crime victim, fear of terrorism, and fear of gun control. Annual revenue for the gun and ammunition industry in the United States topped $15 billion in 2015 and it continues to increase each year. Gun manufacturers are producing twice the number of guns they did only five years ago. The latest data available from the Bureau of Alcohol, Tobacco, Firearms and Explosives (ATF) is from 2013 with 10,847,792 reported weapon sales: 4,441,726, pistols, 3,979,570 rifles, 1,203,072 shotguns, 725,282 revolvers, and 495,142 miscellaneous firearms. The bulk of these guns are sold in this country, only a small percentage is exported, and ammunition was a great contributor to the profit margin. In 2012, the industry made almost as much on small arms ammunition as it did on the guns themselves.

Ironically, President Obama's election and his efforts to expand gun control have caused gun sales to surge even higher. Speculation is that buyers were fearful of gun-control laws under his administration; it might even have something to do with the "take our country back" rhetoric we've heard for seven years. Nonetheless, analysts on the subject have called Obama "the best thing to happen to the firearm industry." During the first term of the Obama administration, the FBI conducted close to 50 million background checks for gun purchases, 23 million in 2015 alone. The firearm business is so good that the number of licensed gun dealerships have risen for the first time in two decades.

Wal-Mart is one of the stores that has taken advantage of the boon. In 2011, in response to dwindling sales the retailer expanded gun sales to half of its 3,982 locations nationwide. Wal-Mart is now the top seller of firearms and ammunition in the country with 400 guns available in its store or catalog. An article by George Zornick noted the success Wal-Mart has had in the gun market. Freedom Group Inc., the largest gun maker in the U.S., revealed that 15 percent of its sales in the last year came from Wal-Mart. The Bushmaster AR-15, the weapon used in the Sandy Hook Elementary School massacre, was a very popular item in Wal-Mart. "They've been selling faster than manufacturers can make them," a gun store owner commented. Wal-Mart pulled the firearm from the website three days after the shooting. Mass shootings give the biggest boost to gun sales. On the Saturday after the Newtown massacre, an estimated 120,000 to 130,000 guns were sold.

Gun Ownership

Despite the growth in the number of guns being made and sold across the nation, the number of households being gun owners has continued to decline. American households having firearms is at the lowest reported level in the last 40 years. General Social Survey data shows the number of households owning guns has fallen from above 50 percent to around 32 percent presently. That means guns are being concentrated in fewer hands with the rise in gun purchases being driven by current gun owners adding to their collections. According to 2013 survey data from the ATF, there are an estimated 8.1 firearms in the average gun-owning household, that number is almost double the 4.2 guns in the average gun-owning household in 1994.

Gun ownership varies from state to state. A published study in *Injury Prevention* by researchers at Columbia University and Boston University found the lowest gun ownership in Delaware with 5.2 percent and the highest in Alaska with 61.7 percent. Dr. Kalesan's research credited state laws, culture, and social norms for the variance. Only a small percentage of women own guns. The average gun owner is a white male, over 55 years old, is either married or divorced, and has a high income. White households are more likely to be gun owners than any other racial group, and gun ownership is usually higher in rural communities. Data from the Pew Research Center shows that while black people are significantly more likely to be gun homicide victims, they are half as likes as whites (41 percent) to have a firearm in their home. Latinos are less likely than blacks to be gun homicide victims but they are also half as likely to have a gun in the home.

The General Social Survey found that conservatives are more likely to own firearms, "half of Republican live in households with at least one gun, which is twice as high as ownership among Democrats or independents." The study also noted the correlation between high gun ownership rates and high gun death rates. Alaska, Louisiana, and Arkansas ranked high among states with greater gun ownership and gun deaths. Hawaii and Massachusetts have the lowest gun ownership rates, the strictest gun control laws, and lowest number of gun deaths in the country.

Gun Laws

States across the country are weakening their gun restrictions and permitting guns to be carried in more public places. Guns are being allowed in schools, churches, restaurants, and other public buildings. Conservative lawmakers would like to further relax gun regulations where they would be allowed in bars, airports, sports arenas, and day care centers. Hidden guns are allowed in all 50 states and Alaska doesn't even require residents to have a permit to carry concealed firearms. Idaho, Mississippi, and West Virginia have approved the carrying of concealed weapons without a permit or firearm training, while Texas allows their residents to carry guns openly.

In response to the tragic shootings on college campuses, ten states have policies allowing guns to be carried on campuses. Tennessee joins the list with Gov. Bill Haslam allowing Tennessee's campus-carry bill to become law without his signature. Full-time faculty, staff, and other employees at public Tennessee colleges will be able to carry their state-issued licensed handguns on campus. Students are not allowed to carry guns on campus under this law, however, Rep. Andy Holt (republican) who sponsored the bill said that would be the "important next step. He was quoted in the Tennessean, "These are adults. We need to stop talking about college students as children. They have the same constitutional rights as others."

According to the Associated Press, guns will be continued to be banned at school-sponsored events such as football and basketball games, and hospitals or offices where medical or mental health services are provided. Guns will also still be banned at daycare centers and elementary schools. Joe DiPietro, president of the University of Tennessee, criticized the law in *The Tennessean* saying, "Our position has been and continues to be that we do not support, as a general premise, any measure that would increase the number of guns on college campuses other than already are allowed by law."

Governor Nathan Deal of Georgia is currently assessing a rule that would allow anyone over 21 years of age to carry a firearm on public campuses. Republican state lawmakers are proposing and passing more legislation that expands gun rights and permits the carrying of firearms in gun-free zones. Opposition to the push for more guns in public has strong support from law enforcement officials who say that more guns carried by civilians expose police to more danger. Nevertheless, there are six places where federal law pre-empts state law and guns are not allowed: federal court facilities, U.S. Post Offices, federal prisons, Ranger stations, national cemeteries, or aircrafts.

Dissenting Arguments Regarding Gun Control

The NRA and other gun rights groups argue that gun controls only hurt law-abiding gun owners, criminals don't care about gun laws; they don't buy them, they steal them. They refer to the 2004 expiration of the ban on assault weapons and the substantial decline in violent crime. John R. Lott, Jr., president of the Crime Prevention Research Center and author of *More Guns, Less Crime*, affirmed that states with the largest gun ownership have had the largest drop in violent crime. He attributes this to the notion that criminals are reluctant to attack potential victims who might be able to defend themselves.

Gun control supporters advocate limiting weapons to effectively drive down gun related crimes. They allude to the response in Australia after the 1996 Port Arthur massacre that left 35 people dead and 23 wounded. Australia enacted strict gun ownership laws and initiated a "buy-back" of 643,000 firearms at a cost of $350 million. From that time there have been zero mass shootings in Down Under, and gun homicide and suicide rates have plummeted. Gun control advocates feel this might be an effective model for the U.S. to follow.

Immediately after the 2012 Sandy Hook shootings in Newton, 58 percent of Americans were in favor of stricter rules regarding gun control in a Gallop Poll. Just a few years later, and after more mass shootings, the number has fallen to 47 percent. In 2015, A Pew Research Poll showed 85 percent of Americans favor expanding background checks for gun buyers. Even in this atmosphere Congress has failed to make any meaningful changes to current gun policy. An enormous amount of money is poured into the troughs of politicians who support gun rights. In 2015, gun rights groups spent $8.4 million on gun lobbying: seven times more than control groups' $1.2 million. A December article in the *Pacific Standard* by Francie Diep reported that for the 2016 election cycle, gun right supporters have contributed $701,084 to political candidates compared to $300 donated by gun control supporters.

In a *Huffington Post* article, Shannon Watts, the founder of Moms Demand for Gun Sense in America, gave her position on the recent wave in states weakening of control laws, "Make no mistake; Whether it's guns on campus, lowering or elimination permitting requirements for concealed carry, or pushing for open carry of handguns, it's just an attempt by the gun lobby, and the lawmakers who carry out their wishes, to put more guns in places, no questions asked." Most of the gun lobbyists she spoke of are paid by the National Rifle Association (NRA). Watts' determination was evident when she said, "For a decade, the gun lobby has pushed state legislators for laws that profit gun manufacturers, but now Moms Demand Action is pushing back in all 50 states, so that these attempts no longer go unchecked."

Gun control critics cite that many of the 298 mass shooting in 2015 happened in gun-free zones. John Lott, Jr. wrote in a Phill.com blog post, "If the media regularly reported when a shooting occurs in a gun-free zone, more people would realize that gun-control laws don't deter criminals who are looking for select targets where people can't fight back."

Gun Violence

Gun violence in the U.S. has caused more deaths than all the war conflicts in the history of this country added together. According to Politifact, there were 1.2 million deaths from the War of Independence to the Iraq War, compared to 1.4 million firearm related deaths during the same period. Even while this country spends above a trillion dollars every year to fight terrorism, terrorist attack deaths amount to only a fraction of the gun violence deaths.

According to the Center for Disease Control's most recent data of 2013, 33,363 persons were killed as a result of gun related deaths, 21,175 were suicides, and 84, 255 were shot non-fatally in the U.S. Mass shootings, defined as an incident involving multiple victims of gun violence, make up only one percent of gun deaths. Mass Shooting Tracker data reports there were 372 mass shootings in 2015, 475 were killed and 1870 were wounded. Fifty-three percent of mass killings are family related. The Mother Jones magazine calculated the direct and indirect costs of firearm-related incidents to be around $229 billion annually.

An article in the Annals of Internal Medicine by Dr. Darren B. Taichman and Dr. Christine Laine said, "It doesn't matter whether we believe that guns kill people or that people kill people with guns—the result is the same: a public health crisis." They refer to the strategies to eliminate polio, to reduce automobile related injuries, even to decrease tobacco related deaths, and ask why there are no research studies or initiatives to focus on the public health threat of firearms. Seven national physician organizations joined by the American Public Health Association and the American Bar Association have united for more research and prevention of firearm injuries and death. They have recommended universal background checks, elimination of privacy laws that stop them from discussing issues related to health safety including guns, and restricting the manufacture and civilian sale of military style weapons and high-capacity magazines.

The reasoning that we do nothing in terms of gun control because criminals will find a way to get guns is not consistent with our War on Drugs policy. Criminals have and will find illegal ways to get drugs and yet we continue to spend billions on this problem. Maybe there should be a War on Guns or re-evaluate how we treat illegal drugs as well. For some the argument may be about their freedom and rights but I suspect that for those who protest too much, this is more about money.

Global Warming

Global Warming

In a 2012 speech, Obama referred to global warming as "one of the biggest threats of this generation," and we're stuck on immigration and terrorism. Seventy percent of Republicans don't believe climate change is real or a serious threat to the world. Our legislators want to ignore the issue of climate change and dismiss it as a problem for future generations to deal with. James Hansen, a NASA climate scientist, testified before Congress in 1988 to warn the world on the dangers of climate change caused by pollutants in the atmosphere. It was more than fifteen years later before the media reported, "There is general scientific agreement that the most likely manner in which mankind is influencing the global climate is through carbon dioxide release from the burning of fossil fuel." In spite of the naysayers, the majority of Americans have finally accepted that climate change is real; nevertheless, the issue has become politicized.

Global warming by definition is the term used to describe a gradual increase in the average temperature of the earth's atmosphere and its oceans, a change that is believed to be permanently changing the earth's climate. More simply it means that one hundred years of polluting the earth is having a negative effect on the environment and the ecosystem and causing climate change. This phenomenon is of great concern for anyone who inhabits the earth. The global community must join together to find solutions to climate change for the benefit of us all.

Information from the Natural Resource Defense Council notes that over the past 50 years the average global surface temperature has increased at the fastest pace since it has been recorded. NASA has been recording the earth's temperature for 134 years. Their data shows the hottest 16 years in that history have occurred since 2000 with the exception of one, and 2000—2009 was the warmest decade on record. This contradicts the theory that there has been a "slowdown" in rising global temperatures. Recent scientific studies warn that unless we take steps to reduce global-warming emissions the average temperature could increase up to 10 degrees Fahrenheit over the next 100 years.

In an effort to address the concern of climate change the international community came together in 1992 in Rio de Janeiro for the Earth Summit. A treaty called the United Nations Framework Convention on Climate Change (UNFCCC) to limit global temperature increases was signed by 180 countries. Three years later realizing that the emission reductions weren't enough, the international community came together again to negotiate a more stringent response to global warming. In December of 1997, another climate change conference took place in Japan. These negotiations created the Kyoto Protocol which mandated greenhouse gas emission reduction levels for each developed country.

The Kyoto Protocol required ratification by 55 members that represented at least 55 percent of carbon dioxide emissions before it would go into effect. The objective was the reduction of greenhouse gas emissions of the members by a collective 5.2 percent below the 1990 emission levels by 2012. China, India, South Africa, and Brazil were among the developing countries that weren't required to reduce their emissions. In 2001, the U.S. Senate rejected the Protocol in a unanimous vote. The treaty didn't become legally binding until February of 2005 when the 55 percent threshold was reached after Russia ratified the Protocol joining Japan, Canada, and the countries of the European Union. Currently 192 parties have ratified the agreement.

Ten years after the Kyoto Protocol was ratified the United States still hasn't signed the treaty. Some critics say the treaty is a failure on many points, mainly because the two largest emitters of greenhouse gases, the U.S. and China are not held accountable under Protocol. Even with reductions by some participating members, including the European Union, meeting and exceeding the goals, that progress has been wiped out with global emissions rising by almost 40 percent over the last two decades.

The problem is that we are all addicts, hooked on fossil fuels, and like most addicts, we deny the seriousness of our addiction. We dangerously postpone any treatments that might help us get a cure. Oil and mining companies serve as our dealers, not wanting us to find ways to free ourselves from the addiction. They convince us that we don't have a problem; they minimize the damage, and tell us we're not hurting anything. They tell us lies we know in our minds are not true but we stay in denial. We can't go along with the preservation of the earth if it keeps us from getting our fix. Kicking the habit is more than we care to think about.

What Causes Global Warming

The Intergovernmental Panel on Climate Change (IPCC) reported that scientists are 95 percent certain that the primary cause of global warming is human activity. The Environmental Protection Agency has concurred that global warming is a result of high levels of greenhouse gas emissions into the atmosphere. The air pollutants responsible for climate change are carbon dioxide, methane nitrous oxide, and fluorinated gases. These greenhouse gases absorb sunlight and solar radiation from the earth's surface that would normally pass out into space and trap this heat or infrared radiation in the atmosphere creating a greenhouse effect which causes the earth's temperature to rise. Of these greenhouse gases, carbon dioxide is the one that causes most of the global warming.

Carbon dioxide (CO2) is released into the atmosphere when we burn fossil fuels to produce energy. Trees and plants absorb CO2 from the atmosphere, and the oceans absorb a tremendous amount of carbon dioxide in algae and vegetation but the overload of CO2 emissions has caused the seas to become acidic. The acidity and the rising temperatures have diminished the capacity of the oceans to continue absorbing CO2. We have also cleared a massive amount of the world's forests. At this point in time we have pumped excessive amounts of carbon dioxide into the atmosphere from burning coal, oil, and natural gas. The problem is that the natural processes to absorb the gases aren't able to maintain a balance.

In the United States, coal-burning power plants generating electricity are the largest source of greenhouse gas emissions, representing 85 percent or two billion tons of CO2 every year. The second largest source of heat-trapping gases is through our means of transportation, generating 1.7 billion tons of CO2 per year. Additionally, the production and consumption of food, manufactured goods, and buildings contribute to carbon pollution. Solid waste also contributes to greenhouse gas emissions. Trash put out for collection is transported to an incinerator or buried in a landfill. The burning of solid waste produces carbon dioxide and the decomposing buried waste produces methane. Recycling and reducing solid waste are further ways we can reduce greenhouse gases.

Consequences of Global Warming

A mere couple of degrees increase in the earth's average temperature can produce critical consequences. Heat-trapping emissions that cause this global warming are changing climates around the world. These changes include extreme heat, more droughts, stronger storms, more frequent and more powerful hurricanes, heavier rainfall, flooding of beaches and low-lying coastal areas, rising sea levels, and acidifying of the ocean. When the environment and the weather are affected this can pose challenges for agriculture, wildlife, the woodlands, and endanger water resources.

Global warming is evident all around the world. What we used to consider a heatwave is now the norm. Scientists predict that heatwaves will become "more frequent, more intense, and more prolonged." According to Accuweather.com, record breaking temperatures were experienced in Australia, Egypt, across Europe, India, Korea, and most of the Middle East in 2015. Thermostats climbed above 90 degree in Paris in the spring when the temps are usually around 70 degrees. Extreme heat is the deadliest of weather conditions, causing 128,885 deaths around the world. In May of 2015, temperatures rose to 113 degrees Fahrenheit throughout India where more than 2500 died of heatstroke. In June, another 1,229 succumbed in a heatwave in Pakistan. In 2016, the National Academies of Science, Engineering, and Medicine announced that up to 75 percent of the earth's heatwaves can be attributed to climate change.

 We are able to measure the extent of global warming not only by temperature of the earth's surface but by the melting of glaciers, the amount of snow cover, and the distribution of ice. The Glacier National Park in Montana was created in 1910 and was the home of an estimated 150 glaciers. Since that time the number of glaciers has dropped to less than 30, and the remaining glaciers are only one-third of their previous sizes. Daniel Fagre of the U.S. Geological Survey Global Research Program predicts that within 30 years most of the park's glaciers will disappear, if not all. The melting glaciers cause rises in the sea level that can lead to coastal flooding on the Eastern Seaboard and on the Gulf of Mexico.

 Ice is melting on both ends of the earth, from the North Pole to the South Pole. The glaciers in the Garhwal Himalay in India are melting at a fast pace; researchers believe most of them could be gone by 2035. Greenland's two-mile ice sheet is shrinking, and the Arctic sea ice is losing depth. Eighty percent of the famed snow-caps of Kilamanjaro Mountain have melted since 1912. In Peru, the Quelccaya, the world's largest tropical glacier is melting; scientists say it could disappear by the end of the century if it continues to melt at its current rate. A study released in the journal, *Remote Sensing of Environment*, reported that up to 25 percent of the permafrost that lies just under the ground surface in Alaska could also thaw by the end of the century, setting free long-trapped carbon into the atmosphere and worsening global warming.

 The rising temperatures cause the melting of ice glacier and snow caps which flow to the oceans. As the sea levels rise they cover plants, destroy agriculture, and some animals lose their main source of food. The increased temperature of the oceans creates more tropical storms. Increased flooding in Florida and in the Gulf of Mexico damages homes and communities. Droughts cause water shortages and increase the risk of wildfires on the West Coast.

Furthermore, there are health consequences from climate change. The rising levels of carbon dioxide are extending the frost-free season and lengthening the pollen season which contribute to the spread of infectious diseases. The increased amounts of ragweed and air pollution exacerbate the symptoms of allergies and asthma. The flooding and storms increase the mosquito population and create favorable conditions for pathogens to grow and spread infectious diseases like malaria, tick-borne encephalitis, and the Zika virus.

Climate Change Denial

Greenpeace defines climate change denial as "anyone who is obstructing, delaying or trying to derail policy steps that are in line with the scientific consensus that says we need to take rapid steps to decarbonize the economy." There are those all over the world who deny climate change but it is primarily considered an American stance. In most industrialized nations climate change denial is preposterous. Imogen Reed, the London based finance and economics writer stated, "In Europe, climate change denial is seen as the preserve of the crackpot, and few political figures or members of the news media would dream of mentioning it, as doing so often receives the same contempt from the European public as denying the Holocaust."

After the Earth Summit, while the United Nation's Intergovernmental Panel on Climate Change (IPCC) were reporting their findings related to global warming and negotiating emissions reductions, coal trade groups and oil and gas industry leaders were busy disputing the data with contrarian scientists' theories. In 1997, climate change denial groups came out of their neutral corner and began their assault on the scientific data concerning global warming in 1997 during the negotiations leading up to the Kyoto Protocol.

The relentless campaign of climate change denial to sabotage the efforts to limiting greenhouse gas emissions was well-funded by well-concealed donors. A research study by Robert Brulle, an environmental sociologist at Drexel University, explored the maze of the hidden funders and found that "140 foundations funneled $558 million to almost 100 climate denial organizations from 2003 to 2010." Digging deeper, Brulle put together a list of 118 influential denial organizations in the U.S. and attempted to probe their financial records to identify their benefactors. What he discovered was that 75 percent of the income of those organizations comes from unidentifiable sources.

Huge companies like ExxonMobil, the biggest oil company in the world, and Koch Industries, the second largest privately held company in the U.S., had vested interests in denying climate change and seeing that the Kyoto Protocol wasn't ratified, particularly by the United States. It stands to reason that those who strongly deny climate change would be persons who benefit from the sale of fossil fuels. These powerful corporations put their money where their mouth is and spent hundreds of millions to delay policies and regulations that would curb global warming. According to Greenpeace tallies from 2003 to 2007, ExxonMobil spent $30 million on scientists and anti-climate change denial-groups promoting disinformation, and billionaire brothers, Charles and David Koch, owners of the coal, oil, and gas conglomerate spent $79 million.

Peabody Energy Corporation, the nation's largest coal producer is now bankrupt; they filed for Chapter 11 protection in April of 2016 faulting falling coal and natural gas prices, and environmental regulation. The company has been under investigation for two years by the attorney general for violation of New York laws prohibiting false and misleading statements to investors and the public regarding the financial risks of climate change. The company has agreed to file revised shareholder disclosures stating that, "concerns about the environmental impacts of coal combustion ... could significantly affect demand for our products or our securities." Attorney General Eric T. Schneiderman said, "I believe that full and fair disclosure by Peabody and other fossil fuel companies will lead investors to think long and hard about the damage these companies are doing to our planet."

On the other hand, ExxonMobil, also facing federal investigation for possible fraud, is financially sound, but has been morally bankrupt for decades. According to a recently revealed email written by Larry Bernstein, a former in-house climate expert, ExxonMobil knew of the hazards of climate change as early as 1977, before it was a public issue and said nothing. *Inside Climate News* and the *Los Angeles Times* have reported the company was well aware of the connection between fossil fuels and the serious threats of global warming from their own scientific research, yet they continued to fund climate change denial groups up until the mid-2000s. Mr. Kenneth Cohen, Vice President of Public and Government Affairs at Exxon, affirmed that the company had supported climate denial and anti-climate policy advocacy groups because the firm agreed with their goal of keeping the U.S. out of the global climate treaty, not to mention how carbon-cutting regulations could slice into their bottom-line.

Politics of Climate Change

Surprisingly, a 2014 poll conducted by the Carsey Institute of New Hanpshire revealed that climate change or global warming has become America's most polarizing political issue. The survey found that "the divisiveness characterizing the climate debate is so strong it has eclipsed such longstanding hot-button issues as gun control, evolution, the death penalty, and even abortion. Thankfully, a new poll showed that 70 percent of American's now believe the climate is changing. The divide is seen in a new report by the Pew Research Center, 71 percent of Democrats believe the earth is warming due to human activity compared to a mere 27 percent of Republicans.

President Obama's climate change plan committed to an 83 percent reduction in carbon emissions from the 2005 levels to 2050 but partisan politics have left the matter at an impasse. Tea Party Republicans and their supporters are the most zealous in their denial of climate change and distrust of science. Ted Cruz remarked, "Today, the global warming alarmists are the equivalent of the flat-earthers." Of those conservative Republicans who do accept global warming they don't believe it's a man-made crisis. Misinformation by the media and corporate lobbying continue to block efforts against legislative action that would put forth any climate change policy.

The American attitude is problematic in the fight against climate change with most people unwilling to pay higher prices to address global warming. Consumers join corporations in their view that reducing global warming will threaten the economy. The rationale for refusing to ratify the Kyoto Protocol was based on its presumed effect on the economy. In an article written by Imogen Reed she remarked:

> "Tackling climate change in America is seen as a way of stifling the economy, reducing growth, costing jobs, and limiting industry's ability to make money. European politicians take the opposite view…climate change is seen as an economic opportunity, which will open up new doors for trade and industry. Investment in energy efficient technologies, renewable energy generation and other green initiatives is seen as a way of creating jobs and helping economic growth, and the European public is already sold on the idea."

Projected Solutions

Now that the controversy of whether climate change is real has been resolved by irrefutable science, ExxonMobil and Koch Industries have ceased their funding of climate denial groups. The new debates are the causes of the earth's climate change and what can be done about it. Lobbyists are now denying the need for feasible solutions that reduce greenhouse gas emissions, such as penalties for industrial carbon emissions, energy efficiency, and clean energy alternatives to fossil fuels. Despite their interference, carbon dioxide emissions have decreased in the U.S. from 2005 to 2015 with the use of cleaner fuels and energy-efficient technologies.

In August of 2015, President Obama announced the Clean Power Plan that put forth new EPA regulations that require existing power plants to reduce their carbon emissions by 2030. We have made improvements but more has to be done to achieve the reductions in greenhouse gas emissions to prevent worsening consequences of global warming. The U.S. is

Greatness, Nuclear Weapons & War

Psst: Somebody Speak the Truth

Greatness, Nuclear Weapons & War

We swallow greedily any lie that flatters us, but we sip only little by little at a truth we find bitter. ~ Denis Diderot

The desire to be important, distinct, and significant is a part of human nature; it's embedded in our DNA. In our modern society these aspirations are represented in our desire for wealth, honor, fame, and the yearning to be great and powerful. Shakespeare said, "Some are born great, some achieve greatness, and some have greatness thrust upon them." The manifestation of greatness is superiority in a field through performance, physically or intellectually.

Individuals desire to be great, families desire to be great, organizations desire to be great, and nations desire to be great. Evidence of greatness is represented by individual or collective achievements. It's measured by the extent of the contributions to the world and mankind. Winston Churchill said, *"The price of greatness is responsibility."* Unfortunately in the beginning of the 21st Century, greatness is now defined by many as military might, despite the fact that none of the monumental contributions that changed our world included a bomb, a fighter jet, or a missile.

Power has become an acceptable substitute for greatness. Power can be earned, transferred, or pilfered. However, a nation's greatness is not in its ability to intimidate, dominate, or kill. Those aren't admirable or honorable goals. It's much more impressive, enviable, and profitable to dominate in intelligence, technology, development of new energy resources, transportation, cutting edge research, and medical care. Can we include compassion for the disadvantaged? The list continues in the arts with literature, visual arts, poetry, and architecture. Is replenishing the nuclear arsenal actually at the top of the list?

The reality is that military domination is done; it's over, no matter how much you spend on weapons, aircrafts, and submarines. It would be more feasible to plant a vegetable garden on Neptune than to spread Democracy in another county. Change comes from within, whether it be inside one individual or a land of one billion. The days of the English roaming the globe, conquering and colonizing underdeveloped countries will never be seen again. There are places on this earth where there is barely enough food for simple survival yet there you can find an automatic weapon, possibly even a surface to air missile. Efforts to rule another man with a boot on his neck leaves the wannabe ruler hobbling.

Why do we feel the need to control the four quadrants of the world instead of tackling our inner challenges of income inequality, crumbling infrastructure, and climate control? President Obama has reiterated that the United States is not the "world's policeman," yet we still have more military bases around the world than any other country costing this country an estimated $156 billion or more every year. Even more bases were built following the 9/11 terrorist attack. It's seems these are not enough for some, for them there will never be enough.

The NATO Watch Committee and the International Network for the Abolition of Foreign Military Bases have revealed that the U.S. operates and/or controls between 700 and 800 military bases worldwide. An article by David Vine in *The Nation* said, "Seventy-two years after World War II and 62 years after the Korean War, there are still 174 "base sites" in Germany, 113 in Japan, and 83 in South Korea, according to the Pentagon. Hundreds more dot the planet in around 80 countries, including Aruba and Australia, Bahrain and Bulgaria, Colombia, Kenya, and Qatar, among many other places." These bases represent our need to dominate the bulk of the world with military might.

The justification for the military bases is to maintain peace and keep us safe from terrorist organizations, "to fight them over there so we don't have to fight them here." Fifteen years into the "War on Terror" there is no end in sight and the terrorist groups have multiplied. Either they keep changing their names or there's a new one every six months. As a result of strategic changes and budget costs, the Obama administration is moving forward to close some military bases in Europe in a plan to reduce its military footprint in the United Kingdom. Luke Coffey, director of the Douglas and Sarah Allison Center for Foreign Policy, objected to the policy of shrinking our military presence in the world writing, "These cuts are sending the wrong signal on America's commitment to transatlantic security and will embolden U.S. adversaries in the Euro–Atlantic region. Most importantly, the cuts will reduce the ability and flexibility of the U.S. to react to the unexpected in Eurasia and the Middle East."

Terrorism raises much fear in our hearts because its randomness and ability to infiltrate our borders. Our fear makes us irrational in attempts to fight the phantom. In contrast to the words inscribed on the Statue of Liberty we deny solace to refugees, divide families in the deportation of immigrants, and drop bombs indiscriminately. De Tocqueville wrote, "*It has been remarked that when danger presses, man rarely remains at his habitual level; he elevates himself well above or falls below…Instead of elevating a nation, extreme perils sometimes succeed in pulling it down' they stir up its passions without guiding them, and far from enlightening its intelligence, cloud it.*"

Now is the time for the citizens of this country to be honest as we reassess who we are and the direction in which we desire to go. I, for one, don't desire to become one of the terrorists of the world who kill innocent people justified by beliefs of what is right in my own mind. Make no mistake that when hundreds of bombs are dropped there are innocent people taken out in the process. There are no winners in war, only the extent to which all involved have lost, be it life, liberty, or money.

In so many instances the exorbitant resources spent on military expansion and wars drained the resources of classic empires, the Roman, Han Dynasty, Egyptian, Spanish, and the French. The common threads were the cost of the military, unequal taxation, and class warfare. So much spent and in the end peace still has to be negotiated. The intelligent thing would be to attempt diplomacy first. In his September 25, 1961 address to the United Nations General Assembly, President J.F. Kennedy said: "*Let us call a truce. Let us invoke the blessings of peace. And as we build an international capacity to keep peace, let us join in dismantling the national capacity to wage war.*"

Greatness, Nuclear Weapons & War

Nuclear Weapons

John F. Kennedy cautioned the world as he stated the perils of nuclear weapons in his September 1961 address to the United Nations General Assembly:

> Today, every inhabitant of this planet must contemplate the day when this planet may no longer be inhabitable. Every man, woman and child lives under a sword of Damocles, hanging by the slenderest of threads, capable of being cut at any moment by accident or miscalculation or by madness. The weapons of war must be abolished before they abolish us. And men may no longer pretend that the quest for disarmament is a sign of weakness—for in a spiraling arms race, a nation's security may well be shrinking even as its arms increase.

There is no other weapon on earth more destructive than a nuclear weapon. A single nuclear bomb can annihilate an entire city, blasting and killing every living thing in its range with fire and radiation. The environment of the city will be destroyed and the after-effects are catastrophic for decades to come. We know this is true because we've witnessed the devastation after the U.S. bombed Hiroshima and Nagasaki with nuclear weapons in 1945, killing an estimated 200,000 people. Four years later the Soviet Union detonated their first atomic bomb, the United Kingdom in 1952, France in 1960, and China in 1964.

The Nonproliferation Treaty (NPT) was negotiated in 1968 in an effort to prevent the list of nuclear states from growing longer. Signed by 190 states in 1970, including Russia, the U.S., China, France, the UK, and non-nuclear-weapon states, the treaty covers disarmament, nonproliferation, and the peaceful use of nuclear energy. By the time the NPT was enforced, the stockpiles of nuclear weapons in the United States and Russia had run up to the tens of thousands. The two countries later negotiated several bilateral arm agreements to reduce the size of their nuclear arsenals. India, Israel, and Pakistan never signed the treaty and are currently pursuing new ballistic missiles, cruise missiles, and sea-based nuclear delivery systems.

Public protests led to the Limited Nuclear Test Ban Treaty in 1963, signed by the United States, the Soviet Union, and Great Britain, which prohibited the testing of nuclear weapons in outer space, underwater, or in the atmosphere. The Comprehensive Nuclear Test Ban Treaty which prohibited "any nuclear weapon test explosion or any other nuclear explosion" was adopted by the United Nations General Assembly in 1996 and signed by over 180 nations. President Bill Clinton was the first to sign the treaty; however, the U.S. Senate rejected the treaty in 1999 citing it would damage the safety and reliability of America's nuclear arsenal.

Hans Kristensen and Robert Norris of the Federation of American Scientists have estimated that there are a total of 15,375 nuclear weapons stockpiled in the inventories of nine countries; Russia, the United States, France, China, the UK, Pakistan, India, Israel, and North Korea. Russia and the United States possess 93 percent of the world's nuclear weapons, most accumulated during the Cold War. Twenty years after the end of the Cold War both nations have 2000 nuclear weapons on high alert for immediate launch. The U.S. hasn't built any new nuclear weapons since the 1990s but has refurbished several to extend their lifetime.

In 2015, the U.S. had an estimated 7,300 nuclear weapons. Robert

Alvarez, in his *Bulletin of the Atomic Scientists* column, put the average per-unit cost around $1.8 million per-warhead, and in 2016, the National Priorities Project reports taxpayers in the U.S. are paying $2.19 million every hour for nuclear weapons. Dr. Lisbeth Gronlund, Senior Scientist & and Co-Director of the UCS Global Security Program, explains the price tags: "*Assuming the DOE and DOD plans move forward, and the United States makes further modest reductions in its deployed and reserve arsenal (to a total of 3,000 weapons) the United States will spend some $250 billion on new nuclear warheads and delivery systems in the next few decades.*"

Nuclear weapons are not practical. A war between two nuclear states would be mutual destruction, and still money is spent to modernize nuclear delivery systems. We the People are told that these weapons act as a deterrent but we have more than the amount needed for a cataclysmic end to life on earth as we know it. The Ploughshares Fund objects to the $1 trillion to be spent on a new generation of nuclear weapons over the next 30 years, "These are not what our soldiers need. Terrorists are not deterred by nuclear weapons. Every dollar spent on this obsolete arsenal is a dollar less for our true defense needs."

In truth, the real threat is from a nuclear accident, a moment of irrational panic from a country that moves them to push the nuclear button, or the theft of a nuclear weapon by a rogue terrorist group. The danger from nuclear weapons comes from the fact that they exist. The real solution to eliminate the risk of nuclear weapons and the probability that they may be used by terrorists is disarmament, to get rid of the weapons all together along with the materials used to make them.

There are also the serious issues of environmental and indirect health effects from the production, stockpiling, and testing of nuclear weapons. Greenpeace has reported that accidents at military reactors and civilian nuclear power facilities have polluted the environment with carcinogenic and mutagenic isotopes for over 60 years. The nuclear accidents of Three Mile Island in 1979 and Chernobyl in 1986 have spread radiation across North America and Europe. Costs for clean up for the U.S. are projected to be more than $300 billion through 2070.

Disarming the Danger

One year after it came into existence, the United Nations began its mission to eliminate weapons of mass destruction. In 1946, the first resolution adopted by the UN General Assembly established a Commission to work on problems related to atomic energy and other concerns, and make proposals for "the elimination from national armaments of atomic weapons and all other major weapons adaptable to mass destruction." Secretary-General Ban Ki-moon referred to this resolution in his October 2008 address to the East-West Institute in New York. An excerpt from "The United Nations and Security in a Nuclear-Weapon-Free World" states:

> The very first resolution adopted by the General Assembly, in London in 1946, called for eliminating "weapons adaptable to mass destruction". These goals have been supported by every Secretary-General. They have been the subject of hundreds of General Assembly resolutions, and have been endorsed repeatedly by all our Member States.
> And for good reason. Nuclear weapons produce horrific, indiscriminate effects. Even when not used, they pose great risks. Accidents could happen any time. The manufacture of nuclear weapons can harm public health and the environment. And of course, terrorists could acquire nuclear weapons or nuclear material.
> Most states have chosen to forgo the nuclear option, and have complied with their commitments under the Nuclear Non-Proliferation Treaty. Yet some states view possession of such weapons as a status symbol. And some states view nuclear weapons as offering the ultimate deterrent of nuclear attack, which largely accounts for the estimated 26,000 that still exist. Unfortunately, the doctrine of nuclear deterrence has proven to be contagious. This has made non-proliferation more difficult, which in turn raises new risks that nuclear weapons will be

used. The world remains concerned about nuclear activities in the Democratic People's Republic of Korea and in Iran. There is widespread support for efforts to address these concerns by peaceful means through dialogue.

There are also concerns that a "nuclear renaissance" could soon take place, with nuclear energy being seen as a clean, emission-free alternative at a time of intensifying efforts to combat climate change. The main worry is that this will lead to the production and use of more nuclear materials that must be protected against proliferation and terrorist threats.

The obstacles to disarmament are formidable. But the costs and risks of its alternatives never get the attention they deserve. But consider the tremendous opportunity cost of huge military budgets. Consider the vast resources that are consumed by the endless pursuit of military superiority. According to the Stockholm International Peace Research Institute, global military expenditures last year exceeded $1.3 trillion. Ten years ago, the Brookings Institution published a study that estimated the total costs of nuclear weapons in just one country, the United States, to be over $5.8 trillion, including future cleanup costs. By any definition, this has been a huge investment of financial and technical resources that could have had many other productive uses.

Seven years later we seem to be emphasizing the identical points in the argument against the use of nuclear weapons as deterrents and the threats they impose. The solution for nuclear proliferation from nuclear states is to tell non-nuclear states, "Do as I say, not as I do." It's difficult to talk peace with an olive branch in one hand and the other poised above the nuclear fire button. Pope Francis alluded to the inconsistency when he appeared in his first address before the UN General Assembly and said:

Any ethics and law based on the threat of mutual destruction—and possibly the destruction of all mankind—are self-contradictory and an affront to the entire framework of the United Nations, which would end up as "nations united by fear and distrust." There is urgent need to work for a world free of nuclear weapons, in full application of the non-proliferation Treaty, in letter and spirit, with the goal of a complete prohibition of these weapons."

Protests

An estimated one million people demonstrated in New York City on June 12, 1982 against nuclear weapons and called for an end to the arms race that began with the cold war. This was the largest political demonstration in American history. This powerful protest should have prompted some change, stirred our consciousness, influence our leaders, but nothing changed.

The movement to eliminate all nuclear weapons has been revived by the International Campaign to Abolish Nuclear Weapons (ICAN). This coalition is comprised of 440 non-governmental organizations in more than 98 countries. Their mission is to rally governmental support to "prevent a humanitarian catastrophe by banning nuclear weapons." In the spring of 2016, activists gathered in Geneva to negotiate proposals for a legally binding treaty for the ban of nuclear weapons. ICAN's executive director, Beatrice Fin, noted the renewed commitment from governments to address the threat of nuclear weapons, "We hear a majority of states right now will start in 2017."

Meanwhile, Republican presidential candidate, Donald Trump, entered the conversation of nuclear weapons advising that the U.S. should not try to stop nuclear proliferation. In a town hall meeting moderated by Anderson Cooper, when asked about proliferation he said, "It's going to happen anyway." It sounds similar to the rationale for allowing everybody to have guns because the bad guys are going to get one anyway.

Once believers that nuclear weapons could be used in a limited strategic options, former secretaries of state Henry Kissinger and George Shultz, along with former Chairman of the Senate Armed Services Committee Sam Nunn, and former Defense Secretary Bill Perry, reversed their past positions in a January 2007 *Wall Street Journal* op-ed article, affirming that nuclear weapons don't make the world safer, that they have become a continuing source of extreme danger. They wrote: "While the four of us believe that reliance on nuclear weapons for deterrence is becoming increasingly hazardous and decreasingly effective, some nations will hesitate to draw or act on the same conclusion unless regional confrontations and conflicts are addressed.

War

> "War appeals no longer as a rational alternative. Unconditional war can no longer lead to unconditional victory. It can no longer serve to settle disputes. It can no longer concern the great powers alone. For a nuclear disaster, spread by wind and water and fear, could well engulf the great and the small, the rich and the poor, the committed and the uncommitted alike. Mankind must put an end to war—or war will put an end to mankind."
> ~President Kennedy, UN Assembly, 1961.

Fifty-five years later and we still haven't gotten the message. Even as President Obama clashes with liberals who want total withdrawal now and conservatives who never wanted military drawdowns, he struggles to fulfill his plan to end the wars in Iraq and Afghanistan. Further complications to the scenario are war hawks who speculate on war in North Korea, Iran, Syrian, and even hint at conflicts with Russia and China. In the last year of his presidency the urgency to act looms greater as Obama picks and chooses his battles. He said, *"As you are well aware, I do not support the idea of endless war. I have repeatedly argued against marching into open-ended military conflicts that do not secure our core security interests."*

Talks and preparations of endless war raise anxiety levels and disturb the peace. The May 2016 U.S. opening of a $800 million missile defense system in Romania recently prompted Russia to suggest that it jeopardized their security and raised the risk for nuclear war. The United States and NATO have attempted to diffuse the acrimony stating that the shield is only for protection against "rogue" states and does not protect Europe or the U.S. from Russia's arsenal, and their strategic nuclear deterrent has not been undermined. Still there have been leaks that their response to the missile defense system is a nuclear-armed drone submarine.

Somehow we can't stop fanning the flames of the possibility of war. We keep interjecting ourselves in the world's skirmishes. Some say it's because of the basic principles of America that we can't turn our backs away from humanitarian tragedies, we have to intervene. Most of the fervor is the fear of not having a leading role in every event on the world's stage. We don't always have to act; we can sit and watch the production sometimes. Some events have to play themselves out and we have to live with the ending whether we like it or not.

It seems obvious that quite a large number of our political leaders are suffering from control issues when they insist we must send ground troops somewhere or carpet-bomb a country. Goodtherapy.com defines control as—exerting influence over one's environment or the actions or behaviors of another person—is sometimes used excessively by those who fear the unpredictable and ambiguous, feel they need to prove themselves, or fear losing control. An incessant need for control may become overwhelming and exhausting, wreaking havoc on relationships and overall quality of life.

If you could actually go to war, at a designated place, and fight terrorism, we would have celebrated that victory a long time ago. Terrorism is dynamic, the enemy is ever changing, and each confrontation breeds new hidden soldiers. All the things we see now are reactions to actions. Yes, you can second-guess and Monday-morning quarterback, but the only truth is that you can't predict the outcome of war. There are no guaranteed instructions for success.

We don't need to escalate.
You see, war is not the answer
For only love can conquer hate
---Marvin Gaye (What's Going On)

Iraq & Isis

Iraq & Isis

"Nothing in the world is more dangerous than sincere ignorance and conscientious stupidity."
~ Martin Luther King, Jr.

The two very serious questions pertaining to war are: when to commence and when to cease. The rule of thumb is that war should be the absolute last resort; all other avenues toward a peaceful resolution must have been explored. Unfortunately, this was not the protocol for waging the Iraq War. This was a preemptive war, defined as the use of U.S. military force to eliminate credible and imminent threats to U.S. interests before enemy attacks occur. As citizens we would like to think that every option has been examined before we are asked to sacrifice the lives of our sons and daughters. We need to be assured that the danger to our country is real, not exaggerated.

President George W. Bush's National Security Strategy (NSS) from September 2002 said:

> "The greater the threat, the greater is the risk of inaction—and the more compelling the case for taking anticipatory action to defend ourselves, even if uncertainty remains as to the time and place of the enemy's attack. To forestall or prevent such hostile acts by our adversaries, the United States will, if necessary, act preemptively."

At this moment in time the perceived threat was from terrorists. The 9/11 attacks stunned and horrified the United States, not only for the lives that were lost, but for the realization that this country was vulnerable to terrorists attacks on our own land. Two weeks later, the FBI had identified and connected the hijackers to the terrorist group, Al-Qaeda. This circumstance called for a strong response. We had to put our enemies on notice that this type of aggression would not be tolerated. Retaliation was certain but against whom. Within three days of the investigation the Bush Administration was making links between Al-Qaeda and Saddam Hussein and 9/11, suggesting that the Iraqi president and the radical Islamic group might conspire to launch additional terrorist attacks on the United States.

If President Bush could brand Iraq as terrorist supporters then that would justify an attack on Iraq.

The political conversation quickly switched from the terrorist group, Al-Qaeda, to "weapons of mass destruction." If Saddam Hussein had such weapons then they were the imminent threat to our safety. Undoubtedly, the aim was to go to war with Iraq, never mind the fact that the entire U.S. intelligence community had dispelled any connection between Iraq and the 9/11 attacks. The National Security Strategy underscored that preemption was their policy of choice in the advent of weapons of mass destruction; "We must adapt the concept of imminent threat [that justifies preemption] to the capabilities and objectives of today's adversaries. Rogue states and terrorists do not seek to attack us using conventional means…Instead, they rely on acts of terror and, potentially, the use of weapons of mass destruction— weapons that can be easily concealed, delivered covertly, and used without warning."

Most of us don't understand the difference between preemptive war and preventive war but there is a distinct difference, specifically, whether the war is justified under international law. This is important for the people to know when they are asked to spill their blood or spill the blood of someone else. No one wants to go to war without a clear reason. By convention, preemptive war, a war of necessity, is initiated to defeat an imminent offensive or to gain a strategic advantage in an anticipated war before that attack materializes. A preventive war, considered a war of choice, is an unprovoked launch to eliminate the potential threat of an enemy when there is no imminent threat or planned attack from that state.

Secretary of State Colin Powell gave a speech before the UN that implied that there was a secret cooperative relationship between President Saddam Hussein and Al-Qaeda from 1992 to 2003. Their rationale for war was based on this assumption. The Bush Administration considered the Iraq War as preemptive with the explanation that the enemy state was arming itself with WMDs. Detractors maintain that it was a preventive war with ulterior motives, immoral, and against international law.

Brief History of Iraq

Iraq, originally known as Mesopotamia, Greek for 'in the midst of rivers,' is considered to be the cradle of civilization. The two rivers are the Tigris and the Euphrates, also the place where the book of Genesis says the Garden of Eden was located. A nation rich with culture and history, this is the place where the first written alphabet was created. True innovators, they were the people who invented the wheel and the plough, developed agriculture, mathematics, and astronomy. The list of well-renown persons from this region is long. Noah is believed to have lived in Iraq and it was where the post-flood civilization was revived. Abraham who is recognized by Muslims, Christians, and Jews as the patriarch of prophets lived in Iraq. Under King Nebuchadnezzar, Babylon was the greatest city-state in the world. The Walls of Babylon and the hanging gardens the king built for his wife are among the Seven Wonders of the World.

The Prophet Muhammad, born in Mecca, Saudi Arabia, was the founder of Islam. There are two sects, Sunni and Shia Muslims, who share faith in the Quran and the Prophet Mohammed's sayings and perform similar prayers; they differ in rituals and their interpretation of Islamic law. Muhammad, allegedly poisoned by his wife, died in 632 A.D., without sons and without a will he left no successor. His closest male relatives were his father-in-law who was Sunni, and his son-in law who was Shiite. Muslims split over who should succeed the prophet and lead the Islamic state. The Sunnis believed that their leader should be elected from the political successors of Muhammad. On the other hand, the Shiites believed their leader should be hereditary, having come directly from the family line of Muhammad. There was civil war between the two factions through which the Sunnis gained control and held it for nine centuries.

Without strategic barriers for protection, Iraq has a long history of being invaded, once even by Alexander the Great who died there. The country was ruled for hundreds of years by the Persians until it was conquered by Muslim Arabs, with Bagdad becoming the cultural capital of the Islamic world. Ghenghis Khan in a Mongol invasion attacked Bagdad in the 13th century, then the Turks, and then Iran who battled back and forth with the Turks. The Turks finally won and Iraq became a part of the expansive Ottoman Empire for five centuries until World War I. The Ottoman Empire accommodated the multiple languages and religions and divided the area known as Iraq into three provinces; the Kurds settled in Mosul, the Shiites in Basra, and the Sunnis in Bagdad.

The British invaded Iraq in 1914 and battled the Turks for two years before they won. They occupied Bagdad until 1932 when they agreed to an independent Arab government. Iraq became a sovereign nation in 1961 with the Sunnis holding the political power. Saddam Hussein came into power in 1979. Territorial disputes with Iran led to an eight year war from 1980 to 1988 after Iraq invaded Iran with the support of the United States. In the end, Iraq declared victory but both sides retained their borders.

Making the Case

The lead-up to the Iraq war started with the threat of weapons of mass destruction. The reports of Iraqi use of chemical weapons against Iran in 1984 and against the Kurds in the city of Halabja in 1988 put them in the hot seat. After Iraq is pushed back from its invasion of Kuwait in April of 1991, the United Nations Security Council passed Resolution 687 which stated that Iraq must destroy its reputed stockpile of WMDs and their ability to produce them. The UN Special Commission was established to oversee the inspection, the destruction, and the monitoring of any chemical or biological weapons. The International Atomic Energy Agency was asked to destroy and document Iraqi efforts to develop nuclear weapons. Iraq accepts the first of many resolutions and so begins the seven year game of hide-and-go-seek.

In January of 2002, in his State of the Union address, President Bush includes Iraq in his international "axis of evil," continuing with his campaign to brand Iraq as an enemy to the United States. He states, *"Iraq continues to flaunt its hostility toward America and to support terror. The Iraqi regime has plotted to develop anthrax and nerve gas and nuclear weapons for over a decade...This is a regime that has something to hide from the civilized world."* As the rhetoric heated up throughout the year, the UN Security Council passed Resolution 1441 which demanded that inspectors be readmitted into Iraq. Saddam Hussein seemed to comply as inspectors returned to Iraq.

In January of 2003, inspectors Han Blix and Mohamed ElBaradei reported their findings to the UN Security Council; no "smoking guns" were found. They didn't discover any biological, chemical, or nuclear weapon activities. The report didn't stop the Bush Administration from throwing out more accusations of Iraq hindering inspections and their attempts to develop nuclear weapons. In February, Secretary of State Colin Powell went before the UN to make the case for war with evidence against Iraq stating, *"These are not assertions. What we're giving you are facts and conclusions based on solid intelligence."* The UN Security Council wasn't convinced and did not pass a resolution authorizing the use of force.

The words "regime change" were banded about as the Bush Administration went on its public campaign to gain support for an invasion. The "evil dictator" needed to be removed and democracy given to the people of Iraq. Saddam Hussein was labeled as an immediate threat to the United States and accused of harboring and supporting Al-Qaeda. Speech outlines from General Tommy Franks stated eight objective of the invasion:

1. Ending the regime of Saddam Hussein.
2. Identify, isolate, and eliminate Iraq's weapons of mass destruction.
3. Search for, to capture, and to drive out terrorists from that country.
4. To collect such intelligence as we can relate to terrorist networks.
5. Collect intelligence related to the global network of illicit weapons of mass destruction.

6. End sanctions and immediately deliver humanitarian support to the many displaced and needy Iraqi citizens.
7. Secure Iraq's oil fields and resources, which belong to the Iraqi people.
8. Help the Iraqi people create conditions for a transition to a representative self-government.

On March 17, 2003, an ultimatum was issued to Saddam Hussein giving him 48 hours to leave Iraq. Leaders in France, Germany, Russia, and countries all around the world supported continued inspections and objected to this end of diplomacy and run-up to war. Three days later the invasion began with a "coalition of the willing" to clear Iraq of weapons of mass destruction. It was a classic case of the ends justify the means, except the predictions were so very wrong.

The Iraq War

The Iraq War, dubbed "Operation Iraqi Freedom," began on March 20, 2003 without any declaration apart from plans to "shock and awe." It started with a series of air strikes directed on government and military installations. U.S. aircraft dropped precision-guided bunker-busting bombs on a complex where they believed President Saddam Hussein was located with his senior staff. The battle with the elite Republican Guard and the intense war that had been anticipated was never realized. Meeting with no serious resistance, U.S. forces moved into Bagdad on April 9 taking over the city. The Ba'athist government collapsed and Saddam Hussein was nowhere to be found.

On May 1, 2003, with the words "Mission Accomplished" as a backdrop, President Bush announced, "Major combat operations in Iraq have ended. In the battle of Iraq, the United States and our allies have prevailed… In this battle, we fought for the cause of liberty and the peace of the world." This was supposed to be the end of combat operations, yet they continued for eight more years. The Shiites and ayatollahs who had fled the country under Saddam Hussein's regime returned. This is when the real war actually started, a civil war, and deadly attacks on U.S.

soldiers. Sectarian violence between Shiite and Sunni militias spread across the country like a wild fire. Killings and chaos within a power vacuum, the fighting between Iraqi insurgents, the Mahdi Army formed by Muqtada al-Sadr, Sunni militias, and the U.S. forces, all contributed to the destabilization of Iraq.

Saddam Hussein was captured in December 2003; he stood trial, was convicted and executed for crimes against humanity. On September 16, 2004, in an interview with BBC news, Kofi Annan, the Secretary General of the United Nations criticized the invasion of Iraq and said, "I have indicated it was not in conformity with the UN Charter. From our point of view, from the Charter point of view, it was illegal."

The Aftermath

President Bush had barely gotten through his victory speech before he appointed L. Paul Bremer Chief Executive Authority of Iraq, making him head of state over 25 million Iraqis. His first order of business was to disband the Iraqi military, and then he fired all the government and administration employees who were members of the Baathist party. Close to 100,000 Iraqis were instantly unemployed. Most of the factories were state owned; when the state went down, millions of Iraqi citizens went down with it. Bremer formed a Governing Council made up of members who supported the invasion, although he retained veto power, and they set about writing an Iraqi constitution. I suppose this is how democracy is spread, with no voice from the people.

Meanwhile, the incidences of attacks on U.S. troops were becoming more frequent, particularly in the Sunni Triangle. This area, northwest of Bagdad has been the center of the violent resistance to the U.S. occupation. Initially the resistance came from those loyal to the Baathist party who had been supplied with weapons by the Iraqi army. Later, religious radicals contributed to the fighting that was called the Iraqi insurgency. The situation continued to move from bad to worse. A year later in July of 2004, the Coalition Provisional Authority was dissolved and Bremer transferred power to an interim Iraqi government. Multi-party elections were held in the following year.

Iraq & Isis

Nouri al-Maliki, a Shiite, was elected as Prime Minister in 2006, with Shiites gaining power in Iraq for the first time in centuries. Sunnis disliked the policies of the new government, feeling disenfranchised, tensions between the two factions intensified. This opened the door for extremists to gain support.

The rebellion against U.S. occupation led to 4000 more U.S. soldier casualties and hundreds of thousands Iraqi death, most of them occurring between 2004 and 2007. The Bush Administration had no idea how deep the rift is between the Sunnis and the Shiites, and the Arabs and the Kurds. The Sunni rebellion of the Shiite government led to the formation of the Islamic State of Iraq.

Was it about Oil?

It was supposed to be about weapons of mass destruction, except the weapons that were searched for were never discovered. It was supposed be about setting the Iraqis free from the evil dictator Saddam Hussein who had gassed his own people, but we took over, set up the government, and the killing continued. It was supposed to drive out terrorist networks; instead, it most certainly gave birth to new ones. Nafeez Ahmed summed it up in a piece for the *Guardian* about the Iraq invasion when he said, "The overwhelming narrative behind the Iraq War has been one of incompetence and failure in an otherwise noble, if ill-conceived and badly managed endeavor to free Iraqis from tyranny."

There were rumblings below the surface about the real reason for the Iraq War: revenge for Saddam Hussein's assassination attempt on George H. Bush, encouragement by the Israeli leaders to help destroy one of their enemies, and urgings by Dick Cheney to gain huge contracts for Halliburton. The truth is that central motivation behind the whole conflict was about oil. The end was there, they just needed the means. In Former Federal Reserve Chairman Alan Greenspan's memoir, he said, "*I am saddened that it is politically inconvenient to acknowledge what everyone knows: the Iraq War is largely about oil.*" Nobody was shocked or surprised. Money is always the source of motivation in a capitalistic society.

James A. Paul, Executive Director of the Global Policy Forum, provided background that explained the reasons for the Iraqi invasion in an article he wrote titled, *Iraq: The Struggle for Oil*. Most of us are not aware that Iraq has the world's second largest proven oil reserves, estimated at 112 billion barrels, along with additional undiscovered reserves that might bring the total above 250 billion barrels. This oil is high quality and cheap to produce, a treasure trove every oil company in the world would love to possess. Chevron CEO Kenneth T. Derr put it plainly at a 1998 speech at the Commonwealth of San Francisco, "Iraq possesses the reserves of oil and gas – reserves I'd love Chevron to have access to."

During George W. Bush's election campaign he said, "As spare production capacity becomes tighter, Iraq is moving into a position to become an important "*swing producer*," with an ability to single handedly impact and manipulate global markets." In the year before the 9/11 terrorist attack, big oil companies, including Exxon, Shell, BP, and Chevron, contributed more money to get Bush and Cheney in the White House than they had in any previous election. There are no doubts about a backroom deal when after one week in office Cheney formed the National Energy Policy Development Group. Within 90 days the group was reviewing maps that completely outlined Iraq's oil producing capacity.

A May 2001 National Energy Policy report on "energy security" commissioned by Cheney warned of an impending global energy crisis. The problem was the rising global demand for energy exceeding production, which leaves the world vulnerable to disruption and energy price volatility. What was needed from Middle East countries was for them "to open up areas of their energy sectors to foreign investment." Then there was Iraq with their oil industry nationalized and closed to Western oil companies. Plans for a military invasion of Iraq were now on the table.

The first session of the Future of Iraq project working on Oil and Energy convened in December of 2002. At the end of their meeting in 2003 they agreed that Iraq "should be opened to international companies as quickly as possible after the war." Representatives from the West's largest oil companies met with Cheney's staff to discuss plans for Iraq's postwar industry. ExxonMobil, Shell, BP, Chevron, and Halliburton were among the oil companies and oil service companies that made their way into Iraq. According to an article by Antonia Juhaszm, after the Iraq invasion and during the next decade, "former and current executives of western oil companies acted first as administrators of Iraq's oil ministry and then as "advisers" to the Iraqi government." In 2007, General John Abizaid, former head of the U.S. Central Command and Military Operations in Iraq stated, "Of course it's about oil; we can't deny that." Defense Secretary Chuck Hagel corroborated, "People say we're not fighting for oil. Of course we are."

It's disturbing to think that we are the kind of country that would sink to the level of doing something this dastardly. That we would sacrifice so many lives, not for the security and benefit of this country as a whole, but to satisfy the greed and avarice of money-hungry oil companies. We're supposed to be better than that, we supposed to be the beacon that the world looks up to. We're supposed to have changed our evils ways from the days of slavery and moral indebtedness. It saddens me that politicians sell us a sorry bill of goods and we fall for it over and over again. They operate for big business exclusively. Why can't we open our eyes and see they don't have our best interests at heart.

Was it Worth It?

The Iraq and Afghanistan debacle are humbling and embarrassing. Even after being advised by credible world leaders not to start the "shock and awe" the Bush administration refused to listen to reason. And so Pandora's Box was opened releasing the evils of war and hate and then shutting it back leaving "hope" as the only thing not to escape from the contents. Now with more ills and confusion we can't fix or make go away, it gets worse every day. What the United States feared and accused others of attempting to do, we have done. We destabilized the Middle East for no apparent gain. It cost us trillions in blood and butter. The only success counted was for the war profiteers whose coffers were filled under the guise of spreading democracy.

The United States formally withdrew all combat troops from Iraq at the end of 2011. There was no noteworthy evidence found to substantiate the Bush administration's claims about weapons of mass destruction. Estimates to the number of Iraqis killed in first four years of the conflict are 150,000 to 650,000. As of the end of 2014, 4486 U.S. soldiers were killed in Iraq, 2345 were killed in Afghanistan, and one million were wounded.

Among the tragedies of the Iraq war was the tremendous loss of ancient biblical artifacts. U.S. armed forces have been accused of looting the National Museum after the collapse of Bagdad, but the troops contend the looting was done before they arrived to protect the museum. Mobs and thieves had ransacked and plundered 15,000 treasured items dating back to the dawn of civilization in Mesopotamia. The staggering losses included mankind's earliest written documents, heads of sculptures, and other works of art.

Iraq Civil War

The growing sectarian violence amid the different ethnic groups and the insurgency against the American-led military coalition in Iraq was labeled a civil war in 2006. There is definitely rancor between the Shiites and the Sunnis and they are both fighting for control in Iraq. Put in power after the collapse of the Baathist rule, the Shia government which is the majority, hasn't been willing to share the power, and the Sunni, who are in the minority, have revolted against their authority. The U.S. military came to the aid of Maliki in the fight against the Sunni, supplying the government with equipment. However, the feeble efforts to form a national unity government that the Kurds, Shiites, and Sunnis would all favor were unsurprisingly unsuccessful.

The terrorist group, Al-Qaeda, saw the anger of the Sunnis as an opportunity to find common ground in Iraq. They formed the AQI (al Qaeda in Iraq) to fight against the U.S. troops in Iraq. In the spring of 2007, there was infighting among Sunnis in Bagdad. With the promise of more power in the central government in Bagdad, the Sunnis joined the U.S. troops in the battle against the radical Jihadists in the AQI. This turnaround was called the Sunni Awakening. The AQI was defeated and pushed out of Iraq. The Al-Qaeda group returned to Syria to expand their position in the Syrian conflict. They re-named themselves the Islamic State of Iraq and Syria.

Adding to the chaos, Maliki was battling rival Shiite militias in several mainly Shiite cities. A U.S. troop surge helped to quiet things down some for a while but as the American troops were drawn down the violent conflicts escalated, and after the withdrawal of all U.S. troops in 2011 the situation in Iraq had reached crisis proportions. It's not hard to recruit members in radical groups when they have been exposed to so much killing, when they don't have jobs, and when they have no hope.

In the summer of 2014, members of the Sunni rebel group who joined Al-Qaeda in Syria, now called ISIS, launched an attack where they drove the Iraqi army out of Mosul and major areas of Northern Iraq, connecting the Iraq conflict to the Syrian civil war. Their goal was to establish an Islamic State in both countries. Then it got really ugly when ISIS fired shells filled with mustard gas landed on Kurdish positions near Makhmour. The U.S. began supplying the Kurdish brigade with heavier equipment to defend themselves; even so there have been complaints that the Shia is holding it up because of fears the equipment might be used later when the

Psst: Somebody Speak the Truth

Kurds fight for their independence. Inevitably, whenever the push against ISIS to retake Mosul begins the situation in Iraq will continue to worsen as more blood is spilled.

This situation in Iraq is more of a quagmire of violent attacks than a civil war, there is infighting among the Sunnis, infighting among the Shiites, then there are suicide bombings and clashing between the Sunni and the Shiites, there is fighting between the secular and the conservative, there are militias fighting Christians, the U.S. is fighting ISIS, and the Kurds are trying to maintain their autonomy through all of it. How can the U.S. military intervene without choosing a side? Dropping bombs, sending troops and withdrawing troops, is a costly never ending rollercoaster ride. The U.S. can't stay in the region forever, the ones we're fighting live there, they have time to wait, and the U.S. doesn't have the connections to build a rebel force in another country.

Now What?

It's been thirteen years since the U.S. invasion of Iraq and what we left behind is still a mess. The level of violence is up and down but shootings and bombings have become a part of everyday life in this country. The political leaders are no less corrupt or brutal than the Saddam Hussein regime. Democracy that is satisfactory to the people is a far off possibility. The near 30 percent unemployment rate among young men makes them susceptible to radical militant groups and criminal gangs. Basic services for the people: clean water, electricity, and medical care are not consistently available. The only assurance the Iraqi have is there will be more violence and death to contend with.

In a *Frontline* interview with Sheikh Gazi al-Essawi, a Sunni Arab leader, he answered Martin Smith's questions about his reaction to the American invasion and presence in Iraq and the philosophy of "A tooth for a tooth," when he said, "In our tribal society, this principle is applied…A lot of the problems resulted from acts of revenge…They killed innocent people who do not have anything to do with anything, nothing to do with the resistance or any other problems. Ideally, they should solve the problem politically and not militarily. Because the military action only calls for reactions." Near the end of the interview he asked, "Why did they have to destroy things? Do the Americans intend to turn me into a friend or an enemy?"

Reviewing all the issues that are before the American people and the important decisions that have to be made, we have to re-evaluate our priorities and determine what is most important for the citizens of this country as we move forward. Will the needs of the people come first or will they be superseded by the needs of corporations, or the needs of nation builders? The final answer does not sit with politicians who are influenced by lobbyists, we the people must speak, and speak loudly. We have to let our vote do the talking. We have to support leaders who have the best interest of the people at heart and send the rest packing.

Capitalism and big business now run this country; they deny climate change, deny athletes' rights to benefit from their own talents, sell guns of war to civilians, make money oppressing the poor, and all without conscience. Let's consider all the companies that profit greatly from government contracts that overburden the taxpayer. It's as if the government is a massive cow with big business constantly sucking the milk out of the teat and nobody sees this as a problem. It only becomes an issue for our legislators when it's the least advantaged of the country wanting a drop from the udder.

Christopher Halloran / Shutterstock.com

The Barack Obama Presidency

The Barack Obama Presidency

Church folks say, "What God has for you, no man can take it from you." Evidently it was meant to be. The whole win was fascinating. It has taken some time for me to fully understand how it was accomplished as the end of his second term approaches. Simply put, he mobilized many of those who prior to that time were non-voters, proving that we do have power whenever we decide to use it. It was so profound that his campaign manager was hired by the Conservative Party of Britain as a campaign strategy adviser. Surely if he could get a black man re-elected as president in the United States, getting them elected in Britain would be mere child's play.

Our first national encounter with Barack Obama was during his speech at the 2004 Democratic Convention as the Senator from Illinois. It was an inspiring speech as he began with a reflection on his unprivileged background and family and how his presence there was unlikely. If that circumstance of the "skinny kid with the funny names" was improbable, what were the odds that he would become president only four years later? Not as farfetched as you might think. He offered the American people something they hadn't had in a long time, hope instead of fear. Not a hard choice if you think about it. The foundation of his hope was in unity, e pluribus Unum, out of many, one, realizing that our greatest strength is in working together for the good of us all.

With a vision and agenda of hope and change, the 44th President of the United States began his first term with serious challenges. His most formidable foes were not the financial crisis or the wars in Iraq and Afghanistan; they were his fellow political leaders who committed themselves from day one to undermine any legislation passed by the Obama administration. Most might find it unbelievable that elected officials, senators, representatives, and governors, would subjugate and sacrifice the wealth and welfare of their constituents and citizens of the nation to sabotage the presidency because a black man is in power, but trust and believe that's what they intended. Thankfully for the American people they were unsuccessful.

The First Year, 2009

The first things on the agenda were the request of a temporary halt to Guantanamo Bay Trials of suspected members of terrorists group. There were reports and supporting evidence of torture, acts that were cruel and inhuman, and degrading treatment of prisoners. President Obama pledged to shut down the military prison located in Cuba because he saw it as a recruiting tool for terrorists and too costly to maintain. Up to this date Congress has resisted any option for the closing of the prison that involved moving the detainees into the United States. Obama has been successful in reducing the number of detains from 273 down to 100, along with the order that interrogations of detainees by all US intelligence agencies will adhere to the 19 methods in the US Army Field Manual. In addition, he ordered that the 'black sites" or secret prisons operated by the CIA outside of the US in European countries be closed.

From the start it seemed as if President Obama wanted to run a clean operation, be above board, and transparent. He would have a big job in washing all of the dirty laundry from the Bush administration. His next order of business was to sign an executive order on ethics, establishing a new code of practice for his executive personnel in reference to lobbyists and lobbying at the end of their appointment. It's hard to be a cohesive team if members have hidden agendas. Once again, this scripture applies, "No one can serve two masters. Either you will hate the one and love the other, or you will be devoted to one and despise the other." Matthew 6:24 KJV.

The first piece of legislation passed by President Obama was the Lilly Ledbetter Fair Pay Act. The law overturned the 2007 Supreme Court decision that said workers only have 180 days to file a discrimination lawsuit. It also prohibits sex-based wage discrimination between men and women in the same establishment who perform jobs that require equal skill, effort, and responsibility under similar working conditions.

The most urgent business was the economy as the country was in the midst of the Great Recession. During periods where private spending has decreased, public spending by the government can save jobs and fuel the economy. Obama signed into law The American Recovery and Reinvestment Act of 2009 after one month in office. His administration declared the act, "is an unprecedented effort to jumpstart our economy, create or save millions of jobs, and put a down payment on addressing long-neglected challenges so our country can thrive in the 21st century. The Act is an extraordinary response to a crisis unlike any since the Great Depression, and includes measures to modernize our nation's infrastructure, enhance energy dependence, expand educational opportunities, preserve and improve affordable health care, provide tax relief, and protect those in greatest need." Another casualty of the recession was General Motors, the largest automaker in the US, filing for bankruptcy. The Obama Administration invested $62 billion of federal money to buy a 60 percent stake in the new GM.

A proponent to reducing global warming and climate change, Obama set stricter limits with a new auto emission policy to decrease greenhouse gas pollution. The national policy requires US auto makers to manufacture cars and trucks that achieve an average 35.5 mpg by 2016. This should reduce carbon dioxide emissions 30 percent, making it the most effective measure taken so far to reduce global warming. As part of the stimulus bill, $90 billion was invested in renewable technology and "green jobs." He also signed an executive order requiring federal agencies to reduce their environmental impact as well.

The discomfort of some with this president is past irrational at times. There is no better example than the President's address to children on the first day of school. The White House said that the speech would stress the importance of education. Obama urged the students to not let failure define them, that they are the future of America. Yet, the Republicans accused him of trying to "indoctrinate school children with liberal propaganda." The speech became so controversial that some school districts decided not to air it and some parents chose to keep children at home to keep them from seeing it. If you doubt that every move by this president was examined and critiqued, remember the flack by PETA for swatting a fly during an interview.

Undeterred by the opposition and the controversy to his every move, Obama nixes plans for a missile defense shield in Poland and pushes for more cuts in the US nuclear arsenal. His strategy is more radical disarmament between nuclear powers to prevent global proliferation. Sitting as chairman, the first for an American President, Obama pushed through a new United Nations Security Council resolution supporting non-proliferation of nuclear weapons, the reduction in existing stockpiles, and the peaceful use of nuclear energy for everyone. This was one of the reasons cited by the Norwegian Nobel Committee for awarding Barack Obama with the Nobel Peace Prize on October 9, 2009, embracing what he stands for along with his "extraordinary efforts to strengthen international diplomacy and cooperation between people."

Also notable was the historic nomination of Sonia Sotomayer to the Supreme Court, making her the first Latina to serve as a Court Justice in the United States. There were several low-profile issues that were important to the Obama Administration, signing into law the Children's Health Insurance Reauthorization Act of 2009 that expanded the healthcare program to cover another 4 million uninsured children and pregnant women, including undocumented immigrants, and families with low income but too high to qualify for Medicaid. The Family Smoking Prevention and Tobacco Act was also signed into law giving the FDA the power to regulate the tobacco industry, with the aim of discouraging minors and young adults from smoking. There was also credit card reform with the Credit Card Act of 2009, to establish fair and transparent practices relating to the extension of credit, and the Matthew Shephard and James Byrd, Jr. Hate Crimes Prevention Act of 2009, giving the FBI the authority to investigate hate crimes and violence, including violence towards the LBGT community. Obama also signed an executive order removing restrictions on Stem Cell research.

The contentious battle of the year was over the Affordable Care Act. Healthcare had been proposed many times by previous presidents without success with the last major national healthcare reform being Medicare back in 1965. The historic healthcare reform bill was passed by the Senate finance committee, and on Christmas Eve was passed by the Senate to extend health insurance to 30 million uninsured Americans.

Much to the frustration of those whose only mission was to make Barack Obama a one-term president with a failed administration, their pledge was left unfulfilled. President Obama ended his first year in office demonstrating that true leadership is not by fear and intimidation but by example and facilitation.

The Second Year, 2010

Barack Obama started off the second year in his presidency announcing a $100 million emergency aid package for Haiti after the island was devastated by a 7.0 magnitude earthquake. In his 2010 State of Union Address he gives a summary of his accomplishments in the first year and introduced an ambitious plan for the New Year.

In March, President Obama signs into law The Patient Protection and Affordable Care Act, also known as Obamacare, to cover the more than 32 million uninsured Americans. This is the first healthcare reform law in the history of this country. Later in the month he signed the Health Care and Education Reconciliation Act, which among other things, increased tax credits to buy insurance, lowered the penalty for not buying insurance, and offered more generous subsidies to lower income groups. The education reconciliation reform portion ended subsidies to private banks; federally insured student loans will be directly administered by the Department of Education. The Pell grant was increased, and repayment caps were added up to 10 percent of the borrower's discretionary income. The Caregivers and Veterans Omnibus Health Services Act of 2010 was also signed into law to improve healthcare services for veterans and expand caregiver benefits and training. The Department of Veteran Affairs budget was also increased by 16 percent to support the soldiers coming home with serious mental and physical problems. A new GI Bill was signed offering $78 billion in tuition assistance and tax credits to businesses who hired veterans.

In efforts to stimulate job growth, the Hiring Incentives to Restore Employment Act was enacted. It created two new tax benefits for employers who hired unemployed workers or part-time workers in 2010. Employers could qualify for a 6.2 percent payroll tax incentive. If each worker is retained for at least a year the employer can claim an additional business tax credit for up to $1000 per worker. The Unemployment Compensation Act of 2010 was signed to assist the 2.5 million workers who lost their jobs in the recession, unemployment insurance was extended, in July, December, and then again in 2011.

Halfway through the year, President Obama signed the Dodd-Frank Wall Street Reform and Consumer Protection Act. This law, considered to be largest financial system reform since the New Deal, re-regulated the financial sector after its bad practices led to the Great Recession. Following that legislation, the Consumer Financial Protection Bureau was created to protect consumers from unfair practices in loans and credit cards. In other efforts to stimulate the economy the Small Business Jobs Act of 2010 was passed and created a Small Business Lending Fund Program to increase the credit for small businesses.

In a speech from the Oval Office on August 31, 2010, honoring a pledge to the American people, President Obama announced the end of the combat mission in Iraq. Operation Iraqi Freedom was over after nearly a decade of war. Close to 100,000 US Troops were pulled out of Iraq. He stated in his address that *"only Iraqis can resolve their differences and police their streets. Only Iraqis can build a democracy within their borders."* If only our leadership had realized this ten years earlier so many lives would not have been lost.

It is impossible to note all the important legislations for the second year but a few more were the appointment of Elena Kagan to the Supreme Court, the Claims Resolution Act that provided funding and statutory authorities for the Cobell lawsuit and the Pigford II lawsuit, brought by Native Americans and African Americans respectively, and the Healthy, Hunger-Free Kids Act which set new nutrition standards and authorized $4.5 billion in funding for child nutrition programs and free lunch programs for the next five years. At the end of the year, Obama signed the Don't Ask, Don't Tell Repeal Act, ending the policy that allowed gays, lesbians, and bisexuals to serve in the military as long as they kept their sexual orientation a secret. Repealing that policy allowed them to openly serve in the United States Armed Forces.

The Third Year, 2011

President Obama started off the year signing the NewSTART (Strategic Arms Reduction Treaty), a nuclear arms reduction treaty between the United States of America and the Russian Federation. The terms of this agreement call for the number of strategic missile launchers to be cut in half, the number of deployed strategic nuclear warheads limited to 1,550 (a third of what it was under the original START Treaty), and limits launchers for intercontinental and submarine ballistic missiles, and heavy bombers for nuclear armaments. The deal is expected to last for ten years. If anyone is worried about the treaty, rest assured that it leaves both countries with enough nuclear power to destroy the earth several times over.

The economy seems to be recovering, albeit without significant job growth or higher wages. There are many other domestic issues we should be focusing on in this nation but the civil unrest in faraway countries like Egypt and Iraq seem to demand all of the attention. In the midst of Obama's efforts to get the U.S. out of wars we keep being drawn into conflicts. On March 19, the president ordered military air strikes in Libya against Muammar Gaddafi's forces to stem the vicious attacks on civilians and aid the rebel troops in the Libyan Civil War.

In April, President Obama announced his bid for re-election, which was no surprise to anyone. There was no shortage in criticism and blame from the Republicans despite the president's attempts towards a bipartisan agenda. Their biggest argument was the belief that withdrawing US troops will lead to sectarian warfare in Iraq. For those who have obviously kept their heads in the sand, the insurgency that began with the war had already progressed into a civil war before Obama took office. The Bush administration had received numerous warnings and objections from no less than 54 countries that a war in Iraq would compromise peace and cause instability not only in Iraq but spread throughout the Middle East region. How detractors manage to place that baggage on the shoulders of Barack Obama is a complete denial of the truth. America's image as far as the rest of the world is concerned has been greatly improved by President Obama.

Almost ten years after the attack on the World Trade Center, on May 2nd, President Obama announced that Osama bin Laden had been found and killed. The catalyst for the wars in Iraq and Afghanistan was finally dead. It was the result of a successful CIA- led operation by the Navy Seals. In the next month, Obama announced his plans to begin the drawdown of US troops in Afghanistan, starting with 33,000 troops.

There were some important developments on the domestic front that are worth mentioning. One of the results of President Obama's "stealth climate policy" was the closing of a significant number of the oldest and dirtiest coal-fired power plants. The fuel efficiency standards for cars and trucks were raised again. The Food and Drug Administration's budget was increase by 1.4 billion with the expansion of their responsibilities to maintain the quality of food with the FDA Food Safety Modernization Act. The $8 billion in subsidies for landlines was shifted toward broadband internet for lower income rural families. At the end of this third year as president, Barack Obama has served longer than any other president in my lifetime without being associated with a scandal.

The Fourth Year, 2012

The final year in Barack Obama's first term begins with the rejection of the Keystone XL Pipeline, a pet project of Republicans and oil industry leaders. The 1700 mile sand oil pipeline would carry oil from Canada to Texas refineries. The biggest argument is the damage it will have on the environment. Oils sands or tar sands are a blend of clay, sand, water, and a black thick oil called bitumen, and require more processing than regular crude oil. The pipeline route is to pass through the Sand Hills region, an environmentally sensitive area of Nebraska that has highly porous soil and shallow groundwater. The Ogallala aquifer is located in this region and the pipeline might be a danger to the drinking water.

One of the arguments in favor of moving forward with the project was given by Gary Doer, Ambassador of Canada to the United States, in a letter to the *New York Times*:

"Construction of the pipeline is necessary to replace the declining imports of heavy crude from Venezuela and Mexico…The pipeline would substantially reduce American dependence on oil from volatile regions, including the Middle East… The Keystone XL would not appreciably increase global life-cycle greenhouse gas emissions. There are tremendous economic benefits to the United States from an integrated energy strategy. There are more than 900 American companies exporting equipment and supplied to the oil sands; 70 of them are from New York and New Jersey. The construction of Keystone XL would create 20,000 direct and 118,000 indirect jobs, providing the kind of infrastructure stimulus that your editorials have promoted."

The first of two arguments against the pipeline project is from Bernie Sanders:

> "When people talk about this being a jobs program, let's understand that there is no debate that what we are talking about are less than 50 permanent jobs - less than 50 permanent jobs. So to suggest this is some kind of big jobs program is nothing more than a cruel hoax and a misleading hoax to workers in this country who need decent-paying jobs."

The second argument is from a statement by the Natural Resources Defense Council:

> "This pipeline, called Keystone XL, will lock the United States into a dependence on hard-to-extract oil and generate a massive expansion of the destructive tar sands oil operations in Canada. In addition to the damage that would be caused by the increased tar sands extraction, the pipeline threatens to pollute freshwater supplies in America's agricultural heartland and increase emissions in already-

polluted communities of the Gulf Coast... Both forms of tar sands extraction fragment and destroy the Boreal forest, killing nesting migratory birds and many other species. Toxic waste from the mining operations is stored in vast man-made dams—called tailings ponds—that already cover sixty-five square miles...Tar sands oil threatens our air, water, land, and economy, and will increase already dangerously high greenhouse gas emissions and demand for natural gas. Tar sands oil has no place in the clean energy economy."

More controversy and uproar came in June when President Obama announced the executive order that would stop the deportation of illegal immigrants who entered the United States under the age of 16 and have lived here for at least five years. Those who are eligible would be in school, are high school graduates or have a GED, have been honorably discharged from the military or Coast Guard, are under the age of 30, and have clean criminal records.

After more challenges to the Patient Protection and Affordable Care Act, it was upheld by the Supreme Court. President Obama ended the year winning his re-election and beating those who did everything in their power to keep him from gaining a second term as President of the United States. *Time* magazine selected him as the "Person of the Year."

The Second Term, Fifth Year, 2013

Barack Obama goes into his second term as president with similar key themes to the first, improving the economy, immigration reform, climate control, ending the war in Afghanistan, and preserving the Affordable Care Act. In a speech on January 16th, unable to tolerate or overlook the gun violence across the country and the December mass shooting of children at Sandy Hook Elementary, Obama outlines his proposal for gun-control to reduce gun violence. Along with executive actions he calls for Congress to take legislative actions that would ban assault and high-capacity magazines, keep guns out of the wrong hands, and increase access to mental health services. In his speech he said, "If there is even one step we can take to save another child, or another parent, or another town, from the grief that has visited Tucson, and Aurora, and Oak Creek, and Newtown, and communities from Columbine to Blacksburg before that -- then surely we have an obligation to try."

Even while Obama was trying to withdraw troops from Afghanistan there was a growing problem in Syria. Bashar al-Assad has retaliated against the protests against his regime and it has turned into a civil war. It has been said that more than 100,000 people have been killed and millions more are trying to flee the country. The president has tried to resist the calls for military action because of his belief that we cannot solve another country's civil war through force, but that all changed on August 21st when the government of Assad gassed over one thousand people, including hundreds of children. The use of chemical weapons is considered to be in violation of the laws of war because of the agonizing suffering and large-scale casualties they cause.

On August 31st, President Obama, as Commander-in-Chief, explained that even though he had the power to order military strikes, that in the absence of a direct or imminent threat to the security of the United States, he would ask for the support of Congress on the issue to be decided democratically. In his speech he said:

> "I will not put American boots on the ground in Syria. I will not pursue an open-ended action like Iraq or Afghanistan. I will not pursue a prolonged air campaign like Libya or Kosovo. This would be a targeted strike to achieve a clear objective: deterring the use of chemical weapons, and degrading Assad's capabilities. America is not the world's policeman. Terrible things happen across the globe, and it is beyond our means to right every wrong. But when, with modest effort and risk, we can stop children from being gassed to death…"

The year ended with President Obama battling the constant opposition to the ACA and defending his stance on Immigration Reform.

The Sixth Year, 2014

The year starts with the U.S. under intense scrutiny and criticism for the above and beyond level of surveillance perpetrated by the National Security Agency (NSA). Outed by one of their own, Eric Snowden, a CIA contractor, leaked to the media the extent of internet and phone spying by the NSA. To make a long story short, not only was the NSA spying on tens of millions of Americans, they had broken the U.S. privacy rules hacking and monitoring the phones and emails of 35 world leaders and 38 embassies worldwide. What ever happened to "do unto others as you would have them do unto you?" Obama had to clean up the mess and try to mend fences with those who had their right to privacy violated. In a speech he said:

> "The bottom line is that people around the world, regardless of their nationality, should know that the United States is not spying on ordinary people who don't threaten our national security, and that we take their privacy concerns into account in our policies and procedures. This applies to foreign leaders as well. Given the understandable attention that this issue has received, I have made clear to the intelligence community that unless there is a compelling national security purpose, we will not monitor the communications of heads of state and governments of our close friends and allies. And I've instructed my national security team, as well as the intelligence community, to work with foreign counterparts to deepen our coordination and cooperation in ways that rebuild trust going forward."

Low wages have been and continue to be a drag on the economy. Obama spent a good deal of time focusing on the wealth disparity, so much that he was called a socialist on many occasions. In February he signed an executive order to raise the minimum wage for federal contractors.

There were heated debates concerning the Crimea/Ukraine situation in the early part of the year. War hawks were soaring across the news wires attempting to bait the president into a confrontation with Putin over

Russia's involvement. His cooler head prevailed again as he encouraged the opposing sides that a diplomatic solution to the crisis was the best way forward. One thing that stuck in my head was his reference about being open to negotiation, *"but that is not something that can be done with a gun pointed at you."* I could see how that reasoning could apply to the other crises that were on the forefront, in Iraq and Ferguson, Missouri.

The most monumental accomplishment by President Obama in 2014 took place at the end of the year. I would say this would be in the top ten of his notable decisions. It was the restoration of full relations with Cuba. It's makes good sense, common sense even. Charting this new course, as he says, will engage and empower the Cuban people. Fifty years of isolation did nothing to force Cuba into becoming a democratic country, today they are still a communist state. What it did do was isolate the United States from relations with a country a mere 90 miles away. Now both countries can work together on "matters of mutual concern." My question is: if you believe in religious freedom, equal rights for all races, the LGBT community, the disabled, and the elderly, why do we have a problem with a country not choosing to become democratic?

The Seventh Year, 2015

The biggest dilemma of 2015 for President Obama was how to fight terrorism to the satisfaction of Congress, the American people, and the rest of the world. That is not an easy task to fulfill. So many Republicans are calling for troops on the ground to solve every problem while Obama, who still has another war to end, resists sending in combat troops. I agree with the President when he says that *"we don't want to be the world's policeman."* Some argue that this is a war against radical Islam and we can't retreat. The truth is these radical groups don't represent Islam or Muslims. In the president's words, *"ISIL is a terrorist organization pure and simple…They do not threaten our national existence."*

One of the greatest achievements of President Obama, definitely in the top five, would be the announcement of a historic nuclear agreement with Iran on July 14th. This deal is an agreement between the United States, the United Kingdom, Russia, France, China, Germany, and the European

Union. The deal eliminated the threat of a nuclear armed Iran and the risk of more conflicts in the Middle East without using any military action. The objections from the Republican Party are too many to mention but military officials, nuclear physicists, non-proliferation experts, along with over 100 countries around the world have given their support for the deal.

With all the derision in politics and the stonewalling of Congress, Obama seems to take it all in stride. Even with all the efforts to repeal the Affordable Care Act nearly 18 million uninsured have signed up. In other good news, Obama announced that an agreement was made with China to fight Global Warming. He even traveled to the Arctic Circle, the first sitting president to do so, to highlight the changes in the region caused by climate change.

The Eighth and Final Year, 2016

There is one issue where there hasn't been a meeting of the minds, at least not with rational minds, and that is gun control. With each mass killing on top of the daily killings in urban cities across this nation, the need for some resolution becomes more apparent. Frustrated with Congress, seemingly held at gunpoint by the National Rifle Association, President Obama begins the year with an executive order on gun control requiring that those wanting to purchase a gun must undergo a background check. It sounds reasonable to me; I can't buy a car without proof of insurance, or any major purchase with installments without a credit check.

It's an election year and the other major issue thrown about by presidential candidates in the election is the Iran deal. Instead of looking at this major success toward keeping peace in the world, small-minded people worry about what we gave away as Obama lifted some of the economic sanctions on Iran. The reality is that it was their money that had been frozen. We don't have a right to keep it. As far as the prisoner exchange is concerned, both sides gained some satisfaction. Isn't that what it's all about? President Obama stated it best in his final State of the Union Address:

> "We also can't try to take over and rebuild every country that falls into crisis, even if it's done with the best of

intentions. (Applause.) That's not leadership; that's a recipe for quagmire, spilling American blood and treasure that ultimately will weaken us. It's the lesson of Vietnam; it's the lesson of Iraq -- and we should have learned it by now."

In February, Supreme Court Justice Scalia dies, and just when I thought we were at the lowest depth of hate and resentment somehow it goes deeper, past any rationale. The Republican Senate is refusing to have hearings or vote on his Supreme Court replacement stating that they want the people to choose who will name the next judge. In their arrogance they seem to ignore the fact the people have chosen, twice in fact, Barack Obama, and his term does not end until the next president is inaugurated. Unperturbed, President Obama moves forward making amends and improving relations with Cuba, Vietnam, and Japan.

During the final edit of this book more turmoil has spread across the globe. There have been more terrorist attacks with many innocent killed, more senseless murders of black men by police, more retribution towards police officers, more political and civil unrest in the Middle East, and Britain voted to exit the European Union. With all the "rage, rage against the dying of the light," there's no chance for Obama's presidency to "go gently into that good night."

Bibliography

ACLU. (no date given). War Comes Home: The Excessive Militarization of American Police. *American Civil Liberties Union.* Retrieved from https://www.aclu.org/report/war-comes-home-excessive-militarization-american-police

Ahmed, Nafeez (2014, March 20) Iraq Invasion Was About Oil. *The Guardian.* Retrieved from http://www.theguardian.com/environment/earth-insight/2014/mar/20/iraq-war-oil-resources-energy-peak-scarcity-economy

Alexander, K., Alexander, M.D. (2005). American Public School Law. Belmont, CA. *Thomas West.*

American Civil Liberties Union (No date given) War Comes Home: The Excessive Militarization of American Police. Retrieved from https://www.aclu.org/report/war-comes-home-excessive-militarization-american-police

Anderson, Jon Lee. (2003). The Sunni Triangle: Tribes and Insurgents. *PBS Frontline* http://www.pbs.org/wgbh/pages/frontline/shows/beyond/iraqis/sunni.html

Associated Newspapers (2003, April 3) Iraq: the cradle of civilization. Retrieved from https://www.h-net.org/~museum/iraq.html

Bellandi, D. (2006, July 27). "Chicago Council Passes "Living Wage" Act". *The Washington Post.* Retrieved October 12, 2007

Beschloss, M. (2006). Our Documents: 100 Milestone Documents From The National Archives. *Oxford University Press.* pp. 194–99

Bivens, J, Gould, E., Mishel, L. and Shierholz, H. 2014. Raising America's Pay: Why It's Our Central Economic Policy Challenge. *Economic Policy Institute,* Briefing Paper No. 378.

Bogus, C.T., (2000). The Second Amendment in Law and History: Historians and Constitutional Scholars on the Right to Bear Arms. *New York: New Press.*

Boundless. (2015, July 21). "Civil Rights Under Nixon." Boundless U.S. History. Retrieved 09 Apr. 2016 from https://www.boundless.com/u-s-history/textbooks/boundless-u-s-history-textbook/the-conservative-turn-of-america-1968-1989-30/the-nixon-administration-224/civil-rights-under-nixon-1264-6479/

Bureau of Labor Statistics (U.S. Department of Labor) Current Employment Statistics program. Various years. *Employment, Hours and Earnings—National* [database].

Carnevale, A. P. & Rose, S. J. (2004). Socioeconomic Status, Race/Ethnicity, and Selective College Admission, America's Untapped Resource – Low-income Students in Higher Education (Chapter 3). San Francisco, Jossey-Bass Publishers

Clary, B. J. (2009). "Smith and Living Wages:Arguments in Support of a Mandated Living Wage". *American Journal of Economics and Sociology* **68** *(5): 1063–1084.*

Code, Penal, Crime, and Justice No date given) Criminal Law Reform: Historical Development in the United States - *Twentieth-Century Developments.* Retrieved from http://law.jrank.org/pages/881/Criminal-Law-Reform-Historical-Development-in-United-States-Twentieth-century-developments.html

Coffey, Luke (2012, July 11). Keeping America Safe: Why U.S. Bases in Europe Remain Vital. Retrieved from http://www.heritage.org/research/reports/2012/07/keeping-america-safe-why-us-bases-in-europe-remain-vital

College Athletics—History of Athletics in U.S. Colleges and Universities. Retrieved from http://education.stateuniversity.com/pages/1846

Congressional Budget Office. (2015, January 26). "The Budget and Economic Outlook: 2015 to 2025." Retrieved from https://www.cbo.gov/publication/49892

Congressional Budget Office. (2015, January 26). "Appendix B: Updated Estimates of the Insurance Coverage Provisions of the Affordable

Care Act." Retrieved from http://obamacarefacts.com/costof-obamacare/

Cornell, S. (2006). A Well-Regulated Militia: The Founding Fathers and the Origins of Gun Control in America. Oxford; New York: *Oxford University Press*

Criminal Justice Degree Online (November 2015) The U.S. Criminal Justice History Resource Page - Criminal Justice Degree Online http://www.criminaljusticedegree.net/resources/the-us-criminal-justice-history-resource-page/

Curran III, W. J. (2016). Commitment and Betrayal: Contradictions in American Democracy, Capitalism, and Antitrust Laws. *Antitrust Bulletin*, *61*(2), 236-255. doi:10.1177/0003603X16641235

Daily Mail.com. (no date give). Iraq: The Cradle of Civilization. Retrieved from http://www.dailymail.co.uk/news/article-171806/Iraq-cradle-civilisation.html#ixzz499xUVwSk

DeSilver, D. (May 06, 2015). U.S. Voter Turnout Trails Most Developed Countries. http://www.pewresearch.org/fact-tank/2015/05/06/u-s-voter-turnout-trails-most-developed-countries/

DeSilver, R. (2014, October 9) For most workers, real wages have barely budged for decades. *Pew Research Center*. Retrieved from http://www.pewresearch.org/fact-tank/2014/10/09/for-most-workers-real-wages-have-barely-budged-for-decades/

DeWitt, L (2010). The Development of Social Security in America. Retrieved from https://www.ssa.gov/policy/docs/ssb/v70n3/v70n3p1.html

Eisen, Lauren-Brooke, Eaglin, J. (2014, December 2). Poverty, Incarceration, and Criminal Justice Debt. Retrieved from https://talkpoverty.org/2014/12/02/criminal-justice-debt/

Faux, J. (2013). NAFTA's Impact on U.S. Workers. *Economic Policy Institute*. Retrieved from http://epi.org/blog/nafta-impact-workers

Federal Bureau of Investigations. (2011). Crime in the United States. *Uniform Crime Reports.* Retrieved from https://www.fbi.gov/about-us/cjis/ucr/crime-in-the-u.s/2011/crime-in-the-u.s.-2011

File, T (July 2015). *The Congressional Electorate in 2008* http://www.census.gov/content/dam/Census/library/publications/2015/demo/p20-577.pdf

Foroohar, R. (2016). Saving Capitalism. (Cover story). *Time, 187*(19), 26-32.

Fortier, N. (2014, December 8). How the Federal Government Can Reshape Law Enforcement. *Brennan Center*. Retrieved from https://www.brennancenter.org/blog/how-federal-government-can-reshape-law-enforcement.

Funding Bill Includes $122 Billion for Army. (2016). *Army Magazine, 66*(2), 6.

Gertner, J. (2006, January 15). "What is a Living Wage?" *The New York Times.* Retrieved March 19, 2012.

Ghilarducci, T. (2015). Raising the Retirement Age: A Sneaky Way to Reduce Social Security Benefits. The Atlantic. Retrieved from http://www.theatlantic.com/business/archive/2015/09/raising-retirement-age-social-security-benefits/403828/

Glick, D. (No date given) Global Climate Change, Melting Glaciers - National Geographic http://environment.nationalgeographic.com/environment/global-warming/big-thaw/#page=2

Hamilton, M., McConnell, M., Gedicks, F., Stone, G., Volokh, E., Inazu. J. and Neuborne, B. (No date given) Amendment I Freedom of Religion, Speech, Press, Assembly, and Petition. Retrieved from http://constitutioncenter.org/interactive-constitution/amendments/

Hiltzik, M. (2013, March 8). The five biggest lies about entitlement programs Social Security and Medicare are big issues, and not everyone is telling the truth about them. Los Angeles Times. Retrieved from http://articles.latimes.com/2013/mar/08/business/la-fi-hiltzik-20130310

Bibliography

History. (No date given). *Social Security* Retrieved from https://www.ssa.gov/history/ssa/lbjmedicare1.html

Howe, S. (2002). *Empire- A Very Short Introduction. Oxford University Press. p. 67.*

Huma, R., Staurowsky, E.J. ((2011). The Price of Poverty in Big Time College Sports. *NCPAOW.org.* Retrieved from http://www.ncpanow.org/research/body/The-Price-of-Poverty-in-Big-Time-College-Sport.pdf

Ikenberry, G. J. (2016). The Rise of Democracy: Revolution, War, and Transformations in International Politics Since 1776. *Foreign Affairs*, 95(2), 169.

Jaison, R.A., Deitz, R. and Yaqin Su. (2014). Are Recent College Graduates Finding Good Jobs. *Current Issues in Economics and Finance*. Volume 20, Number 1 www.newyorkfed.org/research/current_issues

Jozsa F. P. Jr. (2013). College Sports Inc., *Springer Briefs in Economics*, DOI: 10.1007/978-1-4614-4969-0_2

Jones, C. (1941). Cost of Living of Representative Working Class Families, *University of Liverpool.*

JRank. (no date give). Criminal Law Reform: Historical Development in the United States - Twentieth-century Developments - Code, Penal, Justice, and Crime - *JRank Articles* http://law.jrank.org/pages/881/Criminal-Law-Reform-Historical-Development-in-United-States-Twentieth-century-developments.html#ixzz46tUlMW2u

JRank. (No date given). The Early Years of American Law - Colonial Freedom, Britain's Push For Greater Control, A New Start, A New Criminal Court System. *JRank Articles*. Retrieved from http://law.jrank.org/pages/11900/Early-Years-American-Law.html

Kramer, A. E. (2016, May 12). Russia Calls New U.S. Missile Defense System a 'Direct Threat. Retrieved from http://www.nytimes.com/2016/05/13/world/europe/russia-nato-us-romania-missile-defense.html

Kimball. D. (October 25) Fact Sheets & Briefs. https://www.armscontrol.org/factsheets/Nuclearweaponswhohaswhat

Leo, J. (2012, February 14). Our Sorry Workforce: Blame Bad Parents. *The Fiscal Times.* http://www.thefiscaltimes.com/Articles/2012/02/14/Our-Sorry-Workforce-Blame-Bad-Parents

Lucander, David. (2014). Winning the War for Democracy: The March on Washington Movement, 1941-1946. *University of Illinois Press.* 320 pages

Lynn-Jones, S. M. (1998). "Why the United States Should Spread Democracy." Discussion Paper 98-07, *Center for Science and International Affairs, Harvard University*

MacMillan, A. (2016, March 11) Global Warming 101. Retrieved from https://www.nrdc.org/stories/global-warming-101

Madhani, A. (2016). Ore Makers Ignore Trump, Clinton Crticism, Begin Layoffs in Chicago. USA Today. Retrieved from http://www.usatoday.com/story/news/2016/03/23/nabisco-begins-layoffs-at-chicago-plant-despite-criticism-from-trump-clinton/82159194/

Madsen, N. (2014). Jim Moran Says Only 20 Colleges Make a Profit from Sports. *PolitiFACT Virginia.* Retrieved from http://www.politifact.com/virginia/statements/2014/dec/22/jim-moran/moran-says-only-20-colleges-make-profit-sports/

Martin, P. (2015, October 14). Top 1 Percent Own More Than Half of the World's Wealth. Retrieved from https://www.wsws.org/en/articles/2015/10/14/weal-o14.html

Mass Vote. (2009). History of Voting Rights.

Retrieved from http://massvote.org/voterinfo/history-of-voting-rights

McElwee, S. (2015, July 27). The rise of the donor class and the influx of corporate cash have caused many voters to lose faith in politics. *Aljazeera.*

McMahon, T. (2015, June 18). Average Annual Inflation Rates by Decade.

Retrieved from http://inflationdata.com/Inflation/Inflation/DecadeInflation.asp

Mintz, S. (n.d.) Winning the Vote: A History of Voting Rights. *The Journal of the Gilder Lehrman Institute.* Retrieved from https://www.gilderlehrman.org/history-by-era/government-and civics/essays/winning-vote-history-voting-rights

No author attributed. (1894, February 20). President Eliot"s Report. *The Harvard Crimson.* Retrieved from http://www.thecrimson.com/article/1894/2/20/president-eliots-report-the-presidents-report/

Nocera, J. (2016, January 8). A Way to Start Paying College Athletes. *The New York Times* Retrieved from http://www.nytimes.com/2016/01/09/sports/a-way-to-start-paying-college-athletes.html?_r=0

Patterson, T. E. (2002). The Vanishing Voter: Why Are the Voting Booths So Empty?. *National Civic Review*, *91*(4), 367.

Perry, Charles R. (1997). "Outsourcing and union power." *Journal of Labor Research* 18.4 (1997): 521-534.

Piketty, T. (2014). Capital in the 21st Century. *Presidents and Fellows of Harvard College.*

Pilkington, E. (2012, July 13). "Felon voting laws to disenfranchise historic number of Americans in 2012". *The Guardian.* Retrieved 2016-02-02.

Plous, S. (Ed.). (2003). *Understanding Prejudice and Discrimination* (pp. 206-212). *New York: McGraw-Hill.*

Public Citizen. (1997). NAFTA's Broken Promises: Failure to Create U.S. Jobs. Retrieved from https://www.citizen.org/trade/article_redirect.cfm?ID=1767

Rasell, E. (2009). Social Security and Medicare: Examining Proposed "Reforms." Retrieved from http://d3n8a8pro7vhmx.cloudfront.net/unitedchurchofchrist/legacy_url/1826/SS-entitlements-HO.pdf?1418425340]

Reed, I. (2008). Why European Attitudes to Tackling Climate Change Differ So Much from America's. *Think Global Green*. Retrieved from http://www.thinkglobalgreen.org/IRone.html

Reed, K. (2015). Solution Regarding Paying College Athletes or Not is Simple. *The Huffington Post*. Retrieved from http://www.huffingtonpost.com/news/paying-college-athletes/

"Regents of the University of California v. Bakke." *Oyez*. Chicago-Kent College of Law at Illinois Tech, n.d. Apr 10, 2016. https://www.oyez.org/cases/1979/76-811

Reich, R. (2007). Supercapitalism: The Transformation of Business, Democracy, and Everyday Life. *Alfred A. Knopf*, New York

Reich, R. (1991). The Work of Nations: Preparing Ourselves for the 21st Century Capitalism. *Alfred A. Knopf,* New York

Rhett, Remington, (2015). OutSourcing: The Negative Effects. Retrieved from https://www.linkedin.com/pulse/outsourcing-negative-effects-remington-rhett

Roberts, P. C. (2005, April 23). Outsourcing After-Effects, *The Washington Times*

Rosich, Katherine J. 2007. Race, Ethnicity, and the Criminal Justice System. Washington, DC: American Sociological Association. Retrieved from http://asanet.org.

Saez, E. (2010). "Striking it Richer: The Evolution of Top Incomes in the United States. Retrieved from http://elsa.berkeley.edu/~saez/saez–UStopincomes–2008.pdf

Schlein, L. (2016, May 12). Disarmament Group Renews Push to Ban Nuclear Weapons. Retrieved from http://www.voanews.com/content/disarmament-group-renews-push-ban-nuclear-weapons/3327651.html

Schlosser, E. (1998). The Prison Industrial Complex. *The Atlantic*. Retrieved from http://www.theatlantic.com/magazine/archive/1998/12/the-prison-industrial-complex/304669/.

Bibliography

Schmidt, P. (2001, May 18). Debating the Benefits of Affirmative Action. *Chronicle of Higher Education, 47*(36), A25. Retrieved September 10, 2008, from Academic Search Premier database.

Shapiro, I. and Kogan, R. (2015, July 2). Congressional Budget Plans Get Two-Thirds of Cuts From Programs for People With Low or Moderate Incomes. Retrieved from http://www.cbpp.org/research/federal-budget/congressional-budget-plans-get-two-thirds-of-cuts-from-programs-for-people.

Shapiro, J. (2104, May 19). As Court Fees Rise, The Poor Are Paying the Price. *NPR*. Retrieved from http://www.npr.org/2014/05/19/312158516/increasing-court-fees-punish-the-poor

Sherk, J. (2013). What is Minimum Wage: Its History and Effects on the Economy. Retrieved from http://www.heritage.org/research/testimony/2013/06/what-is-minimum-wage-its-history-and-effects-on-the-economy

Sherman, A., Greenstein, R. and Ruffing, K (2012, February 11) Contrary to "Entitlement Society" Rhetoric, Over Nine-Tenths of Entitlement Benefits Go to Elderly, Disabled, or Working Households. Retrieved from http://www.cbpp.org/research/contrary-to-entitlement-society-rhetoric-over-nine-tenths-of-entitlement-benefits-go-to

Smith, R.K. (2000). A Brief History of the National Collegiate Athletic Association's Role in Regulating Intercollegiate Athletics, 11 Marquette Sports Law. Rev. 9 (2000) Available at: http://scholarship.law.marquette.edu/sportslaw/vol11/iss1/5

Smith, R.K. (1996). When Ignorance is Not Bliss: In Search of Racial and Gender Equity in Intercollegiate Athletics, 61 Mo. L. REv. 329, 367.

Social Security Office of Policy.(no date given). Trends in the Social Security and Supplemental Security Income Disability Programs. Retrieved from https://www.ssa.gov/policy/docs/chartbooks/disability_trends/overview.html

Social Security. (no date). History of SSA During the Johnson

Administration 1963-1968. Retrieved from https://www.ssa.gov/history/ssa/lbjmedicare1.html

Soergel, A. (Aug. 13, 2015) Social Security: The National Disgrace. Retrieved from http://www.usnews.com/news/the-report/articles/2015/08/13/ask-an-economist-whats-wrong-with-social-security

Statistic Brain (August 26,2015). Voting Statistics. http://www.statisticbrain.com/voting-statistics/

Stone, C. Trisi, D., Sherman, A. and DeBot, B. (October 2, 2015) .A Guide to Statistics on Historical Trends in Income Inequality. Retrieved from http://www.cbpp.org/research/poverty-and-inequality/a-guide-to-statistics-on-historical-trends-in-income-inequality

Union of Concerned Scientists. (No date given) Global Warming FAQ. Retrieve from http://www.ucsusa.org/global_warming/science_and_impacts/science/global-warming-faq.html#.VyvmVxvmodU

USA Today. (September 11, 2006) "Mayor vetoes Chicago's 'living wage' ordinance aimed at big retailers." Retrieved September 17, 2010.

U.S. Department of Justice (Updated August 8, 2015). About Section 5 of The Voting Rights Act

Http://www.justice.gov/crt/about-section-5-voting-rights-act

Taichman, D.B., Laine C. (2015.) Reducing Firearm-Related Harms: Time for Us to Study and Speak Out. Annuals Intern Med. 2015;162:520-521. doi:10.7326/M15-0428

The Leadership Conference on Civil and Human Rights. (No date given). Affirmative Action. Retrieved from http://www.civilrights.org/resources/civilrights101/affirmaction.html

The National Association of Manufacturers. (1993). "NAFTA, We Need It: How U.S. Companies View Their Business Prospects Under NAFTA," Washington, D.C., p. 69 Retrieved from https://www.citizen.org/trade/article_redirect.cfm?ID=1767.

Thompson, M. (2015, May 28). How Disbanding the Iraqi Army Fueled

Bibliography

Isis. Time Magazine. Retrieved from http://time.com/3900753/isis-iraq-syria-army-united-states-military/

United Nations Office for Disarmament Affairs. (no date given). Nuclear Weapons. UNODA. Retrieved from https://www.un.org/disarmament/wmd/nuclear/

U.S. Congress Joint Economic Committee. (2010). Income Inequality and the Great Recession. Retrieved from http://www.jec.senate.gov/public/_cache/files/91975589-257c-403b-8093-8f3b584a088c/income-inequality-brief-fall-2010-cmb-and-ces.pdf

U.S. Government Revenue. (2016). Retrieved from http://www.usgovernmentrevenue.com/current_revenue

Vine, D. (2015). "Where in the World Is the U.S. Military?" Politico Magazine.

Wang, S. (2013). The Great Gerrymander of 2012. The New York Timeshttp://www.nytimes.com/2013/02/03/opinion/sunday/the-great-gerrymander-of-2012.htm

Wallis, J. (2016). America's Original Sin: Racism, White Privilege, and the Bridge to a New America. BrazosPress

Wieberg, S. (2008, January 13). Study: College Athletes are Full-Time Workers. USA Today. Retrieved from http://usatoday30.usatoday.com/sports/college/2008-01-12-athletes-full-time-work-study_N.htm

Wolff, R.D., (2012). Democracy at Work: A Cure for Capitalism. Haymarket Books

www.ingramcontent.com/pod-product-compliance
Lightning Source LLC
Chambersburg PA
CBHW071604080526
44588CB00010B/1009